Faulkner

THE RETURN OF THE REPRESSED

Faulkner

THE RETURN

OF THE REPRESSED

Doreen Fowler

University Press of Virginia
Charlottesville and London

Acknowledgments for previously published material appear on pages xxi–xxii.

The University Press of Virginia

© 1997 by the Rector and Visitors of the University of Virginia

All rights reserved

Printed in the United States of America

First published 1997

The paper used in this publication meets the minimum requirements of ⊗ the American National Standard for Information Sciences—Permanence of Paper for Printed Library Materials, ANSI Z39.48–1984.

Library of Congress Cataloging-in-Publication Data

Fowler, Doreen.

Faulkner : the return of the repressed / Doreen Fowler.

p. cm.

Includes bibliographical references and index.

ISBN 0-8139-1727-1 (cloth : alk. paper)

1. Faulkner, William, 1897–1962—Knowledge—Psychology. 2. Lacan, Jacques, 1901–   —Contributions in criticism. 3. Psychoanalysis and literature—Southern States. 4. Repression (Psychology) in literature. 5. Marginality, Social, in literature. 6. Afro-Americans in literature. 7. Doubles in literature. 8. Women in literature. 9. Deconstruction. I. Title.

PS3511.A86Z783248   1997

813'.52—dc21   96-37493

CIP

For my mother,
Mildred Ferlaino,

and in memory of my father,
John C. Ferlaino
(1914–1991)

Contents

Abbreviations viii

Preface ix

Acknowledgments xxi

Introduction
Faulkner's "Heart in Conflict" 1

1. "The Beautiful One" in *The Sound and the Fury* 32

2. The Displaced Mother: *As I Lay Dying* 48

3. Law and Desire in *Light in August* 64

4. Reading for the Repressed: *Absalom, Absalom!* 95

5. Renouncing the Phallus: *Go Down, Moses* 128

Epilogue:
Lacan, Faulkner, and the Power of the Word 167

Notes 173

Works Cited 200

Index 209

Abbreviations

AA	*Absalom, Absalom!*
AILD	*As I Lay Dying*
Écrits	*Écrits: A Selection* (Lacan)
FIU	*Faulkner in the University*
GDM	*Go Down, Moses*
LIA	*Light in August*
LIG	*Lion in the Garden*
MOS	*Mosquitoes*
SE	*The Standard Edition of the Complete Psychological Works of Sigmund Freud*
SF	*The Sound and the Fury*
WP	*The Wild Palms*

Preface

I did not set out to write a Lacanian interpretation of Faulkner. My purpose, when I began, was to explore the role of the marginalized other in Faulkner's major novels. As I examined Faulkner's texts, I observed that Faulkner used women and blacks as doubles for the white male protagonist. John Irwin's classic Freudian study *Doubling and Incest/Repetition and Revenge* investigates doubling in Faulkner's fiction, but Irwin's reading, which links doubling to an oedipal desire for revenge against the father, focuses on male pairings and on an intertextual reading of *The Sound and the Fury* and *Absalom, Absalom!* Although Irwin acknowledges that Caddy Compson functions as Quentin's double, his Freudian revenge-and-repetition theory does not seem adequately to explain Caddy's symbolic meaning as double. Indeed, Irwin, using Freud, seems himself to stage or, to use Freud's term, compulsively to repeat the text's marginalization of Caddy. It was this very marginalization, the crucial margin that makes possible a center, that I wished to explore.

As I studied marginality in Faulkner's texts, a pattern of symbolic meanings began to emerge. Given that often the black and/or female other seems to represent the alter ego of the white male protagonist, it appeared that refused meanings return in the form of these marginalized others; and that in Faulkner's works the repressed other, the site of cultural repression, is identified with the unconscious, the site of repressed meanings. Read this way, these marginalized black and female characters, like Caddy Compson, Charles Bon, or the little Italian girl in *The Sound and the Fury,* represent a disguised return of forbidden desires. In fact, through a character in *Mosquitoes,* Faulkner appears to admit as much. Faulkner's character says: "A book is the writer's secret life, the dark twin of a man" (251). The book is the "other" of the self, a representation, like dreams, of the unconscious.

In this way, I discovered that my project was to decode unconscious meanings that return disguised in Faulkner's texts. Once I identified the subject of my book, my turn to Lacan's theory of the unconscious

ix

was inevitable, because Lacan focuses on language, especially its uses of metaphor and metonymy, as the foundation of the functioning of the unconscious. "The unconscious is structured like language," Lacan memorably writes.[1] With this sentence, Lacan succinctly summarizes his theory of subjectivity and language. In what follows, I will attempt briefly to interpret Lacan's teasing analogy of language to the unconscious. As the language theorist Ferdinand de Saussure first pointed out, language works by exclusion. We assign a single meaning to a word-sign by casting out all other meanings and making an arbitrary connection between signifier and signified. As a result of this process of exclusion, however, a word is trailed by the meanings it excluded to distinguish a single meaning. The "other" that was excluded to establish a meaning is not wholly dismissed; there is always seepage with words signifying not only the one thing we chose. In Terry Eagleton's words, "a signifier . . . may be attached to many different signifieds, and may itself bear the trace of other signifiers which surround it."[2] The divisions that language tries to establish are never absolute. These arbitrary and artificial divisions are but momentary stays against confusion, and confusion—that is, all other repressed meaning—is ever at the door erected by repression. All that stands between meaning and indeterminacy is the door, the bar of repression. In this way, language is structured like the unconscious. Language is not a well defined, clearly demarcated structure of stable units. Rather, as Eagleton eloquently describes it, language is "like a sprawling limitless web where there is a constant interchange and circulation of elements where none of the elements is absolutely definable and where everything is caught up and traced through by everything else."[3] Understood in this way, language accurately reflects the structure of the unconscious mind: like the unconscious, language is constituted of a ceaseless interplay of meanings and is the site of repression and return.

Underlying this poststructuralist definition of language is a deep congruence between the nature of language and the constitution of the self. Quite simply, language reflects the condition of the alienated subject (indeed, Lacan describes the subject as alienated *in* language) because language works by repression, the continual dominance of the signifier, the empty symbol, over the signified, the literal object in the physical world. This relationship of signifier to signified Lacan designates with the formula S/s. Lacan revolutionizes Saussurean linguistics by inverting Saussure's formula, putting the signifier S on top and the signified s under the bar. S/s indicates the dominance of the empty word-sound over the physical world. Whereas, for Saussure, the bar represented a link, for Lacan the bar represents repression: every word indicates the absence of what it stands for. All language involves symbolization, a substitution of an empty sign for an object in the world. Language is based on alienation; and alienation, in Lacan's schema, constitutes subjectivity. As James M. Mellard explains, Lacan's formula refers not only to the word but also to the psyche: "Saussure's implied algorithm becomes most useful to Lacan, therefore, in large part because it symbolizes the alienation of the human subject, not only from its world, but also from itself."[4] Lacan implies a fundamental similarity between the structure of language and the constitution of subjectivity when he writes that "the unconscious is the discourse of the Other."[5] Malcolm Bowie lucidly enunciates these similarities: "both are articulations of difference; neither has a centre, both involve endless displacement, neither has a point of plenitude or stasis."[6] Terry Eagleton goes so far as to say that language *is* the self: language, he writes, is "not merely a covenient tool I use," rather language is "something I am made out of."[7] Language, then, reflects the psyche, and the text is the proper field of study of the psychoanalytic critic. Elizabeth Wright explains that the "new psychoanalytic structural approach centres on the workings of the text as psyche, based on the theory that the unconscious is structured like language."[8] In accordance with this understanding of the nature of the psyche and the text, my book takes for its subject Faulkner's texts and attempts to decipher the disguised return of repressed meanings, or what Lacan calls the "sliding of the signified beneath the signifier."[9]

In adopting a Lacanian methodology, I make my book liable to a number of charges that are commonly leveled against Lacan. Because Lacan is an intimidating theorist who seems almost to court controversy and misapprehension, it might be well at the outset to attempt to dispell a number of misconceptions that readers might bring to a Lacanian reading of Faulkner. First, I have adopted a Lacanian methodology for the reasons outlined above. My turn to Lacan is not meant to suggest that Lacan provides a master code that takes priority over other ways of reading a text. In an age of poststructuralism, when surely every literary critic understands the instability of meaning and interpretation, such a disclaimer would seem to be unnecessary. Certainly a Lacanian critic would be the last to assert any ultimate authority. According to

Lacan, truth belongs to the inaccessible register of the Real and must always elude us. We look to the Other to guarantee meaning, but, Lacan writes, "there is no Other of the Other";[10] that is, there is no fixed or transcendental meaning that imbues with meaning the endless chain of signifiers. Signifiers only point to other signifiers. In Lacanian theory, the subject, driven by desire, endlessly chases the ultimate signifier, the phallic Other. But this signifier does not exist. In the words of Jacqueline Rose, the phallus is a "fraud."[11]

As if to sign that Lacan is not for me the theorist of theorists, I do not use Lacan exclusively. While my approach is largely Lacanian, I also draw frequently on other literary and psychoanalytic theorists. At various points in the book, I cite Lacanian revisionists like Nancy Chodorow, Luce Irigaray, Julia Kristeva, and Margaret Homans. In chapter 3, I incorporate Erich Neumann's Jungian theory; in chapters 4 and 5, I frequently cite Freudian concepts. My terminology may also sometimes carry overtones of Derrida's deconstructive strategy. Obviously there are differences among these theoretical models, but they also complement and supplement one another and, as I read these theoretical positions, the points of convergence are far more numerous and meaningful than their often overdetermined distinguishing differences. Each represents a revisionary rereading of the narrative of the constitution of the self. For example, as I attempt to show in chapter 3, Neumann's Jungian narrative of the rise of consciousness transposes into mythic terms the story Lacan tells in terms of the advent into language. Similarly, Derrida's deconstructionist practice seems to be compatible with Lacanian theory. As Elizabeth Wright helpfully explains, a deconstructionist interpretation decenters the text in much the same way as Lacan decenters the subject: the single authority, whether it is called author, subject, or absolute truth, is revealed to be unstable, and is dispersed along a chain of signifiers. Indeed, it might be fair to say that Lacan uses Derrida's and Saussure's insights about the nature of language and applies them to the psyche. My occasional recourse to Freud should seem natural enough. Lacan's indebtedness to Freud, I think, cannot be overstated. There are of course significant differences between Freud and Lacan; chief among these differences is that, whereas Freud saw himself as a biological scientist, Lacan uses not biological but cultural models, like language.[12] In effect, Lacan rewrites Freud's oedipal relationship in terms of language. But Lacan's theory builds on Freud's, and in some instances I have turned to Freud when his description of a certain drive or desire appears to have more explanatory power than Lacan's corresponding notion. In particular, I find relevant to Faulkner Freud's notions of the death instinct and the repetition compulsion.

My critical practice, then, is to use Lacan and related theorists as interpretive mediums through which to read Faulkner's texts. I draw on Lacan and others in my study in much the same way that John Irwin, in *Doubling and Incest/Repetition and Revenge,* applies Freud, Nietzsche, and Rosolato to Faulkner. In his introduction to that seminal study, Irwin stresses that he "understand[s] Faulkner, Freud, and Nietzsche to be related specifically as *writers*" and that he "treat[s] the work of all three as literary texts." Anticipating objections, Irwin explains that his purpose in juxtaposing Faulkner with these other writers is "not to explain or reduce or simplify Faulkner's novels but to make them more problematic, richer and more complex" and that he reads these writers in light of one another because they "were writers who addressed themselves to many of the same questions, and that at numerous points their works form imaginative analogues to one another."[13] Following Irwin's example, I propose to read Lacan's narrative of the unconscious as a text that intersects with Faulkner's texts. As I mean to show, Faulkner and Lacan are analogous writers: they share many of the same preoccupations; indeed, while their approaches and methods are widely divergent, ultimately both address the problems of the self in language. Thus my project is an intertextual reading. I read Faulkner through Lacan and Lacan through Faulkner because not only has Lacan enriched my understanding of Faulkner, but Faulkner's narratives, by providing living models, have enabled me to decipher Lacan's knotty concepts.

In discussing my adoption of a Lacanian methodology, I should also note that Lacan poses formidable obstacles to literary interpretation; namely, the opacity of Lacan's own rhetoric. Whereas most theorists, Freud foremost among these, strive for clarity, Lacan cultivates obscurity. Because of the difficulty of his prose, Lacan has been largely regarded as a recondite, inaccessible theorist or, alternately, as a willful obscurantist. In either case, the sheer difficulty of attempting to draw a coherent meaning from Lacan's writing has caused many literary critics to avoid or dismiss Lacan, and the critic who adopts a Lacanian approach runs the risk of being similarly dismissed or, alternately, of introducing into her interpretation an inscrutable theory. In what follows, I propose to discuss the reasons for Lacan's notorious obscurity and to propound my own strategy for coping with Lacan's mystifying rhetoric; for, while I use Lacan, who writes for the few, it has always been my goal to write a book accessible to all those who read and cherish Faulkner's undying prose.

First of all, Lacan's opacity is not motivated by sheer perversity. Rather, Lacan writes as he does for a purpose. Malcolm Bowie identifies this purpose: "Lacan came to view, in the early fifties, that his own theoretical language had to sound like the unconscious of which it spoke, or at least to bear a prominent trace of the uncanny company that his clinical practice obliged him to keep." In his discourse, Lacan deliberately attempts to mimic the working of the unconscious. Bowie observes that Lacan "attempts to teach by example."[14] In mimicking the unconscious, Lacan uses language to disguise his meanings. He indulges in wordplay, wit, punning, irony, and ambiguity in an attempt to reflect the interplay of meaning in the unconscious. Madan Sarup compares Lacan's prose style to a rebus: "A rebus, like a dream, is a sort of picture-puzzle which looks like nonsense but, when separated into elements and interpreted, makes sense."[15]

Although I do not judge Lacan's rhetorical move, I also do not choose to imitate his practice. My position is simply stated. The unconscious is always at work in all discourse. The "repressed," Lacan writes, because it is repressed, "reappears."[16] It is the ever-present subtext, the other-meaning that has been incompletely expelled to make possible the illusion of meaning. Thus, I argue that it is not necessary willfully to court the other, for the other inheres in every word-symbol.

This brings me to my own Lacanian practice. I attempt to make Lacan's gnomic pronouncements clear, insofar as clarity is ever possible. My practice throughout my book is to use a series of modifiers and to move gradually from Lacan's mysterious term to a term that will delimit and define Lacan's meaning. In adopting this method, I anticipate that I will be accused of oversimplifying Lacan. My answer is that Lacan's riddling prose needs to be interpreted, as the scores of Lacanian commentators seem to corroborate, and that I have not simplified but clarified Lacan's meaning. True clarity, a single meaning, of course always eludes us; it is for this reason that Lacan chooses to surrender to the free play of meaning. I elect the alternative path: I choose the repression of meaning in an attempt to produce an illusory order.

In the task of explicating Lacan's thought, I have been aided immeasurably by a number of Lacanian critics. In particular, I am indebted to Juliet Mitchell, Jacqueline Rose, Jane Gallop, Margaret Homans, James M. Mellard, Malcolm Bowie, Richard Boothby, Elizabeth Wright, Jonathan Scott Lee, and Madan Sarup. While I also cite other interpreters of Lacan's theory, the reader of my book will observe that, in the main, I draw heavily on this group of scholars for elucidations of Lacanian concepts. I turn to these particular Lacanian experts for two reasons. First, these critics, in my opinion, have successfully located the core of coherence behind Lacan's riddling phrases without sacrificing the complexity of his thought. Second, these readers of Lacan focus on issues that are crucial and determining to my reading of Faulkner. My psychoanalytic purpose is to read Faulkner's texts as sites of a conflict between oedipal accommodations to the symbolic and narcissistic desires for a return to the other of the imaginary plane. In pursuing this goal, I found that many Lacanian theorists were not helpful, because they concentrate on the symbolic order, the realm of language and social exchange, and make only passing references to the imaginary. Interestingly, this marginalizaton of the imaginary register in their discourse appears to reenact the psychic entry into language and alienation, which hinges on the displacement of the imaginary, or identifications with the maternal, by the symbolic, or what Lacan calls the Law of the Father. But, as Richard Boothby cautions, "there is a danger . . . in putting too much stress on the linguistic side of Lacan." Boothby continues, "For all its importance in Lacan's thought, his notion of the symbolic and its role in the unconscious must be understood in its dynamic relation to his earlier and seminal concept of the imaginary."[17] Because the subject of my book is Faulkner's representation in his major novels of this "dynamic relation" between the imaginary and symbolic, I cite those commentators who acknowledge the signal importance of imaginary identifications with the maternal.

It may be well also to state at the outset my rationale for selecting for analysis, out of all of Faulkner's large canon, these five novels, *The Sound and the Fury, As I Lay Dying, Light in August, Absalom, Absalom!,* and *Go Down, Moses.* Quite simply, it having always been my purpose to apply a psychoanalytic method to Faulkner's major novels, I analyzed these five because, in my estimation, these are Faulkner's greatest novels. Obviously, this is a subjective judgment. There is, however, wide agreement among Faulkner scholars that the period of Faulkner's greatness begins in 1929 with *The Sound and the Fury* and ends in 1942 with *Go Down, Moses*. Of course, this generalization, too, is debatable, but I am convinced that before 1929 Faulkner was an apprentice writer and that after 1942 Faulkner was a writer in decline; for this reason, I begin my study with the luminous *The Sound and the Fury*, the novel Faulkner "felt tenderest toward"[18] and close with *Go Down, Moses*, the novel that Karl Zender claims is about "a diminishment in Faulkner's creative drive."[19] As I have argued in *Faulkner's Changing Vision*, I find a gradually developing line of questioning in the novels between 1929 and 1942.

Of course, between *The Sound and the Fury* and *Go Down, Moses*, Faulkner wrote eight novels, *As I Lay Dying* (1930), *Sanctuary* (1931), *Light in August* (1932), *Pylon* (1935), *Absalom, Absalom!* (1936), *The Unvanquished* (1938), *The Wild Palms* (1939), and *The Hamlet* (1940). Since, of these eight, I have elected to analyze only three, the question arises: why these three? For purely practical considerations, I could not analyze all ten novels, and some principal of selection needed to be applied. I chose to analyze the novels that seem to me most powerful, most profoundly moving, and most abundant in psychological meanings. To avoid misunderstanding, I should also add that I do not mean to say that Faulkner's other novels are devoid of psychological meanings. In my view, all of Faulkner's novels are immensely rich in psychoanalytic implications, and they are all amenable to a psychoanalytic interpretation. For example, in the first chapter of *Sanctuary*, Popeye, whom Horace sees as his reflected image, seems to represent a disguised return of a repressed desire for the missing phallic signifier; in *The Unvanquished*, Bayard Sartoris's refusal to kill his father's killer arguably signifies a rejection of phallic desire; in *The Wild Palms*, Harry's and Charlotte's attempt to give up the world for love can be read as an expression of a desire to return to a former mother-child dyadic unity, a dyad that is transformed into the triad of the mother-father-child symbolic relation when Charlotte becomes pregnant. I could cite other illustrations, but I think that these examples are sufficient to demonstrate that all of Faulkner's novels can be read fruitfully through psychoanalytic frames.

CHAPTER SYNOPSIS

Thus far I have dealt with overarching issues of the purpose and methodology of *Faulkner: The Return of the Repressed*. In concluding,

I turn now to a more specific description of the contents of each of the chapters in the book. In the introduction, I attempt to provide a clear and readable account of Lacan's narrative of identity. I lay out the essential steps in the constitution of subjectivity, and I define key Lacanian concepts: the imaginary, the symbolic, the Real, the mirror stage, the other, the Other, the phallus, symbolic castration, *objet petit a*, and other such terms. I attempt to show that, for Lacan, there is one moment that matters—the moment when an imaginary unity identified with the mother is surrendered, and a metaphoric substitution takes place as "the prohibition of the father takes up the place originally figured by the absence of the mother."[20] I argue that the traumatic entry into language and identity creates a conflict within the subject between Desire and Law, or, in Freudian terminology, between Eros and Thanatos. The myriad representations of aspects of this central trauma in Faulkner's major novels are examined in chapters 1 through 5; in the introduction, I focus on Faulkner's biography and trace reflections of this dialectical tension in Faulkner's life.

In chapter 1, " 'The Beautiful One' in *The Sound and the Fury*," I begin with Faulkner's stunning pronouncement that *The Sound and the Fury* originated in a sense of loss and that he created Caddy Compson to replace two female absences: the sister he never had and the daughter he was fated to lose in infancy. In Lacanian terms, Faulkner's statement can be interpreted to mean that Caddy Compson functions as a substitute to cover over or sign the lack incurred at the constitution of subjectivity. I read Faulkner's admission in light of the work of feminist Lacanian revisionists, particularly Jane Gallop, who contend that the male's own sense of lack as a subject alienated in language is projected onto women, and I propose that Caddy Compson evokes for her brothers a sense of their loss of the mythical phallus that might reconnect them with the lost first other.

In chapter 2, "The Displaced Mother: *As I Lay Dying*," I propose that the Bundren family's journey to bury Addie in Jefferson represents the passage from the imaginary to the symbolic plane. Town, Jefferson, emblemizes the symbolic order, the register of language and social exchange. The burial of Addie's body ritually reenacts the disruption of the mother-child symbiotic relation in the imaginary, a disruption that accompanies and makes possible the entry into the symbolic. Ceaselessly in *As I Lay Dying*, Addie Bundren is renounced and the resulting absence is covered over with a sign—what Lacan calls *objet petit a*.

xvii

In my reading, Faulkner's novels before 1932 focus on women as representatives of a forbidden former imaginary unity. Beginning with *Light in August* and continuing in subsequent novels, Faulkner explores how the racial other, like the female other, is identified with the totalizing images of the imaginary. In chapter 3, "Law and Desire in *Light in August*," I argue that Joe Christmas's racial indeterminacy (Joe does not know if he is black or white) becomes a symbol for the indeterminacy of the preoedipal stage, when child and mother are a sealed circuit. Joe is a man in the middle. He refuses to internalize the Law of the Father and submit to symbolic castration; as a result, he is not fully assimilated into the symbolic and remains enmeshed in the imaginary.

In chapter 4, "Reading for the Repressed: *Absalom, Absalom!*" I propose that Charles Bon represents a forbidden libidinal relation with the mother and that, for this reason, he must be repressed. Further, I contend that Bon is not only stopped from entering Sutpen's house; he is excluded as well at the level of narration. Miss Rosa, Mr. Compson, and, for a time, Quentin and Shreve also conspire to murder Bon by refusing to read his meaning. But repressed meanings always return—"repressed, it reappears," Lacan writes[21]—and, throughout the three narrations, Charles Bon's meaning returns in disguised forms.

In chapter 5, "Renouncing the Phallus in *Go Down, Moses*," I interpret Ike McCaslin's renunciation of his patrimony, which was prefigured by his refusal to kill the old bear, Old Ben, as a figuration of his renunciation of the missing phallus, the object of desire. While Ike submits to the Law of the Father and accepts the loss of the symbolic phallus, the copula that might connect him with the lost first other, he also finds in the wilderness a substitute for the forbidden maternal relation. The wilderness, for Ike and Sam Fathers, is a disguised figure for the lost m(other), and as long as this meaning is concealed, Ike can ritually reenact a return to a former imaginary wholeness by returning each year to his beloved wilderness.

Finally, in a brief epilogue, I address the issue of the social application of Lacan's seemingly recondite theory. Whereas previously I had used Lacan to interpret Faulkner, in the epilogue I use Faulkner to interpret Lacan. Specifically, I turn once again to Faulkner's immensely rich novel *Light in August* and use the case history of Joe Christmas to lay open the social implications of Lacan's central contention that men and women make themselves in culture through language.

This preface has been largely devoted to a defense of my use of Lacanian theory. Since Lacan is such a controversial and misunderstood theorist, I judged it necessary to explain at some length my turn to Lacan. This emphasis on Lacan in these prefatory remarks, however, may foster the misimpression that my book focuses on Lacan. Let me be absolutely clear on this point: the subject of my book is Faulkner, and, as I have stated previously, I use Lacan only as a tool to help me uncover disguised or residual meanings in Faulkner's texts. Throughout the book, I attempt to foreground Faulkner's texts and to subordinate the theoretical apparatus. Of course, because Lacan's sibylline prose requires explanation, a Lacanian approach always threatens to become itself the subject of analysis. In writing this book, I have been acutely aware of this danger and have worked to avoid what Shoshana Felman calls the "subordination" of the literary text to the higher authority of theory.[22]

No one writes alone, and I owe a great debt to the Faulkner scholars who have preceded me, whose work has made possible this study. In the acknowledgments section of the book, I single out for special recognition scholars whose work intersects with my own project; however, I am indebted as well to countless other readings of Faulkner's works. These "others" also have helped me to construct my interpretation. My one reading of Faulkner is of course exactly that: *one* reading of Faulkner. It is meant to supplement, not supplant, other readings of Faulkner's fiction. In making a case for one way of interpreting Faulkner's novels, inevitably one excludes other possibilities. Ultimately clarity depends on repression. But, as I stated at the outset of these remarks, the other that is excluded to establish meaning, because it is constitutive of meaning, still inheres within a meaning; thus I owe a debt to related and alternative interpretations of Faulkner's novels, and my end notes reflect this indebtedness.

In his preface to *The Ink of Melancholy,* André Bleikasten wisely writes: "Faulkner's work always outraces what might be said about it."[23] With this book, I hope to run a good race and pass the baton to the next runner. My work, I hope, will add to Faulkner scholarship and will help others to see yet other meanings in Faulkner's texts, for his novels will ceaselessly provide grounds for new interpretations.

Acknowledgments

Over the years this book has been in the making, I have incurred a large indebtedness, and I am happy to acknowledge it. As noted in the preface, my book owes a debt to Faulkner scholarship generally, but three texts in particular deserve special mention: John T. Irwin's *Doubling and Incest/Repetition and Revenge,* a brilliant analysis of oedipal relations in Faulkner; John T. Matthews's *The Play of Faulkner's Language,* a sensitive examination of the relationship of language and desire in Faulkner; and André Bleikasten's *The Ink of Melancholy,* a dazzling close reading of Faulkner's texts threaded with relevant insights into history, biography, psychoanalysis, and philosophy. I would also like to single out for special acknowledgments David Galef, Donald M. Kartiganer, and James M. Mellard, all of whom generously and tirelessly supported this project by reading chapter after chapter and making many valuable suggestions. I am grateful as well to the many colleagues who have read or have heard read parts of this book and have offered me advice and encouragement. These include: Jack Barbera, Deborah Barker, André Bleikasten, Robert Brinkmeyer, Deborah Clarke, Philip Cohen, Susan Donaldson, Barbara Ewell, Ann Fisher-Wirth, Alan Golding, Minrose C. Gwin, John T. Irwin, Anne Goodwyn Jones, Ivo Kamps, Richard King, John T. Matthews, David Minter, Alice Petry, Carolyn Porter, Gregory Schirmer, James A. Snead, Jay Watson, Philip Weinstein, and Karl Zender.

The support of the University of Mississippi made it possible for me to bring this book to completion. For summer grants, I am grateful to the Ole Miss English Department and the Graduate School; for a much-needed sabbatical, I gratefully acknowledge the university.

Parts of this work have been previously published. An early version of chapter 1 was presented at the 1991 Faulkner and Yoknapatawpha conference and subsequently published in *Faulkner and Psychology,* edited by Donald M. Kartiganer and Ann J. Abadie (University Press of Mississippi, 1994); and an early draft of chapter 2 was published in the

xxi

Faulkner Journal 4, nos. 1 and 2 (fall 1988 and spring 1989): 113–25. In altered forms, two sections from chapter 3 have appeared, respectively, in the *Faulkner Journal* 9, nos. 1 and 2 (fall 1993 and spring 1994): 139–48; and 10, nos. 1 and 2 (fall 1994 and spring 1995): 55–64. I thank the editors for supporting my work.

Finally, my greatest debt is to my family, to my mother, Mildred Ferlaino, and to my father, John C. Ferlaino, who did not live to see this work completed but who lives in my thoughts, and to Steve and Carina. You anchor me in the world and make it possible for me to write.

Faulkner

THE RETURN OF THE REPRESSED

INTRODUCTION

Faulkner's "Heart in Conflict"

I don't know what I am. I don't know if I am or not.
Jewel knows he is, because he does not know that
he does not know whether he is or not.
—William Faulkner, *As I Lay Dying*

I think where I am not, therefore I am where I do not think.
—Jacques Lacan

*F*aulkner longed for public recognition; at the same time, however, he yearned to keep Faulkner, the man, hidden from the eyes of the world. His frequent declarations of this need for privacy were vehement, even strident: "It is my ambition to be, as a private individual, abolished and voided from history, leaving it markless, no refuse save the printed books; I wish I had had enough sense to see ahead thirty years ago and, like some of the Elizabethans, not signed them. It is my aim, and every effort bent, that the sum and history of my life, which in the same sentence is my obit and epitaph too, shall be them both: he made the books and he died."[1] Moreover, this guardedness about his private life was not limited to the prying eyes of strangers; it extended to close friends and even to family members. All his life, Faulkner engaged in practices that made him elusive even to those presumably closest to him. To avoid exposure, he wore masks, adopted personae, and told lies. Faulkner's well-known fondness for rituals, ceremonies, and traditions was yet another way of distancing others. As David Minter has convincingly argued, Faulkner formalized and stylized his relations with others with the purpose of making intimacy impossible. This yearning to hide his true self from the world also explains his somewhat curious penchant for costumes. Faulkner might dress elegantly or like a vagabond. After World War I he strutted about in his RAF uniform; he specially ordered and wore a pink riding habit; and

I

he insisted that Random House buy for him the tuxedo he wore to the Nobel Prize ceremony. Such costumes served as protective cover. As with costumes, Faulkner also wore personae, fictional characters, behind which he could hide. Thus, when Faulkner, who had not seen any military action in World War I, presented himself as a wounded veteran with a plate in his head, he was posing as a wounded flier. His frequent protestation that he was nothing more than a simple farmer was another pose.[2]

Faulkner not only engaged in strategies to keep the world from knowing him, he also displayed a reluctance to reveal the sources and origins of his fiction. He kept no journals or notebooks, and in interviews he seemed to employ a number of devices designed to allow him to avoid "explaining" the meaning of his work. He sometimes would be provoked by questions; and more oddly, he sometimes gave what appear to be misleading or false answers to questions about his work.[3] He also resisted writing introductions to his novels. He refused, for example, Random House's request for an introduction to the Modern Library volume containing *The Sound and the Fury* and *As I Lay Dying;* and, after writing an introduction to *The Sound and the Fury* in 1933, he sought to suppress it by burning what he believed to be the only existing copy.[4]

Michael Grimwood, who has discussed at length Faulkner's propensity to use fictional personae, interprets this role playing as a confession of literary fraudulence. Grimwood argues that Faulkner—a Mississippi native, who by his own account was "uneducated in every formal sense, without even very literate, let alone literary companions"[5]—was never confident of his literary identity and that his poses reflect his sense of inauthenticity as a man of letters. While I would agree with Grimwood that Faulkner's proliferation of fictional selves registers a sense of being "double," a feeling of "radical discontinuity," I cannot agree when Grimwood attributes this feeling of disjunction to a chasm between Faulkner, the artist, and Faulkner, the product of backwoods Mississippi.[6] After all, as Grimwood himself acknowledges, Faulkner's self-deprecating references to himself as an ignorant farmer marked just another ruse, as false as any of the others. Grimwood is right, I think, when he says that Faulkner's role playing expresses his feeling of being a sham, but I would argue that this feeling of fraudulence was not triggered by Faulkner's rearing in a small town in north Mississippi. Rather, I contend that Faulkner's disguises reflect a deeper disjunction, a psychic disjunction that is universally experienced and universally repressed. His disguises register a sense of the self as split, a sense that the self that speaks is a fiction, and this notion—that the speaking subject is a fiction—is the central tenet of Lacanian theory. Thus, Faulkner's compulsive urge to create impostures can be read in terms of Lacanian theory as a representation of Lacan's fraudulent subject, the subject who is what she (or he) is not.

Faulkner's inclination to cultivate guises has been astutely analyzed by David Minter, too. Minter makes no reference to Lacan or to psychoanalytic theory, but interestingly his interpretation of Faulkner's need for masks also points to the divided subject of contemporary psychoanalytic theory, particularly Lacanian theory. In his impressive biography of Faulkner, Minter attributes Faulkner's need to create poses to an early painful childhood experience:

> Since the implications of Faulkner's kind of cautious variety are subtle and diverse, we must come to them slowly, but both his need and his capacity for such variety can be located. During his earliest years he experienced an unusually strong sense of holistic unity with his family, and especially with his mother. From these years, he gathered a sense of his world as blessed and of himself as virtually omnipotent. Although he suffered no great trauma, he lost this double sense of well-being at an early age and he found the experience painful. Troubled in part by the loss itself and in part by the feeling that those who had bequeathed blessedness had also destroyed it, he emerged from childhood determined to control his relations to his world.[7]

Minter's description of Faulkner's individual experience of loss reformulates the primal experience that, according to recent psychoanalytic theories, originates all identity, consciousness, and culture.

A similar generic or archetypal pattern of the development of human identity is the basic premise of theorists from Freud to Jung to Erich Neumann to Lacan. For example, in *The Origins and History of Consciousness*, Neumann attempts to trace the evolution of human consciousness by examining mythic representations of the ego's origins and development. Neumann maintains that all myths narrate the ego's attempt to distinguish the self by creating boundaries between itself and the natural world and by rejecting its original condition of existence in nature, one with the material world. According to Neumann, this original condition is identified with the mother, because the maternal womb is perceived as the origin of life and the fetus's fused relationship with the womb is analogous to the ego's primal relationship to the natural world. In myth, according to Neumann, the psychic repression of this early fused state is represented by the killing of the mother.

The experience Neumann identifies as defining selfhood in mythic narratives, a break with the mother and the world, is also the defining moment in Minter's narrative of Faulkner's childhood. According to Minter, Faulkner experienced a painful loss in childhood: he lost "a strong sense of holistic unity with his family and especially with his mother." The sense of loss that Minter identifies in Faulkner's individual experience is, according to Lacanian theory, the common experience of all human beings. Loss is the price we pay for being human. According to Lacan's theory of subjectivity, only with the loss of a primal unity and wholeness can we become an I separate from the other: in other words, a break or loss creates the self. Arguably, it is this vacuum or loss at the core of being that Faulkner is attempting to represent, or signify, with disguised representations in both his art and his life. Faulkner may be alluding to this generic sense of loss when he mused aloud to Joan Williams: "Maybe I wrote because I wasn't as tall or as strong as I wanted to be."[8] This remark can be read to mean that by writing he satisfied a deep need to compensate for, or cover over, a primal lack. Similarly, Faulkner may have also obliquely alluded to the hidden psychic origin of his art when he wrote to Malcolm Cowley: "I am telling the same story over and over which is myself and the world."[9] Given that there are few one-to-one correspondences between Faulkner's life and his novels, his comment might seem almost disingenuous, but perhaps he means that his fiction attempted to map the ever-precarious relationship between consciousness and the encroaching material world.

Other signs also point to a remarkable congruence between Freudian and post-Freudian thought and Faulkner's art. For example, both Freud and Lacan hold that repressed material always returns. In his famous essay "Repression" (1915), Freud reasons that repression, by its very nature, leads to exactly what repression was meant to prevent—the return of the repressed: "repression itself . . . produces substitutive formations and symptoms, . . . indications of a return of the repressed." Echoing Freud, Lacan states flatly, "repressed, it reappears,"[10] by which he means that by virtue of being repressed, a meaning always returns; it returns in a disguised form, so as to avoid conscious censors, and surfaces in dreams, in slips of the tongue, and in art.

Although Faulkner seems to have had no formal knowledge of psychoanalytic theory, nevertheless, his statements about the nature of his art seem almost to reformulate in alternative terms the Freudian and Lacanian position that meanings that have been relegated to the unconscious return in art. For example, in the course of conversation with Malcolm Cowley, he uttered perhaps his most revealing statement about the psychic origins of his fiction: "I listen to the voices, and when I put down what the voices say, it's right. Sometimes I don't like what they say, but I don't change it."[11] With these words, Faulkner very nearly admits that unconscious meanings return in his texts. Surely the "voices" that Faulkner heard could only be the voice of the unconscious mind, the voice that most of us tune out. Similarly, Faulkner's admission that the artist is "a creature driven by demons"[12] also seems to point to the psychogenesis of Faulkner's art. Faulkner's demonic image is redolent with meaning: it is a way of naming a forbidden desire to represence the repressed. According to Freud, people who appear to be obsessed by demons are actually exhibiting the repetition compulsion: "in normal persons, [the repetition compulsion] gives the impression of a pursuing fate, a daemonic trait in their destiny." Demonic possession, then, is a disguised image out of the unconscious, an image for an ungovernable urge to repeat "as current experience what is repressed;"[13] and Faulkner's image of the writer as "demon-driven" seems covertly to reflect a feeling that the writer is gripped by unconscious forces and that the writer's text is the site of a disguised return of denied desires.

As the foregoing discussion attempts to point out, both Faulkner's statements about the nature of his art and his apparently tenuous sense of self seem remarkably consistent with the tenets of contemporary psychoanalytic theory—in particular, with Jacques Lacan's reinterpretation of Freudian psychology. To avoid misunderstanding, I should perhaps clearly state at the outset that it is decidedly not my purpose to argue that Lacan "influenced" Faulkner. Faulkner almost certainly did not know the work of Jacques Lacan. Lacan's theories were not widely disseminated in the United States until the publication of *Écrits* in 1966, four years after the death of William Faulkner. It would be surprising if Faulkner had even heard of Lacan. But, as Faulkner himself acknowledged, a writer does not have to have a formal knowledge of a theory for meanings that are interpretable by that theory to figure in his work. Faulkner was explicit in this regard. When asked if Freud's work had influenced his own, he stated flatly, "Freud I'm not familiar with"; at the same time, however, he acknowledged that his texts could be interpreted in terms of Freudian theory: "a writer don't have to know Freud to have written things which anyone who does know Freud can divine and reduce into symbols. And so when the critic finds those symbols, they are of course there. But they were there as inevitably as the critic should stumble on his own knowledge of Freud to discern symbol" [sic].[14] In making this pronouncement, Faulkner is in fundamental agreement with Freud, who frequently reiterated the dictum that poets often "discover" what philosophers and others come to theorize about many years later. Indeed, Susan Stanford Friedman observes that "poststructuralist theory is, in the eyes of many, an extension into philosophy, psychoanalysis, and linguistics of what writers such as Gertrude Stein and Joyce forged in literary discourse."[15] I would add William Faulkner to this list of "prophetic" writers. The post-Cartesian self forever split from knowledge of itself is the subject of both Lacan's theory of the unconscious and of Faulkner's luminous novels. In a sense, Faulkner and Lacan use different methods—one the method of fictional representation, the other of theoretical discourse—to represent a human subject that acquires identity only by virtue of loss.

LACAN'S NARRATIVE OF SUBJECTIVITY

The point of origin, for Lacan, is the imaginary. The imaginary, or preoedipal phase, refers to the condition of the infant prior to symbolization and alienation. Lacan's discussion of the imaginary, writes James M. Mellard, creates a picture of a "plane of immediacy of lived experiences involving the body and affects."[16] Thus, for example, Lacan proclaims that the imaginary "is half-rooted in the natural"[17] and that "the libidinal drive is centered on the function of the imaginary."[18] In this early state of being, the infant exists in an amorphous state, a congeries of parts, that Lacan punningly refers to as l'hommelette (*homme-lette*, "little man"; *omelette*, "shapeless mass of egg.")[19] It is difficult to speak of the imaginary, for the imaginary precedes language and conceptualization; and, for the most part, we have to describe the imaginary in terms of what it is not. The key point that emerges from Lacan's

6

discussion of the imaginary, however, is that, in this early register of being, there is no self and no other and that the two concepts, as Lacan is at pains to show in "Of Structure and Inmixing," come into existence together. In the imaginary stage, the child is, according to Mellard, "an uncognized, material, somatic existence in which, Lacan theorizes, all objects appear to belong to the same object—the baby's or the mother's body."[20] In other words, in this early phase there are only two—the child and the mother—and these two form a single dyad. The child exists as a part of one continuous totality of being. Because of this unbroken mother-child circuit, feminists often describe the imaginary as a blissful state of plenitude. Thus Toril Moi writes that in the imaginary "there is no difference and no absence, only identity and presence."[21] But it should be remembered that there is a price to pay for merging. Because there is no difference in the imaginary, no separation or distance or lack, there is no self. Thus it is possible to read the imaginary in two ways. At one level, the infant in the imaginary possesses no identity; that is, the child has no sense of separate, individual identity, and does not exist as a subject.[22] At another level, however, it is possible to say that the infant possesses completeness of being (although not identity, in the sense that we understand identity) precisely because the child perceives no lack of any kind.

For Lacan, there are two crucial moments in the development of human subjectivity. One is the mirror phase, and the other is the oedipal complex. In the mirror phase, the next stage of development in Lacan's narrative of the self, the infant, who still exists in the imaginary plane, begins to have an incipient sense of self. The mirror phase, while a function of the imaginary, is a step in the transition from imaginary to the symbolic register of being. While still identifying with the mother, the child begins the process of constructing an I. Indeed, we may say that in the mirror phase it is by identifying with the mother that the child locates a self. The mother is the mirror or identificatory imago in which the child finds a reflection of an integrated self-image. Richard Boothby specifies the salutary functions of the identificatory imago: "The imago of the fellow human being functions to provide coordination in the midst of the infant's internal anarchy, to produce homogeneity out of an original heterogeneity, to establish organization in the field of primal discord."[23] It should be remembered that Lacan stresses that at this early stage a blurring of self and mother, subject and object, still obtains. Thus Lacan writes: "We have only to understand

7

the mirror stage *as an identification,* in the full sense that analysis gives to the term; namely, the transformation that takes place in the subject when he assumes an image."[24] Alternately stated, the subjectivity that emerges in the mirror phase is organized strictly within the register of the imaginary.

However, at the same time as the mirror phase takes place within the imaginary register, the mirror imago is also, Lacan states, "a homologue for the Mother/Child symbolic relation."[25] Essentially, the mirror phase anticipates the identity based on alienation of the postoedipal phase because the identity of the *je* (a term Lacan uses to refer to the I of the symbolic order) is founded on something external to the self. Similarly, the identity of the *moi* (a term Lacan uses to refer to the I of the mirror stage) depends on the image of a being outself itself. The mirror stage *moi,* then, prefigures the symbolic *je,* but with a difference, for while selfhood in the mirror stage is mirrored back by some object or person in the world, this object, the mother, is simultaneously outside of the child and not outside of the child. As Eagleton explains, the identificatory imago "is at once somehow part of ourselves—we *identify* with it—and yet not ourselves, something alien."[26]

In the imaginary phase, there are only two terms: the child and the other body, which is usually the mother, and the relation between them is dyadic. But this dyadic structure must give way to a triadic one, and this happens when the father, or someone who represents this role, disrupts the mother-child dyad. This disruption of imaginary unity is the way that Lacan recasts Freud's oedipal complex, and for Lacan, as for Freud, the oedipal passage is the defining moment in the story of the emerging human subject. Ellie Ragland-Sullivan cogently describes Lacan's reinterpretation of Freud's oedipal paradigm: "Freud defined the Oedipus complex as the organized ensemble of loving and hostile desires felt by the child toward her or his parents. This has been recast by Lacan to account for the evolution that, little by little, substitutes the father for the mother."[27]

Before Lacan, psychoanalysis concentrated on the mother-child relation. Lacan's revolution was to rewrite psychoanalysis so as also to emphasize the role of the symbolic, which is identified with paternal law.[28] The centerpiece of Lacan's narrative of the development of subjectivity is a moment of rupture, and this moment, which introduces the child into the symbolic order in which every individual subject must take up his or her place, is Lacan's version of Freud's oedipal crisis. The

8

rupture occurs with the intervention of a third term, the father or paternal metaphor, into the mother-child symbiotic relation. With the appearance of the father, the child is ushered into the symbolic order; that is, into a sign system that is based on difference and absence. For the child to acquire language, to acquire a separate identity, the child must become aware of difference. Identity and meaning come about only as a result of difference, only by exclusion, since, as Ferdinand de Saussure first pointed out, a sign's meaning depends solely on its difference from other signs. The father represents difference: he is sexually different from the mother. The father also ordains difference by decreeing the separation of the child from the maternal body: he prohibits the merging of mother and child. It is at this moment, the pivotal moment in the constitution of the self, that the child, in obedience to the Law of the Father, performs a symbolic self-castration. Under the threat of castration, the child renounces the maternal connection, and a gap, or *béance,* opens up. This gap is the distance between subject and object, between signifier and sign. It is this absence, the absence of the mother, that makes identity and subjectivity possible.[29]

The moment of splitting is also the moment of primary repression. Eagleton writes that "the first appearance of the Law, and the opening up of unconscious desire, occur at the same moment." More, Eagleton explains that the guilty desire for a lost totality "just *is* what is called the unconscious."[30] Prohibition forces underground a desire for a return of the lost being, a desire for a return to the origin. This desire is what Lacan calls the desire of the Other. Lacan defines the Other as the site of the constitution of the self, the always posited but never grasped original signifier of being; "the Other," Lacan writes, "is thus the place where is constituted the 'je' which speaks with the one who listens."[31] Lacan pointedly distinguishes between the Other (*Autre*) with a capital *O* and the other with a small *o*. The other that is designated with the lowercase *o* originates with the mother, the first figure in whom the subject identifies itself, as well as the first from which it splits off. The use of the same word, changed only by the use of the upper- and lowercase first letter, calls attention to the metonymic substitution that takes place in the oedipal moment. As the mother is excluded, (made other), an Other, the father as imagined originator of being, is substituted for her and becomes the object of desire: "Man's desire," Lacan writes, "is the desire of the Other." The desire for the mother, however, is never totally excluded, only repressed and re-articulated, for the desire of the Other is also the desire to be what the mother desires; that is, to possess the phallus, which is the desire of all lacking subjects. Thus Lacan writes that "the desire of the mother is the phallus, and the child wishes to be the phallus in order to satisfy that desire."[32]

My account of Lacan's theory of subjectivity has heretofore made no mention of the phallus. The omission has been deliberate. The phallus is one of the more difficult concepts in Lacanian theory. Confusion about this concept persists because the term exists in the language and carries meanings that Lacan does *not* mean. Jane Gallop discusses this confusion. She notes that, in language, the phallus is commonly confused with the penis and cites as an example a definition of the phallus as "virile member."[33] But Lacan expressly distinguishes the phallus from the penis. He writes that "the phallus in Freudian doctrine is not a fantasy. . . . Nor is it as such an object. . . . It is even less the organ, penis or clitoris, which it symbolizes." Despite Lacan's explicit declaration that the phallus is not the penis, because of the phallus's imagined function—that is, because we imagine it can reconnect us with the lost mother—the phallus inevitably is confused with the penis. But the phallus decidedly is not a physical organ. Rather, as Lacan clearly states, "the phallus is a signifier." Thus the phallus is merely a symbol, but, Lacan tells us, it is a "privileged signifier" because it signifies loss of being and, paradoxically, the hope of a return of that lost being.[34]

The phallus, in Lacan's lexicon, is identified with the paternal signifier. For instance, James Mellard defines the phallus as "the symbol of the authority Lacan assigns to the concept of Law and localizes in the Name-of-the-Father."[35] The phallus, then, at one level, is a way of naming the paternal function; namely, the separation of mother and child. This identification of the phallus with the paternal role further fosters the misimpression that that phallus is a synonym for the penis, and this false identification would seem to "naturalize" authority in the male body; therefore, it needs to be pointed out that the authority associated with the paternal signifier is lacking equally to all subjects—male and female. Juliet Mitchell helpfully describes the phallus as "the necessarily *missing* object of desire at the level of sexual division," and Jane Gallop insists that all subjects lack the phallus as the price of human subjectivity: "The phallus, unlike the penis, is lacking to any subject, male or female. The phallus symbolizing unmediated, full *jouissance* must be lacking for any subject to enter the symbolic order, that is to enter language, effective intersubjectivity."[36]

The phallus, then, is the lost object and the object of all desire. It refers to what was lost at the moment of the constitution of the self at the behest of the Law of the Father, and we identify it with that seemingly powerful Law that decreed lack and that, we imagine, could also confer completeness of being. Jonathan Scott Lee defines the phallus as "the imaginary object of the Other's (and the mother's) desire, that extraordinary object that fully satisfies all possible desire." But, as Rose observes, "this is the ultimate fantasy." The phallus cannot guarantee our being; it cannot make good our loss. The phallus represents the moment of symbolization; in fact, Rose defines the phallus as a symbol "for the moment of rupture." That rupture, which opened up a space for the sign to have meaning, heralded our entry into the symbolic order, the world of social ordering. In this sense, the phallus, which stands for that pivotal moment, created us as human subjects, but the price of subjectivity is loss. In the words of Rose, that moment, that place "is both constitutive and empty."[37] There can be no identity and wholeness precisely because identity in the symbolic order depends on absence.

At the moment of the constitution of the self, we entered into the world of language, and language works by absence. As Eagleton explains, "Words have meanings only by virtue of the absence and exclusion of others."[38] More specifically, a sign has meaning only by excluding all other meanings and assigning to it a single meaning. Thus, for example, A is not $B, C,$ or any other letter. Words only point to other words within a signifying chain, and their meaning is arbitrarily fixed. In the symbolic order, then, we exist not within a world of stable meanings, but within a world of signifiers that take up their meaning not by any external token, any signifier outside the chain, but only by their relationship to other signs and by social agreement. There is no phallic signifier that stands outside this artificial ordering and imbues the chain with meaning.

According to Lacan, at the moment of symbolization, the moment we submit to the Law that decrees lack, we enter the symbolic order and become human: "If one has to define the moment at which man becomes human, we can say that it is the moment when, however little it be, he enters into the symbolic relation."[39] Human subjectivity, then, is predicated upon privation, and what we lack is the presumptive unity with the mother of the imaginary stage. At the moment of alienation, the mother becomes the first other (to be followed by the colonized other, the racial other, and so on), and it is this otherness that allows for boundaries and identity. Following this moment, the newly articulated subject enters a world of substitution; we supply signifiers for what has been displaced. These substitutes Lacan calls *objets petit a*, with *a* here standing for *autre* (the other) with a lowercase *a*. Thus *objet petit a* is obviously meant to contrast with capital *A, l'Autre,* French for the Other. (And indeed Lacan has even instructed his translators not to translate this phrase, as though it was an algebraic formula.)[40] But *objet petit a* is not so much a signifier for the mother as it is a symbol for the mastery of her loss, as Lacan indicates by drawing a parallel between Freud's grandson's *Fort-Da* game and *objet petit a*. Lacan specifically compares the reel that Freud's grandson repeatedly throws away and retrieves to the *objet petit a*. He writes that the reel "is not the mother reduced to a little ball . . . it is a small part of the subject that detaches itself from him while still remaining his, still retained . . . . To this object we will later give the name it bears in the Lacanian algebra—the *petit a*." The reel is an example of *objet petit a*. It is a substitute formation that originates in loss but signifies the mastery of loss. With the retrieved reel, the child is not symbolizing his mother's return so much as he is signaling his own power to expel and recall her.[41]

Loss, however, can never be mastered. We can never lay claim to the mythical phallus. We can never assume the dominant position with relation to the mother that we attribute to the father-become-Father. That position is forbidden by the Law of the Father, the Law that both confers identity even as it decrees lack. This is the fundamental dilemma of human subjectivity. Rose articulates the dilemma this way: " 'having' only functions at the price of a loss and 'being' as an effect of division." The subject that emerges from the oedipal moment is hollowed out; this subject, writes Boothby, is not so much a being as a *"manque à être,* a want of being."[42] In other words, loss is the condition of human subjectivity. Indeed, to describe the extremity of the loss suffered by the I in the oedipal moment, Lacan even uses the term *castration*—a term Gallop calls "phallic," "sexually unreasonable," and "unbalanced." And it is Lacan's use of this term for the condition of the postoedipal subject that leads Gallop to state bluntly that "our human lot is castration."[43]

Lacan's theory of psychoanalysis offers no solution to this fundamental dilemma of human subjectivity. Juliet Mitchell writes that the problem is "insoluble," that "psycholanalysis cannot give the human subject that which it is its fate, as the condition of its subjecthood, to do without." Rather, Lacan's theory advocates that we learn to accept our ineluctable fate. "The ultimate Lacanian goal," Gallop explains, "is for the subject 'to assume his/her castration.' " Alternately stated, the subject must give up a vain pursuit of a mythical phallus and recognize that the Other to whom we look to constitute our identity is castrated as well. Jacqueline Rose characterizes the final goal of Lacanian psychoanalysis this way: "The subject has to recognize that there is desire, or lack in the place of the Other, that there is no ultimate certainty or truth, and that the status of the phallus is a fraud." Lacan's theory ultimately points to acceptance and the work of mourning. We must accept that the phallus is lost and that this loss is irretrievable; and, as Jonathan Scott Lee reminds us, we must mourn "not only the object lost but also the human condition of castration."[44]

Lacan's account of the constitution of subjectivity lays out almost the same narrative for males and females. He holds that prior to the moment of symbolization there is no difference. Gender difference, like all difference, arises at the moment of splitting; and, at that traumatic moment, culturally established roles are assigned to subjects on the basis of the presence or absence of the penis. We must be sure to note here that Lacan is *not* saying that gender roles originate in biology. Rather, as Rose stresses, for Lacan, gender "is something enjoined on the subject." The only meanings that we have access to are culturally produced; that is, the product of arbitrary associations between a meaning and a sign. So it is with gender identifications. The penis signifies insofar as a meaning is culturally assigned to it; that is, it symbolizes the phallus, which is itself another symbol. In other words, anatomical difference does not create gender difference, but anatomy is used to figure difference. Safouan makes this point when he writes that "anatomy is not destiny, but that does not mean that anatomy does not figure," and, quoting Safouan, Rose adds, "but it *only figures* (it is a sham)."[45] Thus anatomy is used by culture to assert an ordering, a hierarchy that subordinates female to male.

My discussion of Lacan's narrative of the emergence of human subjectivity is still not complete. There remains to be explained an important Lacanian concept, the Real. I have deliberately left the Real until last because it is arguably the most difficult of Lacanian concepts and because, in my opinion, we can only apprehend this concept when we have a firm grasp of the imaginary and symbolic registers of being. Lacanian commentators refer to the Real as "unspeakable" and "impossible." It is impossible and unspeakable because we exist as creatures of the symbolic, and the Real exists outside this register. "The Real," writes Madan Sarup, "is the domain that subsists outside symbolisation. It is what is outside the subject." This is the key point that Lacan stresses about the Real: it always eludes us. We can never approach the Real through our arbitrary system of signification. It is a realm, writes Mellard, "outside human control or being." The Real, then, is a mystery; it is what we cannot know with our system of signification. Mellard associates it with light and space, and Sarup relates it to "the dimension of sexuality and death." What is important about the Real is that it posits the possibility of meaning outside of the arbitrary cultural orderings of the symbolic order. This "real" meaning may be nothing more than the reality of brute existence and death or it may be the transcendental meaning that we so desperately desire (but it is not to be confused with the phallus, which, it must be remembered, is a symbol, a construct of the symbolic order). As creatures trapped in language, we cannot know; however, Lacan implies that the Real is implicated in the subject's encounter with death.[46]

READING FAULKNER'S BIOGRAPHY

According to Lacanian theory, every subject is a battleground. In the words of Jonathan Scott Lee, "That the human subject is essentially a place of conflict between the *je* and the *moi*, between the symbolic and the imaginary, will remain one of Lacan's central theses throughout his career." The subject, in Lacanian theory, is driven by competing desires for ego subjectivity in the symbolic and for the fantasy of completion in the imaginary. Because, as Toril Moi states, "the speaking subject is lack," the subject is driven by a desire to recover a former totality of being identified with the mother of the mirror stage.[47] At the same time, we are compelled by what Jane Gallop calls an "ethical imperative" to "break the mirror" and "to disrupt the imaginary in order to reach the symbolic." There is no resolution to this dilemma. To exist as subjects in the symbolic is to experience loss; the alternative, to remain in the imaginary, is, as Toril Moi points out, "equivalent to becoming psychotic and incapable of living in human society." Consequently, according to Lacan, every human subject is the site of a conflict between two drives, toward subjectivity and toward loss of subjectivity. It is to this conflict that Lacan alludes when he writes: "The ego is frustration in its essence."[48]

This conflict between Law and Desire, between Oedipus and Narcissus, Lacan contends, characterizes every human subject. For whatever reason, perhaps because of his artistic sensibility, in William Faulkner's life the signs of an epic struggle between contradictory impulses are strikingly evident. Faulkner seems to allude to these conflictual compulsions when he characterized himself as "a heart in conflict." Even a cursory reading of Faulkner's biography reveals a man at war with himself, and David Minter's perceptive biography of Faulkner stresses inner strife as a central theme of Faulkner's life: "All of his life, at least all of it that is recoverable, Faulkner was driven by conflicting urges: the urge to avoid life and the urge to explore it; the urge to disguise his thoughts and feelings in a thousand ways and the urge to disclose them in a single sentence. Out of this conflict, he fashioned a life of more than usual interest and an art of the rarest power."[49]

I propose to read Faulkner's deep ambivalences in terms of Lacan's reformulation of Freud's psychoanalytic theory. In attempting a psychoanalytic reading of Faulkner's often contrary behaviors, I do not mean to reduce Faulkner's life to a series of psychological frames; rather, by applying psychoanalytic principles, I hope to render meaningful what might otherwise appear meaningless. My project here is to read Faulkner's biography as a text side by side with Lacan's narrative of subjectivity. The point of such a reading is to offer one way—by no means the only way—to account for Faulkner's vacillations. In pursuing this speculative reading, certainly it is not my purpose to use Faulkner's life to "prove" Lacan's theory. First of all, a case study that takes as its subject only one person obviously proves nothing. But more important, talk of proof predicates a scientific methodology and a Western epistemological tradition that run counter to Lacan's thought. Underlying the notion of proof is the confidence that the human being is essentially a unified, autonomous subject and that human knowledge can be grounded in self-knowledge. Lacan's theory undermines such a confidence. Jonathan Scott Lee explains Lacan's move away from Cartesian rationalism: "In place of empirical science rooted in data whose certainty rests on the epistemological preeminence of the subject, Lacan offers us a vision of knowledge as caught up in an ever-changing dialectic between the data derived from a subject's experience and that subject's complexly mediated identity that shapes the very nature of the data."[50] In other words, the notion of proof posits a knowable world, a stable subject, and ultimate authority; and Lacan challenges all such notions. On the other hand, even as we post-structuralist critics acknowledge the instability of meaning and the impossibility of certainty, in accordance with the theories of Derrida and Lacan, it is nonetheless true that anyone who writes does so because of a sense that she or he has something worthwhile to say. As James Mellard wisely observes, "Any use of language involves the presumption of mastery," but given "our lack of signifying authority" we should "make our interpretive claims . . . in all humility."[51] Ultimately, the worth of any interpretive strategy should be judged on the basis of its explanatory power. In the following discussion of Faulkner's life story, I hope to show that Lacan's theory of the divided subject goes far toward explaining Faulkner's "heart in conflict." Looking specifically at his relationships with family members, his romantic attachments, his binge drinking, and his attitude toward death, I propose to demonstrate that Faulkner's life, like his art, reflects conflicting impulses that can be read in terms of a dialectical tension between desires for paternal interdiction and for maternal identification.[52]

To begin with, Faulkner's relationship with his mother shows signs of a deep-seated ambivalence. On the one hand, he appeared to be devoted to her. When he was in Oxford, he visited her every day and sometimes more than once a day. This was a private time set aside for just the two of them, and, accordingly, his wife Estelle never accompanied him on these visits.[53] Whenever he was away from Oxford, he wrote to his mother conscientiously, often two or three times a week. These letters are filled with terms of endearment that might seem more appropriate in a letter to a sweetheart.[54] This prolonged maternal attachment can be read in terms of a desire to reenact a mirror-stage identification with the mother. On the other hand, Faulkner also showed signs of an opposite desire—one to deny a maternal connection. For example, his frequently cited statement about robbing the mother during his interview with Jean Stein in 1955 seems an explicit rejection of the maternal tie: "If a writer has to rob his mother, he will not hesitate; the 'Ode on a Grecian Urn' is worth any number of old ladies."[55] While this remark seems to be Faulkner's clearest disavowal of a maternal bond, his hostile comments about marriage—although less obviously—have a similar intent. According to Nancy Chodorow, the wife is a substitute for a lost preoedipal attachment to a man's mother.[56] Thus, Faulkner's bitter remarks about wives suggest a disguised repudiation of the mother of the imaginary plane. Of these comments, perhaps the clearest expression of a deep resistance to identification with the mirror-stage imago is this reference to Hemingway's three marriages: "Poor bloke, to have to marry three times to find out that marriage is a failure, and the only way to get any peace out of it is (if you are fool enough to marry at all) keep the first one and stay as far away from her as much as you can, with the hope of some day outliving her. At least you will be safe then from any other one marrying you—which is bound to happen if you ever divorce her. Apparently man can be cured of drugs, drink, gambling, biting his nails and picking his nose, but not of marrying."[57] With statements like this, Faulkner voiced a desire for alienation even as his lament that men cannot "cure" themselves of marrying ruefully admits a conflicting desire. Such unconscious narcissistic yearnings for maternal identification, however, must be banished, because mirror-stage identifications pose the threat of reincorporation. This threat is perhaps most explicitly stated in Faulkner's second novel, *Mosquitoes,* when a character specifically links the maternal body to an obliteration of male identity: "She devours him during the act of conception" (320).[58] A fear of maternal identification also can explain much of Faulkner's enigmatic behavior. For example, his frequent refusal to attend school after the fourth grade may signify a desire to distance himself from his mother, who highly valued education, and to align himself with his father, who had been a poor student. A yearning to disavow a maternal relation may also have prompted his curious description of his childhood to Malcolm Cowley, an account that seems to have been formulated with the express purpose of erasing his mother's presence: "I more or less grew up in my father's livery stable. Being the eldest of four boys, I escaped my mother's influence pretty easy, since my father thought it was fine for me to apprentice to the business."[59] Also relevant here are Phil Stone's comments that all the Faulkner boys "were tied to their mother and resented it" and that Faulkner's devotion to his mother was at least partly responsible for "an animosity toward women" that Stone observed in Faulkner.[60] While Stone may not be an unbiased witness, since Susan Snell's biography of Stone reveals him to be a man given to inveighing often against his own mother,[61] nevertheless it is interesting to note that Stone identifies an animus against women in Faulkner and traces it to an overly close relationship with his mother.

Not only the mother, but also other female relatives evoke the mirror-stage double. The daughter or sister, like the mother, is a female relation, and this combination (female and relation) evokes a preoedipal indeterminacy. I will explain this more fully. Since male identity in the symbolic order depends on female otherness, a female must be other. So Lacan writes: "For the [male] soul to come into being, she, the woman, is differentiated from it . . . called woman and defamed." Clarifying Lacan's statement, Rose explains that woman must be "not" for man to exist: "The woman, therefore, is *not* because she is defined purely against the man (she is the negative of that definition—'man is *not* woman')."[62] A female, then, should be other, but a female relative is not other—she is related. In a sister or daughter, the male sees a reflection of himself. This relatedness to one who must be other recalls the identificatory imago of the mirror stage as well as a preoedipal dyadic unity before the intervention of the third term. Thus mother, daughter, and sister are all apt figures for the first denied other.

Faulkner's selection of the name Jill for his daughter suggests an identificatory relation with his daughter. On the surface, the name Jill seems an odd choice. Traditionally in the Faulkner family newborns were named after some family member, living or dead. For example, Faulkner had named his first daughter Alabama after his great-aunt. But he appeared to break with the family naming tradition when, naming the second daughter born to him and Estelle, he chose Jill—a name without an antecedent in either the Faulkner or Oldham family. I propose, however, that he did name his daughter after a family member—himself. The name Jill rhymes with Faulkner's first name, Bill; and in Mississippi twins are often given rhyming names. The choice of Jill's name signifies that Jill is Bill's double, his female twin. If Jill is understood in this way, then Faulkner's ambivalent attitude toward her can be explained. Jill identified this ambivalence when she revealed that she believed her father cared deeply for her but that "he would have walked on [her]" if she ever got in his way.[63] These conflictual feelings toward his daughter may have reflected his contradictory feelings toward the identificatory imago of the mirror-stage relation.

Similarly, Faulkner's ambivalent relationships with women, particularly with his wife and other lovers, also can be accounted for in terms

18

of conflicting desires toward the imaginary other. The women in Faulkner's life all share certain attributes that make them aptly suited to represent the lost mother of the preoedipal relation. For example, when Jill was questioned about her father's relationships with women, she implied that her father's pursuit of women was motivated by a desire to find a woman *like* his mother: "I think that probably Pappy's idea of women—ladies—always revolved a great deal around Granny. She was just a very determined, tiny old lady that Pappy adored. Pappy admired that so much in Granny and he didn't find it in my mother and I don't think he ever found it in anybody. I think that maybe all of these including my mother were just second place. It's difficult to say."[64] Jill's statement—that the women in Faulkner's life were "second place" to his mother and that his "idea of women . . . always revolved a great deal" around his mother—amounts to an admission that Faulkner sought out other women as mother-substitutes. With these relationships he sought to replace the maternal relation with a substitute relation. In this way, he would signify his desire for the imaginary unity of the preoedipal phase in a way compatible with the Law of the Father.

Such an interpretation would be consistent with Lacanian theory. According to Lacan, a son, having renounced the tie to the mother, represses his desire for the mother and seeks substitutes for her. Clarifying Lacan, Margaret Homans writes, "What the son searches for, in searching for substitutes for the mother's body, is a series of figures: someone *like* his mother." By looking for a substitute, the son satisfies his dual desire: he renounces the mother, as well as the lost referent with which she is primordially identified, but then seeks to cover over the gap with a figure, a substitute, someone like the mother. Terry Eagleton explains, "We are severed from the mother's body . . . . We will spend all of our lives hunting for it. We move among substitutes for substitutes, metaphors for metaphors, never able to recover the pure (if fictive) self-identity and self-completion which we knew in the imaginary." Similarly, Nancy Chodorow maintains that all adults "as a result of being parented by a woman . . . look for a return to this emotional and physical union." Chodorow notes, however, that men and women propose to satisfy this yearning for unity in widely divergent ways. Women attempt to reproduce this union by becoming mothers themselves, whereas men seek not to reproduce but to *represent* their lost preoedipal attachment to the mother by seeking substitutes in the heterosexual relationship.[65]

This unconscious urge to paper over the gap left by primary repression could explain Faulkner's series of relationships with women. Perhaps all of these women were, in the words of Addie Bundren, "a shape to fill a lack" (*AILD,* 158). For example, Estelle Oldham may well have appeared to Faulkner as a sister-figure, given their long childhood friendship. From 1903, when the Oldhams moved into a house on South Street not far from the Big Place, Faulkner's grandfather's house in Oxford, Estelle was Faulkner's childhood companion. During his youth he spent a great deal of time at the Oldham home with Estelle; in fact, he was so often there that Lem Oldham, Estelle's father, said Faulkner was like a son to him.[66] Moreover, when Faulkner married Estelle in 1929, she was the mother of two children by her first husband. As both a mother and sister-figure, Estelle was uniquely suited to represent the mother of the imaginary plane.

Similarly, all the other women in Faulkner's life seem like displaced mother-figures. In some way, each of these women resembled either a mother-, sister-, or daughter-figure. For instance, like his mother, all of the women with whom Faulkner formed attachments were small and had artistic aspirations. Helen Baird, whom he courted in 1925–26 before she married another in 1927, was tiny and a sculptress. But something else about her also deeply attracted Faulkner: she had a terrible scar on her body from a childhood burn.[67] In a complex way, Faulkner may have seen the scar as a sign of kinship. The scar may have identified her, in Faulkner's eyes, with a feeling of irremediable loss. It may have seemed like an outward sign of the psychic wound incurred when the subject is created as lack.

Like Helen Baird and Faulkner's mother, Maud, Meta Carpenter, whom Faulkner met in Hollywood in December of 1935, had artistic aspirations: after sixteen years of study she hoped for a career as a pianist. For a number of reasons, Meta could have struck Faulkner as a daughter-figure. A petite woman—only ninety-two pounds—she was the secretary of an important director for whom Faulkner worked, Howard Hawks. Certainly, as Meta describes her early meetings with Faulkner, she turned to Hawks as a daughter might to her father. For example, when Faulkner, inebriated, first asked her out, she fled to Hawks's office and asked him to decline the invitation for her, much as a daughter might seek her father's assistance in turning away an unwelcome suitor.[68] Also, in the alien environment of Hollywood, Meta, who had grown up in a plantation outside of Tunica just fifty-five miles northwest of Oxford and whose great-grandfather had been a slave owner and a Confederate soldier, would strike Faulkner as a kindred spirit.

Meta reminded Faulkner of home at a time when his letters spoke eloquently of painful homesickness.[69] In Hollywood, he felt adrift, and this estrangement reflects the original alienation that attends the constitution of the subject. If Faulkner unconsciously connected his childhood in Mississippi with the plenitude and presence of the pre-oedipal stage, union with Meta may have seemed to figure a return to the totalizing images of the imaginary. Certainly their relationship helped Faulkner cope with his longing for home, and, for Faulkner, home may have been an unconscious metaphor for mirror-stage psychic fusion. Meta would later say, "I could make him forget for hours on end that he was so far from home. Together we recreated our own South."[70]

Joan Williams, whom Faulkner met in 1949 when he was fifty-two and she was twenty—only four years older than his own daughter—may well have seemed to him like a displaced daughter-figure. From the beginning, he was attracted to Joan's childlike quality. For example, Faulkner, who often could not remember the details of his own novels after he had written them, vividly recalled years afterward that in her first letter to him—a letter that elicited a reply and a relationship that lasted for years—she had mentioned that her dog had been recently killed by a car. Surely he was struck by the guileless innocence of this revelation. Moreover, throughout their relationship, he was mentor or father-figure to Joan, who yearned to be a writer. Even more important, however, Joan's family background seemed in several important ways to correspond to Faulkner's own family, who were troubled by his and Estelle's drinking. In fact, Joan explicitly compared Faulkner to her own father in her first letter to him, explaining that she understood about his drinking because her father, too, drank. Like his daughter Jill, then, Joan also emerged from a family troubled by alcoholism. Indeed, Faulkner identified her with his daughter. For example, on one occasion when Joan visited him in a hospital, he asked her to read aloud to him a letter from Jill. As late as 1991, Joan still recalled the details of Jill's letter. In the letter Jill complained bitterly of the suffering her father's drinking caused her. According to Joan Williams, reading the letter was an extremely painful experience for her because she could so readily identify with Jill's suffering.[71]

Although the main similarity between the two young women was this anguished childhood background, Joan Williams recently told me that Faulkner often noted other correspondences between their families. For example, Faulkner's mother's name is Maud, and Joan's mother's name is Maude; Faulkner's wife's name is Estelle and Joan's father's first wife's name is Estelle; in *The Sound and the Fury,* Mrs. Compson's brother is Uncle Maury, and Joan's uncle, her mother's brother, is named Maury; when Faulkner and Meta Carpenter checked into hotels they used the pseudonym "Mr. and Mrs. Bowen," and Joan's first husband's name was Bowen; and Faulkner's birthday occurred on the day before Joan's.[72] Such correspondences may seem to be the merest coincidences; however, the fact that Faulkner was struck by them and repeatedly remarked them may suggest that they reinforced his unconscious sense that he and Joan shared a connection; that is, that Joan was aptly suited to represent the lost m(other). Quite possibly for this reason Faulkner gave to Joan Williams the original manuscript of *The Sound and the Fury,* the novel that, Faulkner said, originated with the image of Caddy Compson looking in the window at her grandmother's funeral. If Caddy Compson, whom Faulkner alluded to as "the beautiful one," "his heart's darling,"[73] was created as a replacement for the prohibited maternal relation of the imaginary stage, then his repeated assertions that he wanted Joan to have the manuscript of this novel suggest that he unconsciously identified her with the mirror-stage double.

Jean Stein, the last woman with whom he formed an attachment, may also have seemed to Faulkner to evoke or signify what had been lost in the formation of identity. Stein, who was eighteen in 1953 when Faulkner met her—two years younger than his daughter and thirty-eight years younger than the fifty-six-year-old author—surely must have appeared to Faulkner as a daughter-figure. Evidently, he was drawn to Jean Stein, as he had been to Joan Williams, because of her childlike quality, and their relationship seemed to be an attempt by Faulkner to recover a lost childhood. For example, Truman Capote recalled visiting Jean Stein in Paris and, when he left, Faulkner and Jean were playing together on the floor like children.[74] With Jean, then, like Joan, Meta, Helen, and Estelle, Faulkner sought to represent something he identified with the mother and the daughter. Interestingly, Faulkner's wife understood that his relationships with women filled some lack. Referring to Faulkner's liaison with Jean Stein, Estelle wrote to Saxe Commins in November of 1955: "I know as you must, that Bill feels some sort of compulsion to be attached to some young woman at all times— it's Bill."[75] Estelle language here is rich in connotations. Her use of the words *compulsion* and *attached* can be read as the lay equivalent of what in psychoanalytic terms might be called a psychic drive to signify a lost imaginary unity.

A desire for metonymic substitutions for the lost first other goes far, then, toward accounting for Faulkner's attachments with women during his life. And just as Lacanian theory is a useful tool in interpreting Faulkner's relationships with figures of the first other, so also Lacan's theory of the development of subjectivity can shed light on the curious dynamics between fathers and sons in Faulkner's family. In Lacan, the father, like the mother, plays a crucial role in the development of identity and language; moreover, these roles share this similarity: both the mother and father represent a threat to the child's identity. On the one hand, the mother represents the threat of reincorporation; on the other hand, the father, whose appearance denotes prohibition, poses the threat of symbolic castration. The father is identified with the sign of difference, the phallus, but difference is purchased only by the loss of an imaginary wholeness. For, while the phallus is the mark of man's difference from woman, it also figures the means by which the connection between mother and child would be restored. The phallus is a symbol for the authority and completeness of being that the child desires and attributes to the father (who appears to possess the mother). The child can enter the symbolic, can achieve identity, only by accepting lack, by accepting that the phallus, the father's presumed authority and completeness, is indeed lost and can be represented only by a signifier. Thus the symbolic castration that the child experiences upon entering subjectivity is a double loss: it is a loss of the mother as the imaginary other and also the relinquishment of the father's role, the role of the phallic Other. In the words of Jacqueline Rose, "the phallus stands for that moment when prohibition must function in the sense of whom may be assigned to whom in the triangle made up of mother, father, child, but at the same moment it signals to the subject that 'having' only functions at the price of a loss and 'being' as an effect of division."[76]

This identification of the father with the threat of castration and death pervades Faulkner's fiction. Moreover, this fictional identification seems to have a biographical basis. A careful review of Faulkner's family history—the novelist changed the spelling from "Falkner" to "Faulkner"—reveals a pattern of fathers who threaten their sons with some form of emasculation. For example, Faulkner family lore holds that Faulkner's great-grandfather, William Clark Falkner, ran away from home when his father, Joseph Falkner, severely beat him for bloodying his brother's head with a hoe.[77] Both these violent acts—either of which might have been fatal—act out the threat that the father or paternal metaphor represents to the son in Lacanian theory.

Whereas Joseph Falkner seems to have quite literally threatened his son with death, in the next generation, William Clark Falkner would reenact this threat to his eldest son in a symbolic way. When his first wife, mother of John Wesley Thompson Falkner, died shortly after the birth of the child, the Old Colonel gave his son to his aunt and uncle to raise, and then remarried and raised eight children born to him and his second wife.[78] The Old Colonel's decision to live apart from his son and to father another family surely was interpreted as a rejection by his eldest son. This act of disowning, which recalls Thomas Sutpen's refusal to recognize Charles Bon, makes a cipher of the son.

The Lacanian paradigm is symbolically enacted again in the next generation when, in 1902, John Wesley Thompson Falkner sold the family railroad, which his eldest son, Murry, believed would belong to him when his father died.[79] Because the family railroad, built by the Old Colonel and handed down from father to son, seems to have been identified in Murry's mind with paternal power (or the mythical phallus, which "the subject can neither have nor be")[80] the sale of the railroad can be interpreted as a symbolic reenactment of the father's prohibition and the son's dispossession.

In the next generation yet again, the son, blighted by the father, becomes the father who threatens the son with symbolic castration. In the novelist William Faulkner's lifetime, his father, Murry, clearly sought to denigrate his son's achievements and to deny his son's manhood. He called his son Snake-lips, mocking Faulkner's thin lips, which were like his mother's, and he often described his eldest son as "nuts." He dismissed his son's novels at the same time as he loudly professed that he had never read one of them.[81] Murry's frontal assaults on his son's manhood can be interpreted in terms of the Lacanian tenet that, as the child enters the symbolic order, the world of social interaction, he or she must assume a subordinated position in the mother-father-child triad.

Given these paternal threats, it is not surprising that in one generation after another each Falkner son showed signs of resisting the father. At the same time, however, these sons also expressed a contrary need to identify with the father. This ambivalent response is also readily accounted for by Lacanian theory, because, while the father stands for the Law of castration that ordains lack, that same moment of rupture ushers the child into the world of cultural meanings, and grants a provisional identity. The oedipal realization, which is triggered by the appearance of the father become Name-of-the-Father, constitutes the subject, and, for this reason, the lacking subject looks always (and always in vain) to the paternal metaphor or phallic Other for completeness of being. Since the Name-of-the-Father signifies both identity and prohibition, the son has good reason to respond ambivalently toward paternal representatives; and, in Faulkner's family, successive generations of sons vacillated between submitting to the Law of the Father and defying it.

In William Clark Falkner's generation, the son signified his resistance to paternal authority when he ran away from home; however, he simultaneously represented his opposite desire to align himself with the paternal signifier when he sought out a substitute father, his uncle—John Wesley Thompson, after whom he later named his son.[82] If, by leaving his father's house, he expressed his rebellion against what the father represents, by running to his uncle and choosing to live as a son thereafter with a surrogate father, he revealed his conflicting desire for what Lacan calls the paternal metaphor.

Similarly, the next generation's son, John Wesley Thompson Falkner, had a deeply ambivalent attitude toward his father that seems to have determined his divided response to his father's death. When the Old Colonel was shot and killed by Richard Thurmond, John Wesley Thompson Falkner did not attempt to avenge his father's death by challenging Thurmond to a duel. This refusal to duel with his father's killer reflects contrary impulses. On the one hand, by not killing the man who shot his father, the son appears to condone, even to approve, Thurmond's act, as if this murder realized his own repressed murderous urges. On the other hand, as Faulkner's reassessment of his grandfather's act in *The Unvanquished* makes clear, the refusal to kill Thurmond can be read in an opposite way. If we apply an oedipal interpretation to the duel between the colonel and his partner in the railroad, when Thurmond kills William Clark Falkner he has killed the father and taken his place. It follows, then, that if John Wesley Thompson Falkner were to duel with Thurmond (the new father-figure), he would be acting on his oedipal desire to kill his father and to take his place. Thus the son's refusal to challenge his father's killer can be read as a gesture of conciliation with his father.[83]

In the next generation, Murry Falkner's apparent inability to succeed at any career can be accounted for in terms of deeply ambivalent feelings toward his father. Throughout Murry's life, his father used his influence to secure jobs for his son. For example, at one time or another Murry owned or managed a drug company, a farm, a hauling business, a livery stable, a cottonseed processing plant, a theater, an ice facility, a buggy dealership, a coal-oil agency, and a hardware store. All of these businesses were subsidized by his father and Murry failed to make a profit at any of them. Quite possibly Murry unconsciously sought to fail at these business ventures because failure satisfied his contradictory feelings for his father. On the surface, in failing at jobs his father sponsored, he seemed to be rebelling against paternal authority by refusing to meet his father's expectations. However, as Michael Grimwood has persuasively argued, Murry's almost obsessive need to fail could be explained in an opposite way. If Murry succeeded at any of these jobs, he would be fulfilling a repressed desire to supplant the father. In other words, if, without his conscious awareness, Murry associated career success with the fulfillment of an oedipal desire, he, again unconsciously, may have sought failure as an act of submission.[84]

During his adolescence and young manhood, William Faulkner—at that time named Falkner—seemed determined to recreate the pattern of failure established by his father: repeatedly his father and grandfather found for him jobs at which he flagrantly failed. The job at his grandfather's bank is a case in point. Faulkner's father and grandfather set him to work in the family bank when he refused to attend school; but Faulkner further refused to work at the bank job. Years later, Faulkner joked about his unwillingness to apply himself to this work: "Quit school after five years in seventh grade. Got job in Grandfather's bank and learned medicinal value of his liquor. Grandfather thought janitor did it. Hard on janitor."[85] Similarly, when his family secured for him another position, university postmaster (1921–24), he again behaved outrageously and forced the postal authorities to dismiss him. Significantly, it was during these years that Faulkner earned the dubious title Count no 'count. Like his father, Faulkner, in the years before he discovered his vocation as a novelist, seemed deliberately to fail, quite possibly because failure satisfied his divided feelings—a desire both to refuse and to accept paternal authority. Instances of contradictory impulses toward his father are everywhere in evidence in his biography. For example, in the 1932 introduction to the Modern Library edition of *Sanctuary,* Faulkner wrote of his father's "unfailing kindness," and recently published letters written by Faulkner to his parents between 1918 and 1925 eloquently express a deep affection for both his father and his mother.[86] At the same time, however, Faulkner could also treat his father with insolence bordering on contempt. For instance, when toward the end of his life Murry Falkner, in a conciliatory gesture, offered his son "a good smoke," one of his own cigars, Faulkner, who smoked a pipe, took the cigar, broke it in half, and stuffed it into his pipe.[87] With the overt phallic symbolism of this gesture, Faulkner signaled his defiance of what Lacan calls the paternal metaphor.

Faulkner not only exhibited conflictual feelings toward his own father, he also sought out father-substitutes, Phil Stone and Sherwood Anderson, toward whom his feelings wavered demonstrably between a need for paternal acceptance and a deep resentment of paternal control. Phil Stone, for example, functioned for years as a father-figure to Faulkner: he mentored Faulkner, directed his reading, lectured to him, planned his career, and even subsidized his protégé's first publication, *The Marble Faun.* Faulkner responded to Stone's paternal guidance with equal measures of gratitude and defiance. He expressed his appreciation for Stone's influence by dedicating *The Hamlet* to Stone. And, in later years when Stone suffered financial losses, Faulkner repeatedly loaned him money. At the same time, however, Faulkner showed signs of resisting Stone's control, as he had resisted his father's. For example, refusing input from Stone, he kept the composition of *The Sound and the Fury* a secret from Stone until the novel was completed, as if his influence might be deadening or threatening to the creative impulse that generated this work. A statement Faulkner made to a friend in Pascagoula in the summer of 1927 may explain why he avoided mentioning his work-in-progress to his mentor. Confiding to Tom Kelly that he owed Stone several hundred dollars, he added somewhat defiantly, "but I'm not going to be obligated to him. I'm gonna pay that money back. Nobody dictates to me what I can write and can't write."

As his relationship with Stone suggests, even as he sought father-figures, Faulkner resisted the son's subordinate role.[88]

With Sherwood Anderson, Faulkner reenacted his filial relationship with Stone and with his own father. For a time in New Orleans, Faulkner lived like a son with Sherwood and Elizabeth Prall Anderson. Like Stone, Anderson played a paternal role: he encouraged the younger man's writing and promoted his career. More specifically, he introduced the young Faulkner to the literati in New Orleans and recommended Faulkner's first novel, *Soldiers' Pay*, to his own publisher, Horace Liveright. But, as with Stone and with his own father, Faulkner simultaneously welcomed and resented this fatherly presence. Possibly without being consciously aware of it, he expressed an oedipal desire to supplant this father-figure when, with William Spratling, he wrote a parody of Anderson, *Sherwood Anderson and Other Famous Creoles,* a work that hurt Anderson deeply, especially as it appeared just after Hemingway's cruel and condescending *Torrents of Spring*. While these insults externalized one side of Faulkner's ambivalence, his praise of Anderson expressed the other side. Years later, Faulkner would call Anderson "the father of all my generation,"[89] praise that might seem excessive unless his choice of the word *father* is read in the context of Lacan, as an expression of the debt the son owes to the father become Name-of-the-Father or symbolic Other, the site of the constitution of the subject and therefore the presumed originator of being.

Just as Lacanian theory offers a way of reading Faulkner's ambivalent responses toward mother- and father-figures, so also many of Faulkner's enigmatic patterns of behavior can be interpreted in terms of a tension between a Desire of the mother and the Law of the Father. I am thinking specifically of Faulkner's notorious binge drinking. Arguably, Faulkner's epic binges, which were paradoxically both controlled and unrestrained, conform to the pattern I have been describing. Although Faulkner could and did drink socially, he also, at periodic intervals, often after completing a novel, would drink in binges. At these times, he would retire to his bed with a supply of liquor. For days and sometimes for weeks, he would remain in his bed drinking himself into unconsciousness, waking only long enough to drink himself unconscious again. Quite remarkably, he would plan these drinking bouts, naming ahead of time the day he would begin drinking and the day he would stop. During these episodes, he would neither eat nor take nonalcoholic fluids and, by the time he chose to stop drinking, his binge would have reduced him to a condition of complete helplessness. He would lie in his bed, sometimes completely naked, and he would have to be fed and given fluids. Like an infant, he would have to be nursed or mothered.[90]

Faulkner's drinking, then, was both abandoned and controlled. Because he drank until he was unconscious and then, when he waked, drank himself unconscious again, his drinking was unrestrained. On the other hand, because he set the parameters of this drinking, and drank on schedule, as it were, his drinking was also controlled. By drinking in this most curious way, arguably Faulkner was satisfying contradictory impulses for subjectivity and for loss of subjectivity. Faulkner's drinking can perhaps be read as analogous to Freud's grandchild's *Fort-Da* game. Like the child who throws away the reel and then retrieves it, Faulkner seems to be playing with loss and return. Like the child, whom Freud hypothesizes is signifying his mastery of his mother's absence, so perhaps Faulkner is signaling his mastery of absence and loss. At one level, Faulkner's binge drinking, which, in the words of Frederick Karl, "involved almost a complete stoppage of the body's normal needs," reenacts primary repression, the rupture that attends the constitution of the self. At another level, however, this drinking, which infantilized Faulkner and made him dependent on a nurse, seems to recreate in a controlled way the preoedipal fused relationship with the mother. It is interesting to note in this regard that Faulkner's own term for the condition brought on by his binges was "a collapse."[91] This word *collapse*, may reflect an unconscious recognition that these binges symbolized a return to an original undifferentiated existence.

By this willed use of alcohol, Faulkner produced what could be called a controlled loss of consciousness; it was as if Faulkner were attempting to assert control over the unconscious—or perhaps over death itself, for, with his protracted drinking, Faulkner flirted with death. By consuming such excessive quantities of alcohol, Faulkner might well have killed himself. With good reason, Frederick Karl calls these drinking binges "virtually acts of self-destruction."[92] When Faulkner drank until he passed out, his brain activity was reduced and his blood pressure, heart rate, and respiration were depressed. In effect, he was taking a step toward coma.

Faulkner's bizarre drinking practices, which seem almost to prefigure death, lead directly to a discussion of his seemingly ambivalent feelings toward death. Both his fiction and his own life story speak of two contrary impulses: a desire for death and a desire to deny death. Several critics, among them Joseph Blotner, Robert Hamblin, and Warwick Wadlington, have argued persuasively that Faulkner longed to "say no" to death. Faulkner even explicitly acknowledged that this desire fueled his fiction, saying that the writer "knows he has a short span of life, that the day will come when he must pass through the wall of oblivion, and he wants to leave a scratch on that wall—Kilroy was here—that somebody a hundred, a thousand years later will see." But even as his fiction proposes to deny the eventual dissolution of the subject, at the same time, his novels insistently invoke death, as John Dos Passos emphasized in his eulogy of Faulkner: "He had met death before many times in his storytelling. His stories are full of the knowledge of death. He did not meet death as a stranger."[93] In other words, Faulkner's novels are replete with representations of death, or, in Lacanian terms, signifiers for death.

Faulkner's biography also reflects a man deeply divided in his feelings toward death. On the one hand, Faulkner said to Felix Linder in June 1962, "Felix, I don't want to die." On the other hand, as Frederick Karl has observed, Faulkner's repeated self-injuries seem to express suicidal tendencies. For example, an X ray taken in 1952 revealed that he had fractured five vertebrae and that he had been walking around for years with a broken back. On at least one occasion, in October 1952, he fell down the stairs at Rowan Oak, and a visitor reported that "his body [was] bloated and bruised from his many falls." He also repeatedly suffered injuries from falls from horses he was jumping.[94]

A somewhat earlier instance of this self-injury is instructive. In September 1937, he saw Meta Carpenter with her new German husband. That night he drank himself into a stupor and fell unconscious on a steam pipe. When he was found the next day, he had suffered a third-degree burn on his back that penetrated to his spine and caused him excruciating pain. Later he told Meta that seeing her with another man had precipitated his accident. And when asked to explain why he had so endangered himself, he responded, "Because I like to."[95] Faulkner's answer might appear to be merely a spiteful or dismissive evasion. However, Faulkner's answer can be rendered intelligible if we read his words in the context of Lacan's theory. Possibly he "like[d] to" hurt himself because by punishing his body he satisfied conflicting drives. At one level, he reenacts the original rupture that attends the constitution of the self and asserts the power of the signifier over the signified. On another level, however, with these injurious acts he courted death, which would satisfy the opposite desire for reincorporation and return. Ultimately, then, all of Faulkner's self-destructive acts prefigure suicide. Suicide, which restrains the body even as it releases all restraint, represented for Faulkner, as it does for Quentin Compson in *The Sound and the Fury*, the resolution—perhaps the only possible resolution—of the conflicting drives toward the imaginary and the symbolic that, according to Lacan, characterize every human subject. Given the correspondence between Faulkner's life of self-injury and Quentin's suicide, quite possibly when Faulkner so eloquently describes Quentin's rapturous attraction to death, he speaks not only for Quentin but also for himself: "But who loved death above all, who loved only death, loved and lived in a deliberate and almost perverted anticipation of death, as a lover loves and deliberately refrains from the waiting willing friendly tender incredible body of his beloved, until he can no longer bear not the refraining but the restraint and so flings, hurls himself, relinquishing, drowning."[96]

CHAPTER I

"The Beautiful One" in
The Sound and the Fury

*I*n an introduction to *The Sound and the Fury* composed in 1933, Faulkner quite uncharacteristically revealed the impulse that moved him to write his first great novel. The novel originated, he explained, in his desire to create "a beautiful and tragic little girl" who was somehow to replace two female absences: the sister he never had and the daughter he was fated to lose in infancy.[1] Caddy Compson, then, is the central focus of the novel. And yet, as critics have frequently observed, Caddy is never concretely presenced in the way that her brothers are.[2] She is never given an interior monologue of her own; she is seen only through the gaze of her brothers, and even then only in retreat, standing in doorways, running, vanishing, forever elusive, forever just out of reach. Caddy seems, then, to be simultaneously absent and present; with her, Faulkner evokes an absent presence, or the absent center of the novel, as André Bleikasten and John T. Matthews have observed.[3] In Lacanian terms, Caddy, who functions as a mother-figure in the novel, appears to figure the mother/other, the first who was made other. Derived from the Latin word *cadere*, to fall, her name may refer not only to her state as a fallen woman but also to the original fall from a state of plenitude, the fall into language and loss and the symbolic order. In other words, she evokes the primary repression that constitutes the self.[4]

Caddy's brothers, Quentin and Jason, like all subjects in language, exist as lack. They lack the signifier, the mythical copula, that could restore the missing connection with the m/other. In this chapter, I propose to show that Caddy's brothers are obsessed with phallic lack and that they project their loss onto Caddy, who occupies the position of mother in relation to her brothers, a position abdicated by Mrs. Compson. This identification of women, and particularly mothers, with

32

lack can be accounted for in terms of Lacanian theory. In particular, feminist revisionists of Lacan have speculated about the causes of this figuration of women. At one level, women can be perceived as representing lack precisely because they are associated with wholeness. Women, as presumptive mother-figures, recall the imaginary dyadic unity of the preoedipal stage as well as the subsequent identificatory mirror stage in which the self finds itself in the reflecting other, who at this point is usually the mother. At this early stage of development, writes Madan Sarup, the mother is not only "the real witness and guarantor of the subject's existence," she is as well "the M-Other who created it."[5] Thus, on this level, because the identificatory imago of the mirror phase conferred a unified self-image and because that unitary image is now shattered, we identify the mother with loss. At another level, the mother seems to objectify the child's loss because the imaginary dyadic unity with which she is associated threatens identity. In the preoedipal state, which Lacan calls the imaginary, there is no ego identity. In this early stage before the appearance of the sign of difference, Terry Eagleton writes, "the child lives a 'symbiotic' relation with its mother's body which blurs any sharp boundary between the two."[6] Thus the mother is associated with loss of being because, as Gallop explains, she recalls a former dyadic relation that "threatens to undo the achievements of repression and sublimation, threatens to return the subject to the powerlessness, intensity and anxiety of an unmediated connection with the body of the mother."[7] This disturbing projection of loss onto the mother can also be traced to yet another cause. Jacqueline Rose points out that women are defined in relation to the male and that, in a phallocentric culture, this relation is "a denigration."[8] For example, Lacan writes: "For the [male] soul to come into being, she, the woman, is differentiated from it . . . called woman and defamed."[9] Women, then, are also identified with loss, "defamed," in an attempt to distinguish and elevate male identity. Finally, the mother seems to figure loss because she lacks a penis. While Lacanian theory stresses that a penis does not confer any authority or power and that all subjects in language are alienated, that is, symbolically castrated, nevertheless, Lacan, following Freud, holds that the female's lack of a penis appears, to a male viewer, outwardly to sign the lack that is the condition of subjectivity.[10] For all these reasons, then, lack is projected onto women and, in particular, onto the figure of the mother. Both Jacqueline Rose and Jane Gallop make a point of identifying this projection. Rose states: "As the place onto which lack is projected and through which it is simultaneously disavowed, woman is a 'symptom' for the man."[11] Gallop exposes this masculine projection in similarly forceful terms: "Whatever relation of lack man feels, lack of wholeness, lack in/of being, is projected onto woman's lack of phallus, lack of maleness. Woman is the figuration of phallic 'lack'; she is a hole. By these mean and extreme phallic proportions, the whole is to man as man is to the hole."[12]

In *The Sound and the Fury,* the projection that Rose and Gallop describe seems to form the novel's subtext. Quentin and Jason, subjects alienated in language, project their own sense of diminishment on Caddy, the displaced mother-figure. Caddy seems to them to represent their own denied lack of being. In this way, Caddy embodies the return of the repressed. And because she represences the repressed in a disguised form, Caddy becomes the focus of their conflicting desires for incorporation and for alienation. Their latent desire for a return to an imaginary relation with the mother surfaces as a desire for incest with Caddy and their contrary impulse to reenact the moment of the appearance of the paternal metaphor, the signifier of difference, translates into a desire to enclose and confine Caddy. Paradoxically both of these contrary desires lead to feelings of lack. On the one hand, if Caddy's brothers choose to embrace the moment of symbolization, they privilege an empty sign over the physical world and experience existence as absence. On the other hand, if they elect to figure a narcissistic return to a preoedipal state before separation and loss, the subject merges with the other and ceases to exist.[13]

This latter fate is dramatized in Benjy, the third Compson brother. Benjy does not exist within the symbolic order; he does not exist as an I separate from the other. As André Bleikasten has convincingly demonstrated, in Benjy's interior monologue "there is no central I through whose agency his speech might be ordered and made meaningful; in like manner, there is no sense of identity to make his experience his."[14] Even Benjy's body seems like a collection of unrelated fragments that act independently of any central volition. He speaks of his voice, for example, as if he did not control it: "My voice was going loud every time" (72). In other words, he is not aware of his existence as separate or as an agent of action. He is not a speaking subject; rather he is a helpless, inchoate, inarticulate bundle of sensations. And Benjy's condition is directly related to his yearning for Caddy. Throughout his monologue, he obsessively pursues one goal: to restore a lost unity with the banished mother-figure. Benjy has not elected to leave behind the mirror-stage identification with the first other, the mother; rather, he is forcibly separated from the object of his desire by the Law of the Father. The fence in his monologue functions as a concrete token of this Law; it separates him from his pasture, emblem of the signified, the physical world, and from the mother-surrogate, from Caddy, whose name he hears repeatedly called from the other side of the fence. On the one occasion when he finds the gate to the fence unlocked, he seizes his opportunity to act on his yearning to reexperience an unmediated connection with the maternal body. He crosses the boundary established by the father become Father, and pursues the Burgess girl, who figures the lost Caddy, who, in turn, figures the first forbidden other. For good reason, then, Benjy's recollection of running after and catching the Burgess girl merges with his memory of being anesthetized for the operation that deprives him of his male organs. The act of seizing the Burgess girl, representative of Caddy who recalls a lost plenitude, returns Benjy to a former unconscious state: "They came on. I opened the gate and they stopped, turning. I was trying to say, and I caught her, trying to say, and she screamed and I was trying to say and trying and the bright shapes began to stop and I tried to get out. I tried to get it off my face, but the bright shapes were going again. They were going up the hill to where it fell away and I tried to cry. But when I breathed in, I couldn't breathe out again to cry, and I tried to keep from falling off the hill and I fell off the hill into the bright, whirling shapes" (60–61). By passing through the gate and expressing a narcissistic desire for a return to an imaginary dyadic unity, Benjy has violated the Law of the Father, and he suffers the father's punishment—castration—the loss of the male identity that is conferred only by submitting to the law of alienation.

Whereas Benjy yearns to transgress boundaries, both Quentin and Jason strive, with more or less ambivalence, to maintain divisions that, by exclusion, establish difference and define the self. Because these boundaries are externalized in the shrinking Compson square mile, Quentin and Jason struggle to keep Caddy and, later, her daughter within these borders. Above all, Jason and Quentin seek to enforce the paternal interdiction against merging. Thus Quentin tries to prevent Caddy from leaving the house to meet with her lover in the dark woods; and when Caddy returns from her nightly trysts, Quentin fastens the gate behind her in a futile attempt to assert the sign of difference, the phallic signifier. Similarly, Quentin attempts to return the little Italian girl to her father's house.[15]

But because Quentin and Jason see personified in Caddy and her daughter the identificatory imago of the mirror stage, these women are identified with signs of slippage and leakage, fissures in the fence and the house. Again and again Caddy and her daughter are associated with windows, doors, and cracks. Each time Caddy meets to fornicate with Ames, she crawls through the fence that surrounds the Compson house. Through a window, Caddy disobediently views her grandmother's funeral; and through a window Miss Quentin escapes Jason's domination, taking with her his money, which she obtains by breaking through the locked window of his room. When Quentin summons to mind Caddy's lost virginity, he alludes to the loss with the phrase, *"One minute she was standing in the door"* (91). Just as the house and the Compson square mile attempt to assert the integrity of the self, windows, doors, and cracks expose the precariousness of this identity. These fissures metaphorically register what Lacan refers to as "the incessant sliding of the signified under the signifier."[16]

The shifting, uncertain nature of the fractured subject is the given of Lacanian theory. A secure and whole identity, for example, is not within the gift of psychoanalysis. Juliet Mitchell explains: "Psychoanalysis cannot give the human subject that which it is its fate, as the condition of its subjecthood, to do without."[17] The subject is created in a moment of alienation, and indeed exists as a subject by virtue of alienation. Lacan muses over this paradox: ". . . why must he assume the attributes of that sex [male gender identity] only through a threat— the threat, indeed, of their privation?"[18] What identity the subject has, writes Mitchell, "is in fact a mirage arising when the subject forms an image of itself by identifying with others' perception of it," because the subject "can only conceptualize itself when it is mirrored back to itself from the position of another's desire."[19] This shaky subject then finds itself in an unenviable situation. The original alienation opens up desire to be the (always mythical) phallus that is the mother's and the Other's desire. According to Lacan, "the desire of the mother *is* the phallus" and "the child wishes to be the phallus in order to satisfy that desire."[20] This desire, however, is forbidden by the Law of the Father under the threat of castration. And from this conflict emerges castration anxiety, as the child is faced with two choices, both of which lead to a form of castration. The child may either renounce the missing signifier in obedience to the Law of the Father in an act that is tantamount to a symbolic castration or, alternately, the child may defy the paternal interdiction by attempting to represence the missing copula and risk the father's punishment—castration.

Castration obviously poses a more powerful threat to the male child than to the female, since the male child perceives himself with something to lose;[21] and, seemingly for this reason, male sexual identity in *The Sound and the Fury* seems particularly at risk. For example, throughout his section Quentin clearly is trying to align himself with the Law of the Father, which is signified by the phallus, but all his efforts to present himself as a man different from his own weak, ineffectual father fail. Significantly, Quentin characterizes these failures as somehow feminizing him.[22] During his humiliating confrontation with Ames, Quentin is disgusted with himself for behaving "like a girl" (186); that is, for slapping Ames with his open hand before he thinks to make a fist, for fainting, and for rejecting Ames's pistol and horse. Unlike Ames, who selects for their meeting place a bridge, and who has "crossed all the oceans all around the world" (172), Quentin, who loses his footing on the bridge and has to be held up by Ames, cannot bestride the waters of life.

In fact, all of the experiences that Quentin obsessively rehearses seem to culminate in failure. His sister consistently defies his interdicts; he fails to preserve her purity, his task as self-appointed surrogate father; he fails to prevent her marriage to the odious Head; he fails to restore the little Italian girl to her father; he fails to carry out his plan of joint suicide with Caddy; and he fails ignominiously when he challenges Gerald Bland. Given these cumulative failures, it seems safe to conclude that Quentin suffers feelings of masculine inadequacy, or, in Freudian terms, castration anxiety.[23] Such feelings would explain Quentin's preoccupation with phallic symbols: the clock tower, the smokestacks, the gun he refuses, and the knife he drops.

Like his older brother, Jason, too, is haunted by feelings of phallic lack.[24] One manifestation of Jason's threatened masculinity is his precarious ability to drive his automobile: as Jason implies when he refuses "to trust a thousand dollars' worth of delicate machinery" (272) to a black servant, only a "real man" is able to steer such a powerful machine. But in the course of Jason's pursuit of his niece and the showman, it becomes evident that he himself is not "man enough" to drive the car: its gasoline fumes reduce him to helplessness. In addition, the details of the purchase of the car—he bought the car with money given him by his mother for investment in Earl's store—also suggest a certain dependency. Moreover, if we accept Jason's car as the outward sign of his virility, his niece's and the showman's gesture of deflating the car's tires takes on suggestive sexual overtones. In fact, Jason consistently seems to have trouble keeping his tires "pumped up"; when he stops at a filling station, the black attendant tells Jason, "Dis here ti' aint got no air a-tall in hit" (353).

Jason hungers for money for the same reason that he cherishes his car. Money helps him to counter his feelings of anxiety about his masculine identity. For example, when Jason says to Dilsey, "At least I'm man enough to keep that flour barrel full" (238–39), he is using money as evidence of manhood. Money is Jason's substitute for potency: appropriately, then, he selects for a girlfriend a prostitute, choosing a relationship that is clearly based on his ability to pay rather than on any other ability. Money compensates him for a sense of diminishment, the same lack that Quentin feels. This sense of loss is experienced as a castration complex. Such a complex explains Jason's habit of keeping his hands thrust deep in his pockets. With his hands in his pockets he can protect his money, which compensates him for his sense of impotence, but he can also protect his threatened genitals.

If money is Jason's substitute for male potency, then, when his niece steals his money she strikes a blow against that potency. In pursuing his niece and the lost money, he is confronted with phallic symbols— "sheet iron steeples" (354) and "a spire or two above the trees" (356)— that seem to mock his lack. His feelings of impotence are dramatized when, in an attempt to forget his head pain, Jason tries to distract himself with thoughts of Lorraine. By picturing himself in bed with the prostitute, he clearly means to bolster his failing masculinity with an image of himself playing the part of the potent and phallic male, but instead in his imagined scene he is pathetic and impotent: "He imagined himself in bed with her, only he was just lying beside her, pleading with her to help him, then he thought of the money again" (355). The specter of sexual inadequacy inevitably invokes thoughts of the lost money because of the identification in Jason's mind of money with masculine potency.

Jason's failure to regain the lost money, the symbol of phallic power, ends appropriately with a symbolic castration. He challenges an "old man" (357), a father-figure, who wields a rusty hatchet and who causes him to fall and experience a blow to the head—an analogue, according to Freud, for castration.[25] Following this blow, Jason behaves as if he has been emasculated: he abandons his pursuit of his niece and the money, his avenue to masculine power. The ultimate sign of his emasculation is his inability to drive his car. On the trip back to Jefferson, Jason takes the backseat, and a black man drives.

For my purposes, what is most significant about these feelings of lack is the way that both Quentin and Jason attempt to evade them by projecting them on the figure of the first other, the mother. This projection is particularly overt in Jason's monologue. Consumed by a sense of phallic lack, Jason focuses these feelings on one central image, the lost bank job promised by Herbert Head. The job, a position of authority, serves as a symbol for the state of full phallic power that Jason aspires to. Plagued instead by feelings of loss, Jason attempts to evade these feelings by projecting them onto Caddy and, in her absence, onto her daughter. Interchangeably, then, he alludes to Caddy and his niece as "the bitch that cost me a job, the one chance I ever had to get ahead" (351). In this way, the two women become scapegoats on whom, and away from himself, Jason expels his own sense of diminishment and dispossession. In other words, by blaming the two women Jason denies his own lack, and these repressed feelings are projected onto Caddy and her daughter.

Like Jason, Quentin also appears to project lack onto the first identificatory other. In fact, Quentin's frequently quoted phrase "the dungeon was Mother herself" (198) may metaphorically register this identification. In Lacanian terms, the mother might be associated with a dungeon because the maternal body is a reminder of an imaginary dyadic unity before the emergence of identity.[26] In the same way, Caddy, whose eyes drain of consciousness and look "like the eyes in statues blank and unseeing and serene" (187) and whose blood surges uncontrollably when she hears her lover's name, also seems to Quentin to conjure an original fused state prior to the appearance of the sign of difference.[27] Perhaps for this reason, when the adolescent Caddy and Quentin struggle together in the hogwallow, he wipes the stinking mud from his leg and smears it on Caddy, a gesture that reenacts the original displacement and substitution that made subjectivity possible.

But even as this act seems to externalize a drive to enforce otherness, Quentin's incestuous feelings for Caddy suggest the opposite impulse, a desire to merge once again with the identificatory imago. And because in such a narcissistic unity the separate subject as such ceases to exist, sex and death are insistently paired throughout the novel, as they are so often in literature. For example, Caddy looks in the window at her grandmother's funeral and acquires a knowledge of death at the same time as her brothers are introduced to the mysteries of sexuality as revealed in her muddy bottom. When Mrs. Compson sees her daughter kissing a boy, she wears black and announces that Caddy is dead. When Caddy sets out to meet her lover for a tryst in the dark woods, Quentin insists that first they go and look at the bones of the mare Nancy lying in a ditch. Sex and death also seem interchangeable in that both separate sleeping partners: Jason can no longer sleep with Damuddy because she is dying; Benjy can no longer sleep with Caddy because she is sexually maturing. And in Benjy's monologue, sex and death repeatedly merge: a recollection of standing on a box to see Caddy's wedding interweaves through a memory of Caddy climbing a tree to see Damuddy's funeral. The equation of sex and death, apparent even in Shreve's sarcastic remark, "Is it a wedding or a wake?" (93), is insisted upon by Caddy, who repeatedly uses death as a synonym for sexual intercourse: "yes I hate him I would die for him Ive already died for him I die for him over and over again everytime this goes" (173).

This equation of sex and death is extended to include Caddy because, for Quentin, sex with Caddy, a displaced mother-figure, images a return to an imaginary unity before the onset of alienation and identity. Thus Quentin finds particularly applicable to Caddy St. Francis's fond name for death, "Little Sister Death" (87), an appellation that anticipates Harry Wilbourne's expression for another mother-figure in Faulkner's 1939 novel *The Wild Palms*, the "grave-womb or womb-grave" (138). In fact, Wilbourne's notion of womb as grave is even dramatized by Quentin when, his sex play with Natalie interrupted by Caddy, he throws himself into the hogwallow in a ritual imitation of sexual intercourse: "I jumped hard as I could into the hogwallow the mud yellowed up to my waist stinking I kept on plunging until I fell down" (156–57; italics removed). The hogwallow, for Quentin, appears to figure the vagina/birth canal and also the womb, where life is made and in which the light of consciousness has not yet dawned, as if lost in the dark seething tumults of primal, unconscious life. Intercourse, then, is perceived as a return to the womb, a return to an imaginary relation with the mother.

Just as the ritual intercourse with Caddy in the hogwallow is evoked in terms of death—a reversion to primal matter—so also Quentin's abortive attempt at joint suicide with Caddy simulates sexual intercourse: Quentin proposes to penetrate Caddy with his knife. At the branch, Quentin drops his knife and fails to achieve penetration, but he is determined not to fail in his last attempt to fuse once again with the imaginary double who is first the mother. Quentin's suicide simultaneously satisfies contradictory desires for alienation and for reincorporation. At one level, Quentin's death by drowning is, like incest with Caddy, the mother-surrogate, an immersion of self in the dark waters of the unconscious. By drowning himself, Quentin is surrendering to the long denied forces of his own unconscious. Dissolved in water, Caddy's element, he is reabsorbed into the matrix of life, the sea (*mer*), the mother (*mère*), and he achieves the consummation he has both resisted and desired: the union of himself with Caddy, the identificatory imago. Conversely, by willing his own extinction, Quentin is asserting the power of the signifier over the signified, and his death reenacts the repression of the first other—the mother. In other words, by killing himself Quentin is also carrying out his threat to Caddy, "I'll kill you" (181).[28] Seen this way, Quentin's suicide strikes a blow against mirror-stage identification in accordance with the psychoanalytic paradigm that "aggressivity represents a will to rebellion against the imago," and that this rebellion frequently takes the form of a fantasized "violation of bodily integrity."[29]

Quentin's death by drowning, then, successfully satisfies conflicting desires. It expresses both his desire for the totalizing images of the mirror stage and his desire to shatter the mirror image. This proposition is supported by a brief, easily overlooked episode that occurs as Quentin returns to Boston. After his humiliating defeat at the hands of Bland, which merges in Quentin's mind with his failed attempt to challenge Ames, he returns alone to Boston on a trolleycar. As the car moves between dark trees, with their evocation of Caddy, Quentin looks out the window, but sees only reflected images: "The lights were on in the car, so while we ran between trees I couldn't see anything except my own face and a woman across the aisle with a hat sitting right on top of her head, with a broken feather in it" (193). In the glass, Quentin sees reflected himself and his double, or his conscious self and his repressed self. The broken feather is a disguised image out of the unconscious. Like Benjy's broken flower, the outward sign of his castration, the broken feather externalizes Quentin's repressed feelings of emasculation. The woman in the glass, the reflection of Quentin's unconscious, is Caddy, the woman-figure in whom he sees himself reflected, the woman on whom he projects his own lack. Thus, as he speeds toward Boston, intent on death, a long desired and resisted reunion, Quentin is accompanied by Caddy, his double, his sister-self, whose death is his own.[30]

Just as Caddy is Quentin's mirror-stage double, so also is the "dirty" little Italian girl, who pursues Quentin relentlessly as he circles the Charles River. Several critics, among them John T. Matthews and Louise Dauner, have remarked correspondences between Caddy and the foreign child.[31] Most notably, of course, Quentin calls the child "sister"; Quentin stands accused of molesting the little girl, when, in fact, it is his sister Caddy for whom Quentin harbors sexual feelings; and in the little girl, as in Caddy, Quentin sees a reflection of himself. Like Caddy, the child is associated with doors—frames in which the self sees itself mirrored: "She came in when I opened the door . . . . [The bell] rang once for both of us" (145). The bell's one ring pairs Quentin with the little girl, suggesting doubling. More specifically, the little girl, who insistently is associated with phallic symbols—her worm-like fingers, her "stiff little pigtails," the naked "nose of the loaf" (155) pressed against her dirty dress—seems to externalize Quentin's own sense of phallic lack, the lack of substance at the core of the empty signifier. The child, who carries a loaf with an exposed, eroding "nose," reflects Quentin's ever-eroding sense of male identity. And, as Quentin's projected self, she resembles Quentin's shadow, another projection. She "shadows" Quentin, step for step: "She moved along just under my elbow" (152). In fact, she seems almost to become Quentin's shadow: when Quentin runs from the child he loses his shadow; when his shadow reemerges, she suddenly reappears. "The wall went into shadow, and then my shadow, I had tricked it again," Quentin notes. "I had forgot the river curving along the road. I climbed the wall. And then she watched me jump down, holding the loaf against her dress" (153–54).

John T. Irwin argues that Quentin's shadow is his masculine double and Caddy is Quentin's feminine double.[32] Here, however, I propose that Caddy, Quentin's shadow, and the little foreign child are all avatars of the same figure: the imaginary double who is first the mother. So Quentin's attempts to elude the child, his efforts to "trick" his shadow, and his threats to kill Caddy are all manifestations of the same deep-seated need to reenact primary repression; and when, leaning over the bridge railing, looking at his shadow spread out on the water below him, he longs to drown his shadow, it is Caddy, the image of the first identificatory other, that he seeks to drown, even as he yearns to drown in her, to reexperience the lost integration of infancy. Not surprisingly, then, a Caddy-avatar, the little girl, accompanies Quentin on his river walk. Circling the water in which he intends to immerse himself, Quentin is accompanied by the girl, with her gaze "black and unwinking and friendly" (150) as the "dark and still" (158) watery grave itself.

Throughout *The Sound and the Fury,* then, women appear to be identified with a preoedipal imaginary unity that was banished to create identity. Once this identification is understood, certain enigmatic episodes in the novel, which have elicited little critical commentary, are readily interpreted. For example, before Quentin "pairs up" with "sister" on his river walk, he encounters three young boys who carry fishing poles. Insistently, throughout the short scene, the three boys are identified with their long, phallic poles: "Their voices came over the hill, and the three slender poles like balanced threads of running fire" (138). The "slender poles" figure the anatomical difference that is identified with the mythical phallus. The emphatic narrative identification of the boys with the poles leads up to a climactic moment, when one of them, Kenny, lays down his pole, in an outward sign of his emasculation. Kenny's manhood, it seems, is subject to maternal influence, and he is mocked by the other boys as they go off to a swimming hole: " 'Yah,' they said suddenly, 'go on then, mamma's boy. If he goes swimming he'll get his head wet and then he'll get a licking' " (140–41). "He climbed a picket fence without looking back and crossed the lawn to a tree and laid the pole down and climbed into the fork of the tree and sat there" (141). The lowered pole is a symbol of Kenny's diminished virility in a novel full of such symbols: Jason's flat tires, Benjy's broken flower, Quentin's broken leg, the reflection of the woman wearing a hat with a broken feather. All these symbols externalize repressed feelings of lack, and this male failure is attributed to a connection to the mother. Kenny, a "mamma's boy," identifies this connection when he retreats to a tree, with its symbolic evocation of Caddy, and when, arguing with another boy about going to a fishing hole, he says to his friend, "You dont have to go. . . . You're not tied to me"(139). Kenny is not tied to his buddy, but he was tied by an umbilical cord to his mother prior to the moment of symbolization that gave rise to subjectivity. Thus, the mother, a reminder of an imaginary unitary identity, is blamed for the male's sense of lack.

This identification of the mother with loss is reiterated, again symbolically, in a closely related episode. Somewhat later in the afternoon, Quentin, now shadowed by "sister," reencounters two of the boys from the fishing-pole incident, who, without Kenny, have joined other "fellows" at the swimming hole. Swimming naked, the boys object to a female presence and express a desire for alienation: "Take that girl away. What did you want to bring a girl here for? Go on away!" In response to this attempt to expel the girl, Quentin calls out, "She wont hurt you" (157). Quentin's four-word rejoinder provides the key to interpreting not only the boys' resistance to "sister," but also his own:[33] first, Quentin accurately assesses that the boys are threatened by the foreign girl, and, second, his brief retort partially echoes his father's diagnosis of the source of Quentin's own anguish and despair, "It's nature is hurting you, not Caddy" (132). Neither Caddy nor the little girl hurts Quentin or the boys, but these females are dreaded because they are identified with an original imaginary dyadic relation. This male identification of women with a preoedipal fused state is dramatized when the boys hurl water—the primal substance from which all forms arise and to which they return[34]—at the girl who shadows Quentin. Like Quentin's gesture of smearing mud on Caddy, which he recalls as he and the little girl approach the swimming boys, this act of hurling water reenacts the projection onto the other of the male's repressed feeling of slippage, of leakage into the other. Perhaps even more important, the ultimate futility of this projection is also implied in the brief scene, for, even as the boys hurl water away from themselves, they swim naked in the swimming hole in an almost ritual simulation of their preconscious existences in the wombs of their mothers. Nevertheless, because identity depends on absence and negation, men persist in identifying women with their own lack as subjects alienated in language, and so, as Quentin and his female counterpart retreat, Quentin remarks, "Nothing but a girl. Poor sister" (158). At a symbolic level, Quentin's words articulate a tacit male equation of "sister," the mother-substitute, with the "nothing" that gives rise to selfhood.

Perhaps most pernicious about this projection are its effects on women. While Caddy and her daughter struggle against this masculine association, both, nevertheless, show signs of accepting and internalizing the male identification of them with the threat of castration and death that subtends the very constitution of identity. For example, Caddy speaks of a nightmare vision: "There was something terrible in me sometimes at night I could see it grinning at me I could see it through them grinning at me through their faces" (128; italics removed). The "something terrible" that Caddy sees in herself "through them" is the interrelation of death and the constitution of the self, which men project and Caddy internalizes. Caddy's internalization of doom and loss is also evident in the novel's appendix, published in 1946, where Caddy is last glimpsed in a photograph, seated in an expensive sports car, beside a Nazi staff general. Given that the appendix was published just after World War II, when, to an American reader, a Nazi general seemed to be the very incarnation of evil, Caddy's intimacy with the Nazi suggests that she has internalized a male projection of her own corruption. Blamed for and even identified with the subject's alienation in language, Caddy seems to accept this attribution and thus allows herself to be possessed by this avatar of death. If, then, as the appendix claims, Caddy is "lost" (710), her brothers projected this loss onto her.[35]

Caddy's daughter is also doomed by a male projection. Blamed from birth by Jason for his own castration anxiety, Miss Quentin, like her mother, seems to resist but finally to internalize this projection on her of absence, loss, and death; but she goes one step further than her mother and clearly identifies Jason's role in dooming her: "If I'm bad, it's because I had to be. You made me" (300).

In addition, in light of a male identification of mothers with privation, Mrs. Compson's behavior becomes readily explainable. Because she has accepted this male projection, she shuts herself up in her darkened, womb-like and coffin-like room, and repeatedly predicts her death—"I'll be gone soon" (69). But, as an exponent of this male view, Mrs. Compson also intuits and articulates the often unspoken assumption of this construction of womanhood and particularly motherhood: "I know it's my fault," she says to Jason. "I know you blame me" (322).[36]

To sum up: I have examined how in the patriarchal culture of *The Sound and the Fury* men seek to deny the loss that accompanies the constitution of subjectivity by projecting this sense of loss onto the mother, who recalls the blurred identity of the identificatory mirror stage and the narcissistic fusion of the imaginary register of being. Because of this projection, women are identified with the male's own sense of lack. Such an interpretation would account for Quentin's ambivalent response to Caddy; more specifically, it would explain why he alternates between a desire to possess Caddy and a desire to control her.

I have thus far focused my analysis on the psychological dynamics of Faulkner's characters, but, in concluding, I would like to speculate about Faulkner's own psychic investment in *The Sound and the Fury.* More specifically, what is Faulkner's attitude toward this dynamic of repression and projection? Why do his characters practice this projection? And ultimately, what is Faulkner's objective in writing this novel about a lost first other?

To respond to these questions, I refer once again to Faulkner's statement about the original impetus for writing the novel. To repeat, Faulkner explained that he wrote the novel to create "a beautiful and tragic little girl" to replace two female absences, the sister he never had and the daughter who would die days after birth. The novel originated, then, in Faulkner's own sense of loss. It is possible that, for Faulkner, the absence of a sister and the death of his daughter betokened the absence of being that attends the constitution of the self. Given that this loss of being is identified with the preoedipal mother and that feelings for the mother are often displaced onto the daughter or sister, it may be that Faulkner wrote *The Sound and the Fury* out of an unconscious desire to figure the primal lack that he identifies with these figures of sister and daughter.

To support this claim, I turn once again to Faulkner's 1933 introduction to *The Sound and the Fury.* In a recently discovered early draft of the introduction, Faulkner, in an unguarded moment, reveals his own psychic involvement in the novel. While explaining that he wrote the novel to explore his own feelings for Caddy, he admits, too, that he wrote himself into the novel: "I could be in it, the brother and father both. But one brother could not contain all that I could feel toward her. I gave her three: Quentin who loved her as a lover would, Jason who loved her with the same hatred of jealous and outraged pride of a father, and Benjy who loved her with the complete mindlessness of a child."[37] In this startling passage, Faulkner reveals that the Compson brothers' feelings for Caddy are his own, that he projects onto the three brothers his own deeply ambivalent feelings toward the mother-figure.

And in relentlessly analyzing these feelings, Faulkner's text reveals yet another projection: onto mother-figures, particularly onto Caddy and her daughter-surrogate, the Compson brothers project their feelings of loss. In other words, through the brothers, who represent him in the text, Faulkner makes of Caddy the projected image of a repressed desire for completeness of being. Such a projection would account for Caddy's elusiveness in the novel. To satisfy conflicting desires for reincorporation and for alienation, Faulkner imaginatively constructs Caddy as an absent presence, banishing her even as he invokes her. It is no wonder, then, that Faulkner always singled out this novel as the one he "felt tenderest toward."[38] Faulkner spoke so ardently of Caddy Compson—she is his "heart's darling," "the beautiful one"[39]—because she embodies in a disguised form an unconscious desire for the lost first other, for the mother of the imaginary relation.

CHAPTER 2

The Displaced Mother:
As I Lay Dying

~~The~~ woman does not exist.—

Jacques Lacan

*T*he phrase "As I lay dying" seems to have haunted Faulkner. He used it not only as the title of his novel about the Bundrens, but years earlier had applied it to a fragment that he would later recast and publish as "Spotted Horses."[1] When questioned about the source of the title, Faulkner quoted a line from *The Odyssey* that occurs as Agamemnon, in Hades, relates to Odysseus the manner of his death: "As I lay dying, the woman with a dog's eyes would not close for me my eyelids as I descended into Hades."[2] As for the relevance of these words to Faulkner's novel, scholars have frequently observed that Agamemnon's speech stresses the indignity of death, a theme certainly evident in *As I Lay Dying*.

I propose that Faulkner titled his novel *As I Lay Dying* because this allusion to Agamemnon's murder evokes matricide and a mother's revenge. Agamemnon's murder, described briefly in *The Odyssey,* is dramatized in a later text, Aeschylus' *Oresteia*. In the first play of Aeschylus' trilogy, Agamemnon is murdered by his wife, Clytemnestra, to avenge the death of their eldest daughter, Iphigenia, sacrificed to the gods for a wind to sail to Troy. As the eldest daughter, Iphigenia is a mother-surrogate; and, when Clytemnestra kills Agamemnon, she avenges her own foreshadowed death, which follows when Orestes repeats his father's act and slays Clytemnestra. In *As I Lay Dying*, Clytemnestra reappears in the form of Addie Bundren, another murdered mother who demands a price for her death.

According to Luce Irigaray, the myth of the murder of the mother, and not the murder of the father, as Freud claims, is the founding myth of Western culture. In *Le Corps-à-corps avec la mère,* Irigaray contends that when Freud in *Totem and Taboo* writes that human culture is founded on the murder of the father by the primitive horde of his sons, Freud "forgets a more ancient murder, that of the mother," which is represented by the myth of the murder of Clytemnestra by her son, Orestes.[3] Aeschylus' trilogy dramatizes a myth found in virtually all of the texts of our culture: the death or absence of the mother makes possible the construction of patriarchal culture. In Aeschylus, Iphigenia must die so that her father can lead his army into battle.

The work of Erich Neumann too (discussed in the introduction) seems to shed light on the dynamics of feminine repression. In *The Origins and History of Consciousness,* which examines mythic representations of the ego's origin and development, Neumann maintains that all myths narrate the ego's attempt to distinguish the self by creating boundaries between itself and the material world and by rejecting its original condition of existence in nature. This original condition is identified with the maternal womb and, according to Neumann, in myth the psychic repression of the early fused state is often represented by the murder of the mother.

In *Bearing the Word,* Margaret Homans finds that this disturbing myth is central to all of Western culture. She explains that the Freudian theory of the stages and processes of human development is based on Freud's reading of classical myths, in particular the myth of Oedipus, and that Lacanian theory, which derives from Freud, is a psychoanalytic retelling of the myth to which our culture has long subscribed—that the mother's absence makes possible desire, law, language, and the civilized order. As Ferdinand de Saussure first pointed out, a sign's meaning depends solely on its difference from other signs. In other words, identity and meaning come about only by establishing difference. According to Lacan, the father creates this difference by decreeing absence, an absence identified with the mother. His appearance marks the end of an imaginary dyadic relation with the mother, a condition of unbroken union without boundaries between self and other. The father intervenes in this union and prohibits merging. The child must repress the desire for the mother, and "that desire," driven underground, writes Terry Eagleton, "just *is* what is called the unconscious."[4] Under the threat of castration, the child submits to the law of alienation and renounces the phallus, which, as Homans explains, is both "the mark of man's difference from woman" as well as, "paradoxically, 'the-copula' or 'hyphen in the evanescence of its erection' that would restore the connection between children and mother."[5] In other words, the child lacks both the original unity and the means to attain it. A sign is substituted to cover over the mother's absence, and the child is ushered into the symbolic order. Only in this way—by banishing the mother and creating absence—can the child assert the boundaries that identify the self. In Lacanian theory, as in myth, the mother's exclusion is constructed as a positive step toward establishing identity and culture.

Homans interprets this myth more critically and argues that women writers trapped in this cultural myth often attempt to delegitimize the privileged voice of the father and to represence the mother's body over and against the exclusion of it required by the father's law. I propose to show that in *As I Lay Dying* Faulkner creates a feminine voice that is fully engaged in the project that Homans outlines: Addie Bundren issues a challenge to paternal structures of meaning. While Homans's argument does not specifically address the possibility of a subversion of the authority of the symbolic order in the work of a male writer, French feminists like Hélène Cixous maintain that "*écriture féminine,*" writing that "ruins representation," can be produced by men as well as by women,[6] and, in her interpretation of Lacan, Jane Gallop stresses that Lacan "repeatedly specifies that any speaking being *regardless of sex* is free to place itself on either side, the side of *tout* (phallic universalization) or the side of *pas-tout* (non-universalized, castrated, Freud would say)."[7] In *As I Lay Dying,* Faulkner, a white, male writer, the great-grandson of a Confederate colonel and slaveholder, presents both sides: he rewrites a dominant myth of our culture, the mythic identification of the mother's body with castration and death, and he allows the dead mother to speak.[8]

Addie Bundren rebels against the Law of the Father that, in the words of James Mellard, "exists on the side of Thanatos, not Eros":[9] she rejects her father's teaching that "the reason for living is to get ready to stay dead a long time" (155) and locates the meaning of existence in the body and the living world: "I believed that I had found it. I believed that the reason was the duty to the alive, to the terrible blood, the red bitter flood boiling through the land" (161). With these words, Addie sets herself up in opposition to a repressive social order. Whereas patriarchal law identifies life with death, the origin in the mother with the end, Addie lives for "the alive," for the fluid, chaotic, elemental existence that the Law of the Father would repress. She lies awake at night "hearing the dark land talking the voiceless speech" (161); she acknowledges the material world, naming her daughter, Dewey Dell, for the land.

As opposed to patriarchal culture, which repudiates what Lacan calls the imaginary, a state in which the boundaries of the self are lost and all is one, Addie embraces the imaginary. With the birth of her first child, Addie knows "that living was terrible that this was the answer to it" (157). In childbearing, Addie experiences an immersion of self in the other; one with Cash, she says that "the land was now of [her] blood and flesh" (159). The sense of completeness that Addie knows as a mother is readily explained by Nancy Chodorow's theory of maternity (alluded to in the introduction). In *The Reproduction of Mothering*, Chodorow argues that a woman's entry into the symbolic is different from a man's and that, for a number of reasons, the daughter does not enter the symbolic as wholeheartedly or as exclusively as does the son. First of all, the child separates from the mother under the threat of castration, but this threat does not evoke the same terror in the female child that it does in a male. In addition, the Law of the Father forbids a return of the missing phallus that would reconnect the mother and child, but, as Margaret Homans explains, because "of her likeness to and identification with her mother, the daughter does not need a copula such as the phallus to make the connection, as the son does."[10] In other words, the daughter can recover the lost unity with the mother, not by restoring the forbidden signifier but by reproducing the lost attachment to the mother; that is, by becoming a mother herself and recreating with her child the lost tie she experienced with the mother. The woman yearns for babies to recreate the original unity and presence of the imaginary. This, then, is what Addie experiences when she bears her firstborn, Cash: "I know that it had been, not that my aloneness had to be violated over and over each day, but that it had never been violated until Cash came. Not even by Anse in the nights" (158).[11]

Given that Addie embraces a preoedipal period when no difference exists between self and world, it is not surprising that both she and her daughter-double are consistently identified with matter. As André Bleikasten has observed, in this novel "woman's body is one with the world's flesh."[12] For example, to Jewel, Addie's hands look like "two of them roots dug up" (13); according to Peabody, beneath the quilt Addie's body is "no more than a bundle of rotten sticks" (40); and Darl scornfully describes Dewey Dell's breasts as "those mammalian ludicrosities which are the horizons and valleys of the earth" (150). And precisely because the maternal is identified with an imaginary unitary identity, patriarchal law denies the mother's existence. Both this identification with matter and this denial are implied in Addie's statement that she "would hate [her father] for having ever planted [her]" (155). If Addie's father "planted" her, then Addie's mother is the land, in which the seed grows. But the mother herself is never named. She is identified with the repressed referent that imbues all symbols with meaning but is itself absent. Like the connection to matter, the connection to the mother is not spoken, and so Addie's mother is referred to only by a metaphor, an allusion to the land.

This same denial of the mother as matrix is inscribed in *The Eumenides,* the last play of the *Oresteia.* At the conclusion of Aeschylus' drama, Orestes is tried for matricide and, although he has cut his mother's throat, he is found not guilty of a crime on the grounds that "the mother is no parent of which is called her child, but only nurse of the new planted seed that grows. The parent is he who mounts."[13] Here also the mother is both identified with the earth and denied; in the words of Apollo, "no parent." Only the father is acknowledged.

This attempt to assert the primacy of the empty signifier over the signified is the central project of patriarchal culture in *As I Lay Dying,* but nature continually threatens to disrupt symbolization and to restore an original inchoate state. For example, at Addie's funeral, the farmers discuss the rain that will wash out of the earth the seed they have labored to plant.

It's a fact. Washed clean outen the ground it will be. Seems like something is always happening to it.

Course it does. That's why it's worth anything. If nothing didn't happen and everybody made a big crop, do you reckon it would be worth the raising?

Well, I be durn if I like to see my work washed outen the ground, work I sweat over.

It's a fact. A fellow wouldn't mind seeing it washed up if he could just turn on the rain himself. (80; italics removed)

Their seed has been swept away: nothing has been made of their creative efforts. Even more important, however, the comment of one farmer indicates that it is precisely this "nothing" that imbues the symbolic order with meaning. "If nothing didn't happen . . . , do you reckon it would be worth the raising?" "Nothing" is the loss associated with the disruption of the mother-child dyad; and, without this "nothing," their signifiers would have no meaning.

Addie, like the land, represents that "nothing," the denied referent behind all signifiers. After bearing Cash and Darl, she says "I was three now" (159). As her name suggests, Addie is not single, separate, and distinct; she represents a plurality that threatens difference, the difference upon which language, culture, and authority are established. For this reason, time and time again in *As I Lay Dying,* Addie is renounced, signifying the original splitting that attended the emergence of subjectivity. For example, Addie recalls the original severing of the umbilical cord attaching her to the newborn Jewel, a severing that outwardly signs the loss that makes identity possible: "With Jewel—I lay by the lamp, holding up my own head, watching him cap and suture it before he breathed" (162). The physician, representative of the sign of difference, cuts the umbilical cord, severing "Jewel—I" and then he sutures the rupture left in Jewel by his mother's absence. Significantly, the word *suture* is a signal term in film theory and psychoanalysis. In the context of Lacanian film criticism, suture is the supplementation of an absence, the joining of a gap by representation. Jewel has been severed from his mother, and the stitches cover over, represent, what has been lost.

Like the stitches that shore up the gap in Jewel, language is also "a shape to fill a lack" (158), another substitute to cover over the loss that accompanies the entry into the symbolic order. For good reason, then, Addie hates words. Addie recognizes what Saussure has pointed out, the arbitrariness of language, a system of signs that substitutes for an absent referent. She understands that "words are no good; that words dont ever fit even what they are trying to say at. When [Cash] was born I knew that motherhood was invented by someone who had to have a word for it because the ones that had the children didn't care whether there was a word for it or not. I knew that fear was invented by someone that had never had the fear; pride, who never had the pride" (157–58). More, Addie hates language because it is based on separation and difference—"we had to use one another by words like spiders dangling by their mouths from a beam, swinging and twisting and never touching"—and she whips the school children to abolish this distance and difference: "and only through the blows of the switch could my blood and their blood flow as one stream" (158).[14]

53

Lacan states that "there is woman only as excluded by the nature of things which is the nature of words."[15] Jonathan Scott Lee interprets Lacan's comment to mean that "woman finds herself systematically excluded from reality as constructed in terms of the androcentric symbolic order."[16] This systematic exclusion of women in language is also indicated by Lacan's insistence that the feminine article *la* be crossed through in writing, thereby associating women with the bar separating the signified from signifier in Lacan's formulation S/s. Thus woman, through her association with the imaginary, comes to represent what must be renounced in order to enter into language and culture. She is, writes Homans, "primordially identified" with "the lost referent" (9), the object of desire. As a result of this identification, the mother is ceaselessly subjected to symbolization; that is, she is renounced and replaced with a substitute object, which (as noted in the introduction) Lacan calls *objet petit a.*[17] This process of substitution, of turning the mother into an *objet petit a,* is lucidly explained by Terry Eagleton:

We are severed from the mother's body: after the Oedipus crisis, we will never again be able to attain this precious object, even though we will spend all of our lives hunting for it. We have to make do instead with substitute objects, what Lacan calls the "object little *a,*" with which we try vainly to plug the gap at the very centre of our being. We move among substitutes for substitutes, metaphors of metaphors, never able to recover the pure (if fictive) self-identity and self-completion which we knew in the imaginary.[18]

In *As I Lay Dying,* we repeatedly witness this process of substitution. Compulsively, Addie is excluded and replaced with *objets petit a,* small objects meant to replace the true object of desire. In particular, three of Addie's sons have such compensatory objects; for Vardaman, the *objet petit a* is the fish; for Jewel, it is his horse; for Cash, it is the coffin.[19] Vardaman's choice of a symbol—the fish—suggests clearly the elemental threat that is identified with the mother. Because fish inhabit water, according to Mircea Eliade, primitive people believe that fish are infused with water's power to restore an original formlessness;[20] given this association of water and fish with the power of nature to threaten symbolization, when Vardaman kills the fish, he is asserting his control over elemental life: he aims "to show it to ma" (26), evidence of his manhood, his ability to master the physical world. He has plumbed the depths of the water, the source, and captured and killed its inhabitant, emblem of the fluid, transforming powers of nature. Because these powers are also identified with the mother, the slaying of the fish ritually reenacts the renunciation of the first other and the emergence of the speaking subject. Addie, a reminder of an imaginary unity, must figuratively die. Her displacement is a crucial step in the formation of subjectivity; in this way, like the fish that is "cooked and et," she sustains the symbolic order.

Jewel displaces his mother and replaces her with his horse; in Darl's words, "Jewel's mother is a horse" (84). This substitution allows Jewel to act out his conflicting feelings for his mother. On the one hand, when, at fifteen, Jewel purchases a horse by doing without sleep—cleaning up Lon Quick's forty acres of new ground at night after working all day—Jewel is denying the body, and this denial formalizes his assertion of the rule of the empty signifier. On the other hand, as Cash and Darl suspect when they notice Jewel slipping out at night, Jewel is also satisfying his desire for a woman, but not by fornicating with a local girl, as Cash and Darl at first think; with the horse he works to buy, Jewel is satisfying his desire for his mother. He can project onto the horse his conflicting feelings for a lost imaginary dyad. Alternately, he caresses the horse and beats it into submission, expressing his contradictory desires for incorporation and for alienation.

Addie is distanced and replaced yet again by the coffin that Cash builds to "her measure and weight" (80). Like Vardaman's fish and Jewel's horse, the coffin is meant to enclose and dispose of the threat to the symbolic order associated with the mother's body. The building of the coffin externalizes the struggle between the symbolic order and the fluid, chaotic world of matter. Cash carefully calculates all physical forces exerted by Addie's corpse in order to make the coffin "balance." The balance Cash is trying to achieve recreates the ever fragile and precarious construction of patriarchal authority over the natural world, a delicate equilibrium that is particularly threatened by the mother, who is associated with the imaginary. Thus it is motherhood—symbolized by Addie's reversed, head-to-foot position in the coffin like a fetus in the mother's womb, a position imposed by "them durn women" (80)—that disturbs the "balance," and reveals that the Law of the Father is always on the brink of collapsing back into an inchoate preoedipal state.

Each of these erasures and figurations of Addie thinly disguises a desire for her death. The repressed, unspeakable meaning behind these substitutions occasionally erupts in the text. Watching Cash build the coffin for his mother's corpse, Jewel bursts out, "Good God do you want to see her in it" (13). Similarly Darl invades Dewey Dell's "secret self" and confronts her with her own buried desire: "You want her to die so you can get to town; is that it?" (35). In fact, because the symbolic order is built on a pimordial rupture associated with the mother's absence, unconsciously each one of them does desire her death. In a sense, her family members are like the vultures that trail Addie's corpse. Her death makes possible the trip to town, which ritually reenacts their entry into the symbolic order. To acquire language, law, and culture, Addie must become an "it" buried in a hole that is "filled and covered" (220).

All of Lacan's writings, explains Jane Gallop, issue "an ethical imperative . . . to disrupt the imaginary in order to reach the symbolic." In *As I Lay Dying,* the Bundren family can be seen to be obeying this "ethical imperative." The novel can be read as an attempt by the Bundrens to replay the passage from the imaginary, identified with the mother-child relation, to the symbolic, identified with "town"—Jefferson. The problem, however, is that the symbolic develops out of the imaginary. Jane Gallop describes the interrelationship of the two orders: "It could be said that the symbolic can be encountered only as a tear in the fabric of the imaginary, a revealing interruption. The paths to the symbolic are thus *in* the imaginary. The symbolic can be reached only by not trying to avoid the imaginary, by knowingly being in the imaginary." Gallop's explanation of the way the symbolic "is mired in the imaginary"[21] prepares us to interpret Addie's revenge. Addie's revenge on her family for their denial of her (as an emblem of the imaginary) is her funeral journey. At one level, Addie's funeral journey stages a return to the imaginary register of being. At another, related level, the arduous struggle to bury Addie reflects how the symbolic is dependent on the imaginary. The two registers are "bound together," writes Gallop, and the much maligned imaginary, "which is linked to the relation to the mother," has a "positive and necessary function": "the imaginary embodies, fleshes out the skeletal symbolic."[22] In a sense, Addie's funeral journey seems to be expressly designed to objectify the positive and necessary function of what Laplanche calls "the vital order."[23] Addie literally delivers from the original formlessness Cash and Jewel, the children who attempt to represence her body even though it means defying the Law of the Father and risking annihilation. In particular, Addie rescues and is rescued by Jewel, her illegitimate son, whose very existence, because he is her child and not Anse's, exposes the lie of the biological primacy of the father and affirms what patriarchal culture would deny—that the mother is.[24] "And Jewel is," Darl says, "so Addie Bundren must be" (72).

For example, crossing the river, which is swollen like the body of a pregnant woman, externalizes the attempt to cross over from the imaginary register of being to the symbolic. In these threatening waters, boundaries between human and animal and between human and material collapse: Jewel's horse "moan[s] and groan[s] like a natural man" (140); Cash, spewed up on the bank, looks like "a bundle of old clothes" (141); and the current against their bodies feels "like hands molding and prodding at the very bones" (144). The flooded river, then, as Darl observes, is the "original myriad motion," which threatens to dissolve the temporary "clotting" (149–50), which is the self. The bridge over the river functions like language; it is "a shape to fill a lack"; it attempts to bridge the gap over the repressed referent. And by walking over the half-sunk bridge, Anse, Dewey Dell, Vardaman, and Tull avoid—repress—the transformative powers of nature. Darl, Jewel, and Cash, on the other hand, enter the water with Addie; and when Cash fastens the rope to the wagon bearing Addie's corpse and hands one end to Darl and the other to Jewel, he is symbolically reconnecting the severed umbilical cord. Thus, as they enter the flooded river, they are all three ritually immersed, returned to an original formlessness that preceded the emergence of subjectivity.

The log, on which "a long gout of foam hangs like the beard of an old man or a goat" (134) and that Cora calls "the hand of God" (138), figures the paternal metaphor that intervenes in the original imaginary mother-child dyad. When the log strikes the wagon and overturns it, "like it had been sent there to do a job and done it and went on" (139), its "job" is to enact the Law of the Father: the mother is to be renounced and the son who refuses to relinquish the mother is threatened with castration and death. In his role as father become Father, Cash, the eldest son, attempts to enforce this law. He orders Darl to "let the rope go" (134) and to "jump clear" (135). When he unties the rope that connects Jewel to his mother, he reenacts both the cutting of the umbilical cord and the primal splitting that produced the self as lack.

In this reenactment of the primary repression of the first to become other, Darl submits to the law that ordains lack, drops the rope, severs the bond joining him to the mother, and allows her body to be submerged. Jewel, on the other hand, defies the Name of the Father and risks dissolution by recreating the original fused state. He reenters the flood, finds the wagon with Addie's coffin, and reties the rope that joins him to the maternal body. Cash's role is dual. In his role as father-surrogate, he attempts to cut the cord attaching Darl and Jewel to Addie; but, in his role as son, he clings to Addie's body as it is immersed in the primal substance and risks a return to the formlessness of preexistence.

The trial by water ends with the triumph of the "the alive" over the empty signifier of difference. Addie's body is represenced and the cut cord is reconnected. The rope, tied fast once again to the wagon containing Addie's body, signals a return to an imaginary relation with the mother, as Tull's metaphor for the taut rope seems to acknowledge: "Like it was a straight iron bar stuck into the bottom and us holding the end of it" (141).

Throughout the river episode, the value of the material world is asserted. When Addie's family members are engulfed by the furious current, they are saved from being swept away by the ford, "the hard earth" (124), "the vain instants of solidity underfoot" (134). It is the earth that defends their integrity. For example, Jewel, who violates the law of alienation and reenters the "surging heaving desolation" (134), is not reabsorbed into the primal matrix. Rather, as always, Jewel, is "wooden" and "rigid" (168). The son who holds fast to the mother's body emerges unscathed, solid. Cash, who, in his role as father, orders the son to relinquish his bond to the mother and, in his role as son, metaphorically restores the missing signifier, is both punished and saved. He emerges from the flooded river with his identity intact, borne on Jewel's horse, a substitute for Addie, but with a broken leg. His broken leg figures a symbolic castration, the father's punishment on the child who defies the paternal prohibition against merging and restores an imaginary wholeness.

Whereas Jewel emerges with Addie and Cash surfaces with an Addie-substitute, Jewel's horse, Darl arises from this ritual immersion emptyhanded. His empty hands objectify that he has no attachment to the mother-matrix to deny. Unlike his brothers, who have severed the bond to the mother and covered the gap with a symbol—the coffin, the horse, the fish—Darl has no substitute for Addie. Long before he could renounce his mother, Addie renounced him, as Darl recognizes when he says, "I cannot love my mother because I have no mother" (84), and, without a mother to deny and to replace, he cannot say "I am." He says: "I dont know what I am. I dont know if I am or not" (72). The speaking subject defines itself as separate from the identificatory imago, the mother. Identity depends on separation and negation. Without a mother to deny, Darl is not constituted as a subject; he is unbounded, fluid, and he flows into others, invading their secret selves.[25] In this way, by renouncing Darl, Addie objectifies how the patriarchal order depends on her. As Bleikasten notes, because Darl is not grounded in "the sustaining earth,"[26] with disturbing regularity, he observes images of uprooting, reflecting his own disembodied state: "Above the ceaseless surface they stand—trees, cane, vines—rootless, severed from the earth" (127). Without a mother to deny, culture's symbols are not grounded and are as empty as Darl's hands as they emerge from the flood, emblem of the waters of the womb: "empty out of the water emptying the water emptying away" (137).

Because Addie has rejected him, Darl has not been able to pass through the normal phases of development, in particular, the dissolution of the oedipal complex, that, according to Lacan, establishes a normative subject. Thus, when Darl sets fire to the barn containing Addie's corpse, he is attempting figuratively to take possession of Addie and to renounce her. Paradoxically, however, Darl's act, which is intended to enact ritually the oedipal encounter, has precisely an opposite effect: it unleashes the elemental forces that threaten to overwhelm the fragile order constructed by symbolization. The burning barn, like the flooded river, threatens dissolution; and, in the fire as in the flood, Jewel once again violates the paternal prohibition and risks disintegration. In the "dissolving" (204) barn, "enclosed in a thin nimbus of fire" (205), he calls to Darl to help him prevent their mother's body from being consumed: "For an instant he looks up and out at us through the rain of burning hay like a portière of flaming beads, and I can see his mouth shape as he calls my name" (204). Darl, intent on alienation and displacement in accordance with Law of the Father, refuses; and Jewel is left singlehandedly to rescue Addie. Jewel's heroic efforts to recover Addie's corpse represence in a disguised form a repressed desire for reincorporation and return and, because the unconscious is now ascendant, he appears to be flat and one-dimensional, like a shadow, "running against the glare like that figure cut from tin" (204). In this trial by fire, like the trial by water, the child who acknowledges a forbidden desire of the m/other is saved by Addie. Jewel rides out of the conflagration borne on Addie's corpse: "Without stopping it overends and rears again, pauses, then crashes slowly forward and through the curtain. This time Jewel is riding upon it, clinging to it, until it crashes down and flings him forward and clear" (205). Addie's corpse translates into an actual event how the symbolic order is supported by the imaginary: the corpse literally carries Jewel out of the consuming flames. When Jewel escapes the burning barn carried on Addie's coffin, and when Cash rides to Jefferson, again borne on Addie's coffin, Addie objectifies how—to quote Gallop—"the paths to the symbolic are . . . *in* the imaginary."[27] Too late, even Darl admits his desire of the lost first other: in the aftermath of the fire, Vardaman finds Darl weeping, lying on the box that contains Addie's corpse.

When Darl sets fire to the barn sheltering Addie's coffin, he simultaneously enforces the Law of the Father and threatens it. On one hand, by attempting to incinerate Addie's corpse, Darl means "to hide her away from the sight of man" (197), in accordance with the law of alienation. In his role as displaced father, Cash supports Darl's attempt to erase Addie—"And me being the oldest, and thinking already the very thing that he done" (217)—even as he recognizes that Jewel's efforts to recover the maternal body violate patriarchal law: "and it seemed to me that when Jewel worked so to get it outen the river, he was going against God in a way" (216). On the other hand, by burning Armstid's barn, Darl poses a threat to the symbolic order. The barn is a cultural construct and, by setting fire to it, Darl unleashes the power of nature to dismantle the cultural order. For this infraction, in Cash's judgement, Darl must be punished: "Because there just aint nothing justifies the deliberate destruction of what man has built with his own sweat and stored the fruit of his sweat into" (221).

With the burning of the barn, then, the folks who branded Darl "queer" at last have concrete evidence that he poses a threat to the social order. Rejected by Addie, he has never been able to renounce the first other and achieve full symbolization. Ironically, because he has been rejected by the mother, he is like the mother; he, too, is a reminder of an original condition before the advent of the paternal metaphor. His eyes are "full of the land" (23, 32); he sees and represences the signified that patriarchal culture denies and covers over with symbols: "his eyes gone further than the food and the lamp, full of the land dug

60

out of his skull and the holes filled with the distance beyond the land" (23). Darl penetrates the unconscious and makes the conscious mind aware of chaotic, subversive, instinctive forces. He taunts Jewel, for example, by hinting broadly about Addie's adulterous liaison, Jewel's illegitimacy, Jewel's incestuous desire for his mother, and Jewel's figuration of Addie as a horse. Darl's ability to mine the unconscious mind is perceptively analyzed by Cash: "I see all the while how folks could say he was queer, but that was the very reason couldn't nobody hold it personal. It was like he was outside of it too, same as you, and getting mad at it would be kind of like getting mad at a mud-puddle that splashed you when you stepped in it" (220). For Darl, who has not fully internalized the symbolic, the unconscious mind is an open book. He reads the repressed, as we readers, whom Cash directly addresses, read Faulkner's novel. Through no will of his own, but like a mud puddle, which muddies people, Darl restores what culture displaces. Darl, then, like his mother, threatens the foundation of patriarchal culture. Therefore, he suffers the same fate as Addie; he is denied and expelled: "Our brother Darl in a cage in Jackson where, his grimed hands lying light in the quiet interstices, looking out he foams" (236).

When the representatives of the law come to take Darl away and imprison him, even before the state officials can act, Dewey Dell and Jewel hurl themselves on Darl. One of the lawmen must restrain Dewey Dell, while Jewel holds Darl down, saying, "Kill him. Kill the son of a bitch" (221). Dewey Dell's and Jewel's violent attack on Darl can be explained in two ways. At one level, they represent patriarchal culture's repudiation of Darl; that is, they hate him for reading their own denied desire for an unmediated connection with the maternal body. But, from another perspective, this attack also represents the mother's vehement rejection of Darl. Seen this way, Darl, who has attempted to erase Addie's body, enacts the archetypal role of Orestes, the son who murders the mother; and Jewel and Dewey Dell are Faulkner's formulation of the Furies, the maternal spirits, who in the *Oresteia* torment Orestes for the murder of the mother. Both Dewey Dell and Jewel are well chosen as avatars of maternal fury. Dewey Dell, now that she has been denied her abortion, will become the displaced mother; and Jewel, Addie's illegitimate son, born outside of patriarchal law, has proven himself again and again the champion of his mother's body. The dual roles played by Jewel and Dewey Dell, simultaneously representing both patriarchal and matriarchal rejection, are not contradictory but, rather, reinforcing; together, they stress the completeness of Darl's alienation. Darl is renounced by both Anse and Addie, and this double rejection leaves him utterly estranged, as Cash recognizes when he offers in epitaph for his exiled brother, "This world is not his world; this life his life" (242).

From the beginning, Addie's revenge focused on Darl. She formulated her revenge with his birth: "And when Darl was born I asked Anse to take me back to Jefferson when I died" (159). Moreover, his expulsion occurs almost simultaneously with her own final displacement: having just lowered Addie's body into a hole and covered it with earth, the Bundrens permit Darl to be handcuffed and carried away to a state asylum. Addie accomplishes her revenge on patriarchal culture in two ways by rejecting Darl. First, she successfully asserts the value of the repressed referent by denying Darl the opportunity to renounce his tie to his mother's body. Second, like the archetypal avenging mother, Clytemnestra, Addie exacts equal justice. Clytemnestra slays Agamemnon for slaying her daughter-double Iphigenia. Similarly, to avenge her lifelong exclusion, Addie insures that Darl is excluded. Ultimately, Addie's revenge is to make Darl suffer the mother's endlessly reenacted fate: he is sacrificed to insure the continuance of the social order.

In the end, Addie's protracted interment, her revenge on her family for their denial of her, has limited success. During the funeral journey, she succeeds in temporarily reenacting the original mother-child relation, but she is never able to put a stop to patriarchal culture's figuration of her. The symbolic order is built on representation, an endless series of inadequate substitutions for the presence and plenitude experienced in an imaginary symbiotic unity with the mother. With the mother renounced, the family generates substitutes for her. For example, the Tull sisters predict that with Addie's death her sons will marry; these wives will serve as substitutes for the mother, since, as Chodorow explains, men recreate the early bond with the mother with the heterosexual relationship with a wife.[28] Anse also replaces Addie with a wife, the duck-shaped woman, the new Mrs. Bundren, who usurps even Addie's name.

Throughout the arduous journey to bury Addie in Jefferson, even as Addie repeatedly attempts to ruin representation by stripping her family members of their substitutes for her, her family replace their substitutes with more substitutes, reenacting the primal trade—the exchange of the presymbolic dyadic relation for law and language. In the flooded river, for example, the mules that carry them toward their destination—town, with its resonances of the symbolic order—are drowned, and Cash's cherished tools, substitutes for his real desire, are swept away. But the Bundrens are undeterred by this dismantling of representation; they persist in favoring the figurative over the literal. Cash lovingly embraces his returned tools, and the other Bundrens replace the lost mules by swapping their substitutes for more substitutes. For mules to carry them to their cultural mecca, Anse trades their replacements for the lost symbiotic unity: Anse's money for new teeth, Cash's money for a "talking machine," and Jewel's horse. The diminishing nature of their substitutions, how with each trade they trade down, is most clearly demonstrated at the novel's conclusion, when Dewey Dell tries to placate Vardaman by offering him bananas as a replacement for the electric train in the store window: "Wouldn't you rather have bananas?" (233; italics removed). Just as the bananas are an inadequate substitute for the train that made Vardaman's "heart hurt" (199), so also the train is a sorry substitute for an original plenitude with no lacks or exclusions of any kind. In other words, the Bundrens vainly attempt to cover over the gap at the center of their being with one substitute after another. The whole endeavor of patriarchal culture, to disrupt a former imaginary unity and then to cover over the resulting gap with a sign, is ritually reenacted by the Bundrens' trip to Jefferson, as Tull observes with devastating acuity: "They would risk the fire and the earth and the water and all just to eat a sack of bananas" (126). In the end, the ultimate absurdity of the symbolic order's displacement and figuration of what Sartre calls being-in-itself is summed up in the novel's closing cartoon image: with Addie safely underground, the Bundrens munch bananas in their wagon, which stands on the square, the Jefferson courthouse at their back. But the only appreciative witness is Darl: "Dewey Dell and Vardaman on the seat and Cash on a pallet in the wagonbed are eating bananas from a paper bag. 'Is that why you are laughing, Darl?' " (236).

CHAPTER 3

Law and Desire in
Light in August

The manuscript and typescript versions of the text of *Light in August* reveal that Faulkner repeatedly rearranged the order of the chapters of his novel and that only late in the composition process did he decide on the sequence that informs the published novel.[1] Ultimately Faulkner appears to have decided to frame the central narrative, the tragedies of Joe Christmas and Joanna Burden, with two other narrative strands, the stories of Lena Grove and Gail Hightower. Faulkner's novel begins and ends with chapters devoted to Lena Grove. Within this framing narrative is another narrative frame: Hightower is introduced in the second and third chapters of the novel, and he is also the central character in the penultimate chapter. Thus the stories of Lena Grove and Hightower appear to form concentric circles around a horrific center, the murder of Joanna Burden, as if the dark narrative at the novel's core needed somehow to be contained.

In this chapter, I organize my discussion of *Light in August* in a way similar to Faulkner's arrangement of the three narratives; that is, I position Joe Christmas between Hightower and Lena Grove. All three fictional strands can be read as narratives of identity; that is, they seem to render allegorically the way in which human subjectivity comes into being. Indeed, one Lacanian commentator has said that "for Lacan narrative is the attempt to catch up retrospectively on this traumatic separation, to tell this happening again and again, to re-count it,"[2] and in *Light in August* each narration "re-counts" the primal trauma from a different perspective. Because Faulkner confers closing significance on Lena Grove, I, too, close with Lena's narrative, and I begin my interpretation with Hightower.

"I AM DYING": THE OEDIPAL MOMENT

Seemingly unaccountably, Faulkner devotes the penultimate chapter of *Light in August* to the wraith-like, defrocked minister Gail

Hightower. The chapter follows hard on the death of Joe Christmas, and the sequencing appears to be, at best, mysterious, at worst, anti-climactic. Shortly after the fugitive Christmas has been shot and cas-trated in Hightower's kitchen, we find the minister sitting in his study in the fading light of late afternoon "dream-recovering" (487); that is, attempting mentally to recreate his grandfather's fatal Civil War exploit, the moment his ancestor was shot from his horse as he led his cavalry though the Union forces at Jefferson. On the surface, this chapter does not appear to advance the narrative: Hightower merely reflects on his life as he awaits the arrival of his vision.[3] In fact, however, these reflec-tions are revelatory: they explain why Hightower has never assumed his place in the social order. More important, they lead him to take a crucial and long-overdue step in his social development—to pass through the oedipal stage. The oedipal crisis triggers the formation of the subject. To achieve subjectivity, it is necessary to submit to the ultimate au-thority of the Law, to accept castration; that is, the oedipal law of alien-ation into language that embodies Lacan's concept of Freud's castra-tion. Until this time, Hightower has avoided this symbolic castration; consequently, he is not yet a subject, but a subject in the process of constitution. He is as yet inchoate: a ghostly, death-in-life figure. How-ever, as Hightower reconstructs his past, he is moved to take a long overdue step: to recognize the phallic signifier and its meaning as cas-tration. At this time, in his fifties, the minister, who has heretofore existed in a limbo-like state, outside of both the imaginary and the symbolic, negotiates the oedipal encounter and finally comes into being as a subject.

Often *Light in August* seems to proceed by means of flashbacks. For example, chapters six through nine take a backward look at Joe Christmas's childhood years. Chapter twenty functions in a similar way, placing Hightower in the context of his recent and not-so-recent past: as he sits by his study window, awaiting a repetition of his grandfather's gallant death, Hightower recollects his childhood and recalls his mother, father, and grandfather. His thoughts take him back to the very beginning, the preoedipal phase, when he still lived in symbiotic relation with the mother's body. Because at this time he still remained firmly attached to the mother, his earliest memory of his mother evokes the image of the Medusa, the mythic representation of the phallic mother. He remembers her "first and last as a face and tremendous eyes and a spread of dark hair on a pillow, with blue, still, almost skele-

65

ton hands" (475). Like the snaky-haired mythic figure who represents a fusion of male and female, Hightower's mother is a figure of integration: mother and child are a whole. She embraces and contains him; she is like a house, den, or cavern, within which he exists:

[His mother's eyes] were the house: he dwelled within them, within their dark and all-embracing and patient aftermath of physical betrayal. He and she both lived in them like two small, weak beasts in a den, a cavern, into which now and then the father entered—that man who was a stranger to them both, a foreigner, almost a threat: so quickly does the body's wellbeing alter and change the spirit. He was more than a stranger: he was an enemy. He smelled differently from them. He spoke with a different voice, almost in different words, as though he dwelled by ordinary among different surroundings and in a different world. (475)

Into this dyad, the father intrudes, introducing difference. In his place as the representative of the Law of the Father, Hightower's father creates difference by banishing the mother's body and forbidding the child access to her under the threat of castration. In the case of Hightower's mother, this erasure of the maternal body is virtually objectified. She gradually dwindles away before her son's eyes, the victim of a sign, her husband's righteous convictions. More specifically, during the war, while he was absent, she had scarcely enough food to subsist on because of his principles; that is, because he opposes slavery he will not allow her to eat food grown or cooked by a slave, and because she is not able to reciprocate in kind, he will not even allow her to accept the help of neighbors. For Hightower's father, the Law—God the Father—takes precedence over the body's needs. When his wife beseeches him to observe these needs, he tells her, "God will provide." Her response is practical, worldly: "Provide what? Dandelions and ditch weeds?" He replies with a belief: "Then He will give us the bowels to digest them" (467). In other words, the body must conform to the rule of the signifier. So stifled, the maternal body vanishes before their eyes:

If on the day of her death he [Hightower] had been told that he had ever seen her otherwise than in bed, he would not have

66

believed it. Later he remembered differently: he did remember her moving about the house, attending to household affairs. But at eight and nine and ten he thought of her as without legs, feet; as being only that thin face and the two eyes which seemed daily to grow bigger and bigger, as though about to embrace all seeing, all life, with one last terrible glare of frustration and suffering and foreknowledge, and that when that finally happened, he would hear it: it would be a sound, like a cry. (475)

The Law of the Father displaces the mother and imposes a penalty of alienation and ostensibly even death on the subject who denies its authority. As a child, Hightower associates this paternal prohibition with something external, with the much-patched frock coat his father wore instead of a uniform during the war, and, in particular, with one patch, which was "blue, dark blue; the blue of the United States" and which "stopped his very heart" (469). The child, Hightower, would steal into the attic, remove the coat from a trunk, and touch the blue patch "with that horrified triumph and sick joy and wonder if his father had killed the man from whose blue coat the patch came, wondering with still more horror yet at the depth and strength of his desire and dread to know" (470). The coat is a physical representation of the phallus, or paternal metaphor, which mandates loss even as it ushers the child into the symbolic order. Confronted with this representation of the paternal signifier, Hightower's response is, not surprisingly, ambivalent: he feels "sick joy," "horrified triumph," "desire and dread." On the one hand, Hightower is the son who must submit to the father become Father under the law of castration; thus, he identifies with the Union soldier he imagines his father killed. For him, the sign of difference is a threat. Hightower can acquire identity only by submitting to the law of alienation into language (Lacan's version of Freud's castration). On the other hand, however, Hightower esteems the phallic signifier. He glories in the transcendence of the empty signifier; he yearns to exist in the place of the Name-of-the-Father.

Hightower's dual response to the paternal metaphor is also signaled when, gazing at the patch, he feels "a little sick" (469). Nausea, as Bleikasten explains, externalizes the paradox of subjectivity: it signifies a desire for separation even as it denotes immanence.[4] In other words, although he longs to identify with the paternal signifier, at the same time he incarnates the other who must be displaced; that is, he identifies with the slain soldier. Whereas the soldier was killed, Hightower must submit to a somewhat similar fate: he must accept alienation into language; he must give over his identity to the knowledge of castration. Consequently, when Hightower confronts his father at dinner that evening, the child stares at the father "with on his child's face an expression of the Pit itself" (469). Hightower is identified with the pit, an image for the condition of existence prior to the emergence of separate identity, because the child has not yet accepted separation and loss.

Hightower thus faces the dilemma of subjectivity: he longs to identify with the father become Father, but he dreads the rupture, the alienation into language that attends the constitution of the subject. In this instance, the conflict is resolved by a substitution that allows him to satisfy his desire for a representative of the symbolic Other and to evade castration. Hightower achieves this feat by "skip[ping] a generation" (478), by identifying not with the father but with his dead grandfather. The grandfather, like Hightower's father, embodies the heroic aspect of the symbolic Other, but with an important difference: the grandfather poses no threat. For this reason, from his early childhood, Hightower is obsessed with the Civil War exploits of his dead grandfather. As a child, whenever his father left the house, Hightower "would go to the kitchen and say to the negro woman: 'Tell again about grandpa. How many Yankees did he kill?' *And when he listened now it was without terror. It was not even triumph: it was pride*" (470; my italics). To Hightower, the grandfather, whose wartime heroics demonstrate a sublime disregard for the world and the flesh, seems to have achieved an apotheosis; in Lacanian terms, the daredevil raid has transformed him in death into the symbolic Other. By identifying with the dead grandfather, Hightower satisfies his desire for the transcendental signifier without undergoing castration, without the loss of being that would constitute identity, because, unlike his father, his grandfather does not represent a threat to him. Quite the contrary, his grandfather is allied with him in his resistance to the father: the grandfather is "the single thorn in his son's side" (470). This situation conforms to a paradigm that John T. Irwin identifies in Faulkner's fiction. Irwin explains that the father is in the position of being both father and son—both the son who is to be castrated by the father and the father who fears the son's retaliation for castration. As a result of this positioning, the father fears both the father and the son: remembering his own hostile feelings for his father, he fears his son; and he fears the grandfather—his father—who threatens him with castration.[5] As Ernest Jones expresses it: "We doubtless have here the deepest reason for the constant identification of grandson with grandfather; both are equally feared by the father, who has reason to dread their retaliation for his guilty wishes against them."[6]

By this substitution, by rejecting the phallic father, Hightower evades the oedipal encounter. He never passes through what Lacan sometimes calls "the phallic stage,"[7] which puts "the finishing touches on the process of separation that posits the subject as signifiable, which is to say, separate, always confronted by an other."[8] Consequently, Hightower is not yet constituted as a subject. He is inchoate; he has no ego identity. Like Peter Pan, Hightower refuses to grow up, to become a man—in Lacanian terms, to position himself as a man in his structuration as a subject.

Having refused symbolic castration, Hightower could elect to extend the preoedipal stage, to remain fused with the phallic mother. This, however, is not his choice. He rejects not only the phallic father but also the phallic mother, and she, too, is replaced with a substitute: the church. In effect, he attempts to reconstitute himself with a new conception and birth by replacing his parents with safe substitutes. He believes that his adopted mother, the church he enters as a young man, will provide him with a refuge from existence in the world:

> when he believed that he heard the call it seemed to him that he could see his future, his life, intact and on all sides complete and inviolable, like a classic and serene vase, where the spirit could be born anew sheltered from the harsh gale of living and die so, peacefully, with only the far sound of circumvented wind, with scarce even a handful of rotting dust to be disposed of. That was what the word seminary meant: quiet and safe walls within which the hampered and garmentworried spirit could learn anew serenity to contemplate without horror or alarm its own nakedness. (478)

Hightower compares the church to a perfect vase. How are we to interpret this metaphor? Throughout the novel, the urn, or vase, visually represents the preoedipal phase, a preconscious, fused state. For example, the urn is identified with Lena Grove, a mother fused with

69

her child. Given this usage, Hightower's application of the urn image denotes a substitution. He means to replace one vase with another: to substitute the church—"a classic and serene vase"—for another container, his own containment in the world, emblemized by the maternal body. The purpose of this substitution, as Bleikasten observes, is disincarnation.[9] The "intact and on all sides complete and inviolable" vase he identifies with the church will, he is convinced, provide him with boundaries. In other words, by this substitution, he means to escape the threat of incorporation that the preoedipal mother represents, just as, by substituting the dead grandfather for the living father, he means to evade the threat of castration posed by the Law of the Father.

Because Hightower renounces the maternal body and substitutes a sign, he rejects the imaginary; and because he refuses to submit to the greater power of the Law, he is not yet constituted as a subject in the symbolic. Once this Lacanian context is established, Hightower's ghostly condition in *Light in August* becomes understandable. Hightower has "no depth, no solidity" (486); he gives off the "smell of people who no longer live in life" (317–18), because he exists neither in the register of the imaginary nor of the symbolic. His fears of engulfment by the phallic mother and of castration by the phallic father lead him to seize on what he believes is an alternative to generation and death. He fixates on a moment that seems to him outside of time—the moment that his grandfather was shot from a galloping horse while leading a raid on the Union-held Jefferson. But his ploy is a failure, because it excludes a generation: it bypasses the father, the link between himself and his grandfather. Quite simply, because Hightower rejects the father, he cannot come into existence. It is "as though the seed which his grandfather had transmitted to him had been on the horse too that night and had been killed too and time had stopped there and then for the seed and nothing had happened in time since, not even him" (64). Hightower has, as it were, positioned himself outside of generation. His grandfather's seed can only be transmitted to him through the father; by overpassing his father, Hightower cancels out himself. He can never come into being as long as he denies the father in his role as symbolic Other. Paradoxically, he can never attain manhood as long as he evades castration. For as long as he avoids the oedipal encounter, he is like a "enunch chanting in a language which he does not even need to not understand" (318).

Belatedly, Hightower does becomes a subject. He takes the first step toward achieving subjectivity when he acts as an agent of the Law of the Father. It is the father's role to help the child enter the world of culture, law, language, and loss. Hightower assumes this role when he officiates at the birth of a child. His first attempt to act as a representative of the Law is abortive: the child of the black woman whom he aids is stillborn. But in his second attempt, he delivers into the world a living child—Lena Grove's child. In presiding at these deliveries, Hightower is assuming paternal responsibility; he is identifying with the paternal metaphor. Consider, for example, the instruments he brings with him to assist him: a razor and a book. With the razor, he severs the umbilical cord, separating mother and child, introducing the child to loss. The resulting yawning gap in the newly created subject is then covered over by empty signifiers, symbolized by the book. Hightower's identification with the paternal signifer is further signaled when he hopes and expects that Lena will name the child after him, an honor that is often bestowed on the father. Given that he has played the paternal role, his desire for a namesake is appropriate. He has assumed the responsibility of separating the child from the maternal body; he has acted as a representative of the Name-of-the-Father. Fittingly, then, after the delivery, when he returns home and settles down with a book, "he chooses food for a man" (Shakespeare's *Henry IV*) (405).

But to acquire identity, more is required of Hightower. To accede to the domain of the symbolic phallus, he must acknowledge the authority of death, negation, and loss. He must face symbolic castration. This acceptance takes place as Hightower sits by his study window in the gathering dark and reflects on the sum of his past. Mentally, Hightower has relived his life from the beginning to the present. His long retrospection ended, he now sees himself in a new light, and is finally ready to become a subject. As he sits by the window, lost in contemplation, Hightower passes through the successive phases in the constitution of the subject—the mirror stage and then through the oedipal complex, with its attendant acceptance of the loss of that signifier that Lacan calls the phallus.

The mirror stage is the first step in developing an ego—an integrated self-image. At this level of development, the emerging subject arrives at a sense of an I by seeing itself reflected back by some person or object in the world. In the words of Terry Eagleton, "the object is at once somehow part of ourselves—we can identify with it—and yet not our-

71

selves, something alien."[10] This is the first step in alienation—in recognizing the other as other. While a blurring of self and other still obtains, the process of constructing a self has been initiated. This mirror stage of development is represented in the text as Hightower reviews his life and sees his own image reflected in the mirroring faces of others: "And more than that: the faces seem to be mirrors in which he watches himself. He knows them all; he can read his doings in them. He seems to see reflected in them a figure antic as a showman, a little wild: a charlatan preaching worse than heresy" (488).

From the mirror stage, the first step toward establishing a separate identity, Hightower moves toward a recognition of the phallic signifier and its meaning as castration. For the first time, Hightower sees loss in relation to the paternal metaphor. He perceives that the transcendental signifier is an empty marker, signifying only lack: "And I know that for fifty years I have not even been clay: I have been a single instant of darkness in which a horse galloped and a gun crashed. And if I am my dead grandfather on the instant of his death, then my wife, his grandson's wife. . . . . . . the debaucher and murderer of my grandson's wife, since I could neither let my grandson live or die. . . . . . ."(491). This acknowledgement of the missing signifier is the knowledge of castration. Accordingly, as Hightower confronts lack, the imagery that attends these revelations evokes a painful, bloody wounding. For example, the flow of the minister's thoughts is compared to an instrument of torture: "Out of the instant the sand-clutched wheel of thinking turns on with the slow implacability of a mediaeval torture instrument, beneath the wrenched and broken sockets of his spirit, his life" (490–91); and his sweat is metaphorically elided with blood: "sweat begins to pour from him, springing out like blood" (490). This imagery of blood and torture tells us that Hightower is negotiating the painful passage through the oedipal phase.

In the oedipal encounter, the father—or the phallus, that which stands for the father—introduces prohibition, separation and individuation. In this instance, the paternal signifier appears in the form of a composite face. As Hightower observes the wheel of mirroring faces, he is struck in particular by "two faces which seem to strive (but not of themselves striving or desiring it: he knows that, but because of the motion and desire of the wheel itself) in turn to free themselves one from the other, then fade and blend again" (491–92). The two faces that struggle—but not of their own volition—for difference, separation, and identity are those of Joe Christmas and Percy Grimm. Because Grimm plays the role of the father who initiates the oedipal realization, introducing alienation, loss, and subjectivity, Hightower's recognition of Grimm ushers the minister into the symbolic order: "But he has seen now, the other face, the one that is not Christmas. 'Why, it's. . . . . . .' he thinks. 'I have seen it, recently. . . . Why, it's that. . . . . . boy. With that black pistol, automatic they call them. The one who. . . . . . into the kitchen where. . . . . . killed, who fired the—— ' " (492). As Hightower mentally recreates this oedipal moment, he finally accepts the knowledge of castration, and he attains lack. Because this symbolic castration—a cutting off and rejecting of a part of the self—is an act of repression, it is represented in the text by ellipses, which figure the gap in the newly established self. Hightower becomes a subject, but because subjectivity is based on no more than the supposition of symbolic value, his accession to the domain of the symbolic is rendered as a loss of being: "Then it seems to him that some ultimate dammed flood within him breaks and rushes away. He seems to watch it, feeling himself losing contact with earth, lighter and lighter, emptying, floating. 'I am dying,' he thinks" (492). This is the death into being, the acknowledgement of death and negation and loss that constitutes selfhood.

At long last, Hightower achieves full symbolization. Paradoxically that means that he has attained lack: his body is "empty and lighter than a forgotten leaf and even more trivial than flotsam lying spent and still upon the window ledge which has no solidity beneath hands that have no weight" (492). He has emptied himself out "so that it can be now Now" (492), so that he can accede to the place of the signifier of lack, the place of the missing phallus. That place is represented in the text by Hightower's vision of his grandfather's Civil War exploit, the daredevil ride through the streets of Jefferson. All his life, Hightower has identified transcendence with his grandfather's headlong rush into death. Fittingly, then, Hightower's accession into the symbolic is rendered as the vision of the galloping cavalry. As Hightower accedes to the place of the empty signifier, a sign to cover over what is lost, he conjures the reckless ride with images that stress its symbolic aspect, with evanescent, substanceless imagery: "Like a long sighing of wind in trees it begins, then they sweep into sight, borne now upon a cloud of phantom dust" (492). And as Hightower accepts the loss of the phallus, he visualizes a vacuum overtaking the phantom cavalrymen: "They rush past, are gone; the dust swirls skyward sucking, fades away

73

into night which has fully come" (493). Because subjectivity is founded on a void, Hightower's grandfather's ride into death appropriately images the minister's accession to the symbolic order. Like his grandfather's raid, the symbolic order is a gesture of bravado, a gallant but doomed effort to defy death by rushing headlong into the void. Ultimately, Hightower's grandfather's ride into death is analogous to Hightower's entrance into the symbolic order because symbolization is only another form of death.

BETWEEN THE IMAGINARY AND THE SYMBOLIC

After Joe Christmas has been shot and castrated by Percy Grimm, he lies dying on the floor of Hightower's kitchen "with his eyes open and empty of everything save consciousness and with something, a shadow, about his mouth" (464). Joe ends his life as he has lived it: as a split subject. On the one hand, his eyes are open, and he clings to consciousness; that is, he desires subjectivity and representation. On the other, the shadow that plays about his mouth images a contrary desire for the totalization of the imaginary.

Joe is a man in the middle, caught between Law and Desire, between the symbolic and imaginary registers of being. He desires ego-identity; that is, he desires to be an I separate from an other, but, without his conscious awareness, he resists the prohibition, alienation, and lack that attend the constitution of the self. Likewise, at an unconscious level, he desires to restore the plenitude and presence of the imaginary, but he shuns the loss of difference and of subjectivity that such a drive toward completion entails. As a result, he is a subject adrift, and the outward sign of his psychic ambivalence is his racial indeterminacy.[11] Just as Joe does not know if he is black or white, he does not exist on either the symbolic or the imaginary plane. Joe's racial ambiguity casts into stark relief the conflict that exists at an unconscious level in every human subject. To achieve language and subjectivity, the child must undergo symbolization (symbolic castration), but it is also true, as James M. Mellard points out, that "for Lacan the orders of the Real, the Imaginary, and the Symbolic are always inmixed with each other." In other words, the move from the imaginary order to the symbolic is not complete or absolute, and dependency on the imaginary persists even after the subject has acceded to the function and power of the symbolic. Again Mellard offers a lucid explanation: "It must be understood that the 'passage through' the Imaginary to the Symbolic does not mean the subject goes beyond the Imaginary. In the constitution of the subject, the Symbolic enters the subject. Thereafter both registers will persist in the subject's display of itself in behavior and verbal repetitions."[12]

Joe Christmas's story can be interpreted in terms of the play of these two registers of being. In a sense, Joe is the typical Lacanian subject, because he exists as a site of conflict, and Lacan describes the human subject as "essentially a place of conflict between the *je* and the *moi,* between the symbolic and the imaginary."[13] Joe's case, however, is extreme: because he refuses to accept the loss of the symbolic phallus, Joe is never fully assimilated into the symbolic and remains neurotically enmeshed in the imaginary; and this psychic conflict erupts in the form of haunting images out of his unconscious. Lacan writes that "the subject caught in the snares of spatial identification [of the mirror phase] . . . fashions the series of fantasies that runs from an image of a fragmented body to what we may call the orthopedic vision of its totality."[14] Joe Christmas is just such a subject, beset by unconscious images of a repressed desire for an imaginary totality of being.

To decipher the representations of the repressed unconscious in *Light in August,* Jung's philosophy of the unconscious is a useful tool. Because both Jung and Lacan are Freudian revisionists and because both, with Freud, share the basic premise that there is a generic or archetypal pattern to the development of human identity, the two seemingly different psychoanalytic theories have a number of points of convergence. More specifically, while Jung relies heavily on myth and Lacan has recourse to language theory, both Jung and Lacan are identifying a similar narrative about the emergence of ego-identity. In fact, Jung's explanation of the origin of consciousness can be read as a mythic parallel to Lacanian theory. For example, Erich Neumann's Jungian study *The Origins and History of Consciousness,* (already alluded to in the introduction and chapter 2) attempts to trace the evolution of human consciousness by examining mythic representations of the ego's origins and development. Neumann maintains that all myths narrate the ego's attempt to distinguish the self by creating boundaries between itelf and the natural world and by rejecting its original condition of existence in nature. Prior to the emergence of consciousness, the self does not exist: there is only an undifferentiated existence in the cosmos; and this preconscious state is imaged as the circle—in ancient

Egyptian mythology, the uroboros, or circular snake, that bites its own tail, the most ancient deity of the prehistoric world.[15] In Jungian philosophy, this ancient symbol of the round is termed the mandala.

Because the state that precedes the emergence of the ego answers the question, From where does the ego arise? this original condition is identified with the maternal womb and the coupled parents. Like the enveloping world from which the self detaches itself, the womb also is a container from which the individual emerges. Similarly, the child issues from parental sexual intercourse, an act that fuses the opposites, male and female. The joined parents and the maternal womb, then, are also formulations of the uroboros, the initial state, one with and engulfed by natural existence; and this state is often represented visually by images of the containing urn, the pit, and the Medusa, a mythic female creature whose hair is a mass of twisting snakes symbolizing the uroboros and whose gaze turns men to stone; that is, reduces them to matter. From these images of the initial unconscious state, Neumann explains, human beings flee, because "consciousness = deliverance."[16]

Neumann's Jungian interpretation of the human project to establish selfhood seems particularly applicable to Joe Christmas for two reasons: because his racial ambiguity can be read as a form of the uroboros, a sign of the self's continuity with the other and the world, and because Joe is haunted throughout his life by images out of the unconscious, which take the form of pits, containers, circles, and Medusas. At the same time, Lacanian theory, too, applies. In Lacanian terms, Joe's grandfather, Doc Hines, represents the Law of the Father or the phallus—that which comes between the mother and child and decrees alienation. Hines, a white-male supremacist, stands for difference, boundaries, and repression; his life's work can be read as an effort to police the borders between self and other. In the mother-father-child triangle, Hines plays the role of father become Father by separating Joe from his mother and his grandmother and by denying the child the use of the phallus to restore union with the mother. The father's punishment for recreating this union is castration, the annihilation of the self; and Hines exacts this punishment.[17] He kills Joe's father for engaging in sexual intercourse with Joe's mother; and, because Joe, who is called "a white nigger," seems to embody a blurring of racial identity that reflects the original imaginary unity, Hines appears equally intent on destroying his grandson.[18]

Throughout his life, Joe resists the Law of the Father that ordains lack: he refuses to submit to the authority of father-figures like Hines who threaten him with castration and death, and he continues to desire the original lost object, identified with the mother's body. Because he desires a repressed totality of being and because, according to Lacan, a repressed desire insistently returns, Joe is repeatedly confronted with images of a preoedipal imaginary unity. This preconscious state erupts for the first time when Joe, as a small child in an orphanage, inadvertently witnesses a primal scene. As Joe hides in the room of a young woman identified only as the orphanage's "dietitian," he stealthily eats her toothpaste, while, on the other side of a curtain, she and a young intern engage in illicit sex. The dietitian, whom Joe associates with "eating, food, the diningroom" (120), is a mother-substitute, the nurturing female in the house; the young intern, "assistant to the parochial doctor" and "a familiar figure about the house" (121), is a father-surrogate. Because Joe is witnessing the intercourse of parental figures, he is, metaphorically, present at his own conception.[19]

As these parental surrogates copulate, Joe, instinctively swallows the dietitian's pink toothpaste, which seems interchangeable with the "pink and white" dietitian herself, who makes "his mouth think of something sweet and sticky to eat, and also pink colored and surreptitious" (120). The toothpaste, then, figures the dietitian/mother, but it also emblemizes the sexual union of mother and father, for as Joe squeezes the tube, the paste resembles "a pink worm" that "coil[s] smooth and slow onto his parchmentcolored finger" (120). The coiled snake being the uroboros, the ancient symbol for the union of opposites in the unconscious, two forms of fusion, the fused parents and the womb-state, are invoked by this primal scene. As Joe swallows the paste beside the copulating couple he seems to be returned to the womb. Squatting in the dark, "pinkwomansmelling" enclosure, still behind the curtain, swallowing, "automatonlike," mouthful after mouthful of the pink paste, he is the image of the fetus taking sustenance from the mother's body. These figures of fusion—joined parents and womb-enveloped fetus—mirror one another and herald the eruption of Joe's unconscious:

> In the rife, pinkwomansmelling obscurity behind the curtain he squatted, pinkfoamed, listening to his insides, waiting with astonished fatalism for what was about to happen to him. Then it happened. He said to himself with complete and passive surrender: "Well, here I am."

When hands dragged him violently out of his vomit he did not resist. He hung from the hands, limp, looking with slack-jawed and glassy idiocy into a face no longer smooth pink-and-white, surrounded now by wild and disheveled hair whose smooth bands once made him think of candy. "You little rat!" the thin, furious voice hissed; "you litte rat! Spying on me! You little nigger bastard!" (122)

When "the curtain fled back" (122), the division between conscious and unconscious collapses, and Joe is confronted with an image projected out of his unconscious. The dietitian, with her "wild and disheveled hair," assumes the appearance of the mythic formulation of the preoedipal mother, the Medusa.[20] The Medusa aptly figures an original condition prior to the advent of the paternal metaphor both because she is a snaky-haired female creature and because she turns men to stone. With her hair a mass of twisting snakes, symbolizing the uroboros, or round, she externalizes a union of opposites: she is both female and male. She is a female creature, but her snake-like hair, a phallic image, suggests a bisexual nature. In Lacan's rendering of this figure, she represents the phallic or preoedipal mother, a formulation of the child's terror of the imaginary, a terror of incorporation. Because the imaginary is a condition of no lacks, a condition prior to symbolic castration, the mother of the preoedipal phase is presumed by the child to posssses the phallus, the all-powerful signifier. Jane Gallop explains: "The imaginary might be characterized as the realm of non-assumption of the mother's castration. In the imaginary, the 'mother' is assumed to be still phallic, omnipotent and omniscient, she is unique." In other words, because the imaginary is a realm of totalization and because the imaginary "is linked to the relation to the mother,"[21] the mother of the preoedipal relation is presumed to subsume all, including the phallus and the child, within herself. Thus while the imaginary holds out the promise of completeness, it also threatens the child with a loss of difference, as the image of the snaky-haired Medusa signifies.

Joe represses this image leaked out of his unconscious, but it reappears in various forms throughout his life. For example, when, at fourteen, he and other boys hire a black girl to copulate with them, their intercourse, a fusion of male and female, black and white, revives his memory of the toothpaste episode. When it is Joe's turn to mate with the girl, he feels as though "there was something in him trying to get out, like when he had used to think of toothpaste" (156). Joe's repressed desire to restore the forbidden signifier and to be the phallus that the mother lacks is "trying to get out," to erupt in the act of sexual intercourse. As before, when he ate the toothpaste beside the coupled parental figures, he metaphorically returns to the womb; he is "enclosed by the womanshenegro" (157),[22] and, as he leans over the prostrate girl, "he seemed to look down into a black well and at the bottom saw glints like reflections of dead stars" (156). According to Neumann, the well is a womb symbol, but more than a symbol for the individual maternal womb, as Freud theorizes; rather, it is "a primordial symbol of the place from whence we come, the state of being contained in the whole."[23] In other words, Joe is once again confronted with an image out of the unconscious for the condition prior to primary repression. Looking down at the "unaware . . . prone, abject" girl, he sees himself lost in the cosmos, absorbed back into the world. The "glints like reflections of dead stars," appear to be a reflection of his own eyes with consciousness extinguished. The girl seems to be his double, the reflection of the void, the *mise en abime,* he buries in the unconscious, and when Joe strikes her—"He kicked her hard, kicking into and through a choked wail of surprise and fear" (156–57)—he objectifies a desire to exorcise an image out of his own unconscious mind.

Striking out at the black girl, Joe externalizes the psychic strategy of repression. In effect, Joe reenacts the original repression that constitutes subjectivity. And Joe ritually reenacts this repression again when, as an adolescent, he is first told about menstruation. An older boy draws for him and other boys a "picture" of women that "moved them": "the temporary and abject helplessness of that which tantalised and frustrated desire: the smooth and superior shape in which volition dwelled doomed to be at stated and inescapable intervals victims of periodical filth" (185). An exponent of the values of his culture, the older boy teaches that women are vessels containing filth and that they are helpless before physical compulsions. In response to this lesson, Joe performs a ritual sacrifice, reminiscent of primitive rites. He stalks and kills a sheep and kneels and dips his hand in the blood of the dying animal. This ritual act helps him to "live with it, side by side with it": "It was as if he said illogical and desperately calm *All right. It is so then. But not to me. Not in my life and my love* (186).[24]

In this way, Joe denies menstruation, relegating it to the unconscious. Menstruation is a sign of something he refuses to accept. The symbolic meanings of menstruation have been thoughtfully considered by Jane Gallop, who bases her reflections on the work of Freud and Michelle Montrelay. Gallop begins by citing Freud's assertion that "the taboo on menstruation is derived from this 'organic repression,' as a defence against a phase of development that has been surmounted."[25] The phase of development to which Freud alludes Lacan calls the imaginary. Drawing on Freud's insight, Gallop concludes that menstruation stands as a sign of an immediate intense relation with the maternal body, "a state totally threatening to the stability of the psychic economy, that stability which is achieved by means of representations." Citing Montrelay, Gallop argues that we cope with this threat by representation: "representations [are] a way of mastering what is otherwise too intense."[26] Gallop's discussion of representation seems directly applicable to Joe's ritualistic slaying of the sheep. By representing menstruation with the blood of the slain animal, Joe, in effect, brings menstruation under the rule of the empty signifier and restores the balance of power signified by Lacan's formula S/s. The ritualistic sacrifice of the sheep also asserts the power of the signifier over the signified by reenacting the original severing that gave rise to selfhood. The slain sheep is a scapegoat; like the original scapegoat, a goat over which the ancient Israelites confessed their sins and then sent into the wilderness to suffer and die in their place, it is a substitute: it replaces Joe, the subject who comes into being only by a rupture, a castration. But, however many times he reenacts this original displacement of being, Joe cannot completely defuse the threat to ego-identity that the imaginary poses. Indeed, this threat is unmistakably imaged when menstruation is again invoked years later. When his first love, Bobbie, speaks of menstruation, reminding him of what he had "forgotten" (186), he strikes her and runs into the woods where "as though in a cave he seemed to see a diminishing row of suavely shaped urns in moonlight, blanched. And not one was perfect. Each was cracked and from each crack there issued something liquid, deathcolored, and foul. He touched a tree, leaning his propped arms against it, seeing the ranked and moonlit urns. He vomited" (189). On the surface, the "suavely shaped urns" issuing a foul liquid recall the picture of menstruating females sketched by the older boy: the "smooth superior shapes" with their "periodical filth." But the cracked urns with their inner putrefaction also represent Joe's vomiting body. As Joe retches, he is the mirror image of the "suavely shaped urns" with their evocation of menstruation; his body, no less than the female's, is a vessel containing decay and death. Moreover, according to Neumann, like the image of the well, both the cave and the urn are images out of the unconscious for the state of being contained in the whole.[27] The "ranked and moonlit urns," then, are yet another disguised representation of an imaginary preconscious existence.

With Bobbie, who, as "the waitress"—a woman who provides nourishment—is a mother-figure, Joe for a time yields to his desire for reintegration. When Joe makes love to Bobbie, he is what Bahktin calls a body "at home in the cosmos":[28] "He lay naked too, beside her, touching her with his hand and talking about her. Not about where she had come from and what she had even done, but about her body as if no one had ever done this before, with her or with anyone else" (195–96).[29] With Bobbie, Joe fuses once again with the imaginary double, who is first the mother. This violation of the Law of the Father is objectifed when Joe escapes from his adopted father's house by means of a "rope, neatly coiled" (190), a symbol of the round, the uroboros. And because, in the act of intercourse with the waitress, Joe figuratively restores a former unitary identity, he confesses to Bobbie his own fused nature, his racial indeterminacy, as he will every time he has intercourse with a woman.

McEachern, Joe's adopted father and representation of the Law of the Father, attempts to prevent this return to a preoedipal unity: he arrives at a schoolhouse dance intent on dividing Joe from Bobbie. In Lacanian terms, this division restages the oedipal phase: the father become Father separates the child from the mother and ushers the child into the symbolic order. But Joe refuses to submit to the ultimate authority of the law of alienation: he crashes a chair over his foster father's head. With McEachern—the figure of the Law of the Other—fallen, another image out of the unconscious erupts: Bobbie appears, to assume the form of the mythic Medusa. Her hair is "wild with the jerking and tossing of her head" and, like the dietitian before her, Bobbie violently proclaims Joe's lack of difference: " 'Bastard! Son of a bitch! Getting me into a jam, that always treated you like you were a white man. A white man!' "(217). With this apparition, Joe metaphorically returns to a preoedipal phase before the emergence of subjectivity. He is beaten senseless by Bobbie's friends, and as he lies on the floor, unable to speak or move, he exists as if an infant in a preverbal universe. Standing over Joe, his attackers abuse him physically and verbally, taunting him with signs of his fusion—his preconscious symbiotic relationship with the mother and his racial indeterminacy:

> He ought to stay away from bitches
> He cant help himself. He was born too close to one
> Is he really a nigger? He dont look like one
> That's what he told Bobbie one night. But I guess she still dont know any more about what he is than he does. These country bastards are liable to be anything. (219; italics removed)

After his experience with Bobbie, Joe's ambivalent feelings are reflected in his relationships with women. "Beneath the dark and equivocal and symbolical archways of midnight" (224), he sleeps with prostitutes, and, when he does not have money to pay the woman, he confesses to Negro blood and is cursed by her and is sometimes beaten unconscious by other patrons of the establishment. This arrangement satisfies Joe's contradictory impulses. He desires the totalizing images of the imaginary, so he engages in sexual intercourse with figures for the lost first other. Significantly, he chooses midnight—a time between one day and the next—to satisfy his psychic need for merger. Simultaneously, he desires the alienation necessary for the constitution of an ego-subjectivity, so he confesses to black blood, eliciting exclusion and punishment. Joe requires the cursing and the beating, which symbolically recreate the oedipal encounter with the father become Name-of-the-Father.

When Joe Christmas first encounters Joanna Burden, he figures once again a return to a preoedipal formlessness. He enters Joanna's house by crawling through a window, metaphorically reenacting a return to the womb: "he seemed to flow into the dark kitchen: a shadow returning without a sound and without locomotion to the allmother of obscurity and darkness" (229–30). When Joanna appears, Joe is confronted with his double. She stands in a doorway, a frame in which the self sees itself mirrored, and they face each other, reflecting one another: "She stood in the door. They looked at one another for more than a minute, almost in the same attitude: he with the dish, she with the candle" (231). The female holds the candle, symbol for the phallus, signifier of the Law of the Father; the male holds the dish, a symbol, like the urn, for the state of being contained in the whole. This imagery reflects their psychic ambivalence: both Joe and Joanna are divided subjects, torn by warring drives. They both desire subjectivity on the plane of the symbolic; equally, they desire the totality of being of the imaginary. Both have yet to pass through castration or what Lacan sometimes calls "the phallic stage";[30] they are unable to give over their identity to the symbolic and the knowledge of castration.

Like Joe, whose cigarette smoke drifts across his face, dividing it, Joanna, too, is a "dual personality" (234–35). On the one hand, she is a mother-figure. She is an an older woman who sets out food for Joe, "the allmother of obscurity and darkness" (230); and she enters into a sexual relationship with Joe, later desiring to bear a child. On the other hand, she submits to the law of castration. For this reason, when Joe attempts to rape Joanna to "ma[k]e a woman out of her" (236)—that is, symbolically to recreate the primary repression associated with the exclusion of the maternal body—he finds that she has already achieved his goal: "beneath his hands the body might have been the body of a dead woman not yet stiffened" (236).

In Joanna, this conflict between imaginary and symbolic registers is neatly compartmentalized: "It was as though there were two people: the one whom he saw now and then by day and looked at while they spoke to one another with speech that told nothing at all . . . ; the other with whom he lay at night and didn't even see, speak to, at all" (232–33). By day, she is "manlike" (234), and she anticipates the "disposal" of her woman's body: in her safe "reposed the written instruction (in her own hand) for the disposal of her body after death" (234). By night, however, she rebels against the law that decrees lack: "She would be wild then, in the close, breathing halfdark without walls, with her wild hair, each strand of which would seem to come alive like octopus tentacles, and her wild hands and her breathing: 'Negro! Negro! Negro!' " (260). With the imaginary now ascendant, Joanna, like the dietitian and the waitress Bobbie before her, assumes the mythic form of the phallic mother, the Medusa. And like her sister Medusas, she identifies Joe as a figure of fusion: as "Negro," he is a representation of the forbidden other who was first the mother.

Joanna's contradictory impulses reflect Joe's own psychic conflict. He observes her as he would watch his own mirror image:

Anyway, he stayed, watching the two creatures that stuggled in the one body like two moongleamed shapes struggling drowning in alternate throes upon the surface of a black thick pool beneath

83

the last moon. Now it would be that still, cold, contained figure of the first phase who, even though lost and damned, remained somehow impervious and impregnable; then it would be the other, the second one, who in furious denial of that impregnability strove to drown in the black abyss of its own creating that physical purity which had been preserved too long now even to be lost. Now and then they would come to the black surface, locked like sisters; the black waters would drain away. (260–61)

The two figures represent an unconscious struggle within Joanna between a drive toward subjectivity in the symbolic and toward loss of subjectivity in the imaginary. Because Joe, too, is driven by these contradictory impulses, he sees his own image reflected on the surface of the thick black pool, and he senses that he, too, like the sisters, is drowning: "he began to see himself as from a distance, like a man being sucked down into a bottomless morass" (260). The bottomless morass is another pit symbol; it pictures the containing world that threatens to absorb the subject; concomitantly, it is another unconscious representation of Lacan's imaginary register of being.

What Jane Gallop calls "the fantasmatic resolution of differences in the imaginary"[31] erupts into the text once again on the evening of his fatal confrontation with Joanna, as Joe walks the streets of Jefferson. Because of his psychic ambivalence, in "the wide, empty, shadowbrooded street he looked like a phantom, a spirit, strayed out of its own world, and lost" (114). But then Joe enters Freedman Town, the black section of town, and "he found himself" (114). What Joe finds is an unconscious image or imago of the illusory yet sustaining imaginary register. In the black hollow, "not only voices but moving bodies and light itself must become fluid and accrete slowly from particle to particle, of and with the now ponderable night inseparable and one" (114). Again Joe sees himself "as from the bottom of a thick black pit . . . enclosed by cabinshapes" (114). Immersed in the (m)other, as though sucked down in a morass, Joe loses all sense of identity, as if he were returned to a primal state before the emergence of difference: "On all sides, even within him, the bodiless fecundmellow voices of negro women murmured. It was as though he and all other manshaped life about him had been returned to the lightless hot wet primogenitive Female" (115). From this engulfment, Joe runs "with drumming heart and glaring lips" (116), and a short time later he attempts to provoke a confrontation with a group of black men and women. As they pass, Joe yells, "Bitches! . . . Sons of bitches!" (118), identifying the racial other with the mother who is the forbidden first other.

Because Joe and Joanna are both caught between the imaginary and the symbolic, the conflict between them mirrors the conflict within each of them. In other words, their own warring desires are externalized in their treatment of each other. Both experience a drive toward identity and representation. At the same time, both also are driven to fill the gap and restore the missing signifier; and this desire fuels their passion for one another. By means of their lovemaking, they figure a return of the lost object. Juliet Mitchell explains this representation. Following primary repression, she writes, "the girl will desire to have the phallus and the boy will struggle to represent it."[32] It is in the act of sexual intercourse that Joe "represent[s] the phallus, and Joanna appears once again to "have" the lost object of desire. In this way, Jacqueline Rose writes, through sexual union, "each sex com[es] to stand, mythically and exclusively, for that which could satisfy and complete the other."[33]

In the last phase of their relationship, Joanna is intent on returning to the communal order under the law of castration; accordingly, she identifies with the symbolic Other, the locus of the constitution of the self: she wears a garment "that looked as if it had been made for and worn by a careless man," and her hair is "drawn gauntly back to a knot as savage and ugly as a wart on a diseased bough" (275). As a representative of the phallic signifier, the law that ordains alienation, she would have Joe identity himself as a black man; and she demands that he accept the knowledge of castration, the alienation into language, when she commands him to kneel with her before the almighty Father—God, the Other, whom she claims to represent: "It's not I who ask it. Kneel with me" (282). In response to Joanna's ultimatum, Joe thinks, "No. If I give in now, I will deny all the thirty years that I have lived to make me what I chose to be" (265). In other words, Joe's acquiescence would register his submission to the rule of the Law of the Other and his acceptance of the lack of the symbolic phallus.

At the same time as Joanna is the agent of the symbolic Other, the site of language, loss, and the symbolic order, however, she is equally representative of the mother prior to the prohibition that gave rise to subjectivity. For example, when Joe comes at night to see her in this last phase, he "sat looking at her like a stone" (268). This allusion to the Medusa, whose gaze turns men to stone, signifies that Joanna occupies also the place of the phallic mother and poses the threat of incorporation.

Because Joanna represents both the preoedipal mother on the plane of the imaginary and the the Law identified with the Name-of-the-Father in the symbolic, as she raises an ancient revolver, the legacy of her ancestors, its shadow on the wall fuses images of the phallus, the marker of difference, the sign of lack—it is "almost as long and heavier than a small rifle"—with the circular snake, symbol for an undifferentiated existence in the world: "But the shadow of it and of her arm and her hand on the wall did not waver at all, the shadow of both monstrous, the cocked hammer monstrous, backhooked and viciously poised like the arched head of a snake" (282). In killing Joanna, Joe rejects once again both the imaginary and symbolic spheres.[34]

Simultaneously, however, when Joe cuts Joanna's throat he recreates the role of Perseus, the mythic representative of the psychic desire for alienation into language. The myth of Perseus narrates this desire: Perseus beheads Medusa, a representation of the mother before the acceptance of castration detaches the subject from dependence on her. Freud says that beheading is an analogue for castration; hence, this decapitation figures the symbolic castration that attends the constitution of the subject.[35] In Lacanian terms, Perseus plays the role of the father become Father who enforces alienation and the acceptance of the lack of the symbolic phallus: his decapitation of Medusa signifies the fall into the symbolic order. When Joe cuts Joanna's throat, he is another Perseus, another representation of a desire for alienation: the sundering of Joanna's head from her body signals the child's knowledge of the mother's lack of the symbolic phallus—a knowledge that ushers the child into the symbolic order. And later, when Joanna's decapitated body is discovered and her severed head seems to face in the opposite direction from her body, this positioning signifies Joanna's contradictory impulses toward representation on the plane of the symbolic and fusion in the sphere of the imaginary.

In killing Joanna, then, Joe is occupying the place of the Name-of-the-Father. But even as Joe seeks to occupy the place of the symbolic Other, the Law, he also desires the other, the first figure from which the subject splits itself. His opposite drive toward an illusory totality in the register of the imaginary is signified by the shoes he wears. To elude his pursuers, Joe exchanges shoes with a black woman who wears her husband's brogans. Because they are identified with blacks and women, the shoes outwardly sign his desire for the (m)other: "It seemed to him that he could see himself being hunted by white men at last into the black abyss which had been waiting, trying, for thirty years to drown him and into which now and at last he had actually entered, bearing now upon his ankles the definite and ineradicable gauge of its upward moving" (331).

In the last moments of his life, Joe vacillates again, pulled by conflicting drives. These final moments are related by Gavin Stevens, whom Noel Polk has described as an unreliable narrator of these events.[36] Observing Joe behaving in contradictory ways, Stevens interprets this conflict in racial terms. According to Stevens, Joe is alternately driven by his "black blood" and "white blood." Predictably, when Stevens approves of Joe's act, the lawyer attributes it to "white blood"; when Stevens disapproves, Joe acts in accordance with "black blood. While Stevens's construction of these events is demonstrably racist, I think we need to examine his remarks for an unconscious level of meaning. White blood and black blood, here as throughout the novel, can be read as symbols for inward drives toward two epistemic registers, the symbolic and the imaginary. White blood is the symbolic analogue for a drive toward alienation; black blood represents a drive toward the forbidden other who was first the mother. For example, when Joe runs to the Negro cabin, he is driven there by his desire for an imaginary fusion with the other. Alternately, Joe flees the cabin in obedience to an opposite desire to preserve the distinctions that create identity. Seeking the world of representation, he runs to the house of the minister Hightower, driven there by "a blind faith in something read in a printed Book" (449); and when Joe strikes the minister, he rejects symbolic castration, the price of subjectivity and difference. In the end, Joe submits to the Law of the Father and accepts the loss that this Law ordains: "He crouched behind that overturned table and let them shoot him to death, with that loaded and unfired pistol in his hand" (449).[37]

Joe's death represents a long-delayed entry into the symbolic order. At last, Joe submits to the power of the symbolic, represented by Percy Grimm. The paradox is, as James M. Mellard eloquently explains, that one becomes a "subject-as-subject" only through castration; that "the drive toward subjectivity" "is always toward death"[38]—lack, privation, the loss of the symbolic phallus.

Because Joe's death, like Joanna's, represents the triumph of the empty signifier of difference, it reenacts yet again the tale of Perseus, the mythic version of what Lacan calls entry into the symbolic order. In this recreation of the myth, Percy Grimm is Perseus. A representative of the symbolic Other, his face has "that serene, unearthly luminousness of angels in church windows" (462); and he exalts the empty signifier over the signified: "the American uniform," he is convinced, "is superior to all men" (451).[39] The Medusa that Grimm/Perseus slays is of course Joe Christmas. All his life, Joe has refused to be one thing or the other. He desires identity and meaning, but up to the last moment of his life he refuses to accept the Law of that signifier that Lacan calls the phallus. Alternately, he desires totality of being but refuses to accept the consequent loss of subjectivity. Joe is, then, a formulation of the Medusa, a figure of fusion. He transgresses racial boundaries: he will be neither white nor black. And he transgresses boundaries between mother and child: Joe's sexual relationship with Joanna, a displaced representative of the mother, is an attempt to restore the missing phallus and recreate a preoedipal unity. For these violations of boundaries, Percy Grimm exacts the father's penalty: castration and death. Physical castration here represents symbolic castration, the intervention of the paternal metaphor and the separation of mother and child, as Percy himself claims. Flinging aside the bloody butcher knife, Percy cries, "Now you'll let white women alone, even in hell" (439).

The act of castration symbolizes the alienation that creates the self as lack. On the surface, then, it would seem that Joe's long vacillation between the imaginary and the symbolic ends with the victory of the symbolic order. Joe's death signifies his ultimate submission to the authority of the Law that decrees separation and loss. Paradoxically, however, Joe's death is simultaneously the triumph of the imaginary order. The paradox occurs because both the drive toward the imaginary and toward the symbolic lead ultimately to death. In Lacan's economy, one gains subjectivity only by a loss of being—death—and the desire to reclaim that lost being returns one to an original amorphous formlessness—death. Thus, Joe's death, which represents a long delayed entry into the symbolic order, is also the triumph of the contrary drive toward a loss of subjectivity. All his life, Joe has struggled to escape castration and death; in the end, he accepts that the battle is always already lost; that, in the words of Lacan, "this life we're captive of, this essentially alienated life existing, this life in the other, is as such joined to death, it always returns to death."[40]

"YOU CANT BEAT A WOMAN"

Light in August does not possess the kind of unity we ordinarily expect to find in a novel. Faulkner's *Light in August* consists of three almost separate narrative strands—the stories of Joe Christmas, Gail Hightower, and Lena Grove—that are but minimally related to one another. This narrative format has given rise to a critical debate about the nature of, or even the existence of, unity in this work of fiction.[41] Some critics have even maintained that the novel is seriously flawed by a lack of structural cohesiveness.[42] These critics have focused their complaints on the Lena Grove narrative, arguing that, while the stories of Joe Christmas and Hightower do intersect—however tenuously and unconvincingly—Lena does not even so much as cross paths with Joe Christmas.

Is the Lena Grove narrative unrelated to the story of Joe Christmas? Although it is true that Joe and Lena never actually meet, they are brought together by the narrative in ways other than temporal or physical.[43] For example, in a sense, Lena replaces Joe in the narrative: she occupies the space he vacates; at least, when he abandons the cabin behind the Burden place, she takes up residence there and gives birth on the cot that he had slept on. Once installed in the cabin, she looks into the shard of mirror that previously had reflected his image. Moreover, while Joe never meets Lena, they are tied to one another through Joe Brown/Lucas Burch, who is, again in a sense, the "mate" of both of them: Lena calls Lucas Burch her husband, although they are not wed, and the sheriff calls Joe Christmas the "husband" of Joe Brown (321).

These connections provide clues to the relationship between Joe and Lena. Lena takes Joe's place and looks into the same mirror because she is his reflection, the identificatory imago; that is, the mirror-stage double. Lena Grove, a pregnant woman and later a nursing mother, represents the state of being contained in the whole. Because the maternal body is identified with a preconscious loss of difference, she is a living representative of what Ragland-Sullivan calls the "psychic fusion and corporal identification"of the mirror stage.[44] For this reason, Joe and Lena inhabit the same novel. All his life, Joe's psychic conflict— his incomplete entry into the symbolic order—has emerged in the form of images of an imaginary relation with the mother: pits, urns, and Medusas. Lena is yet another avatar of the illusory totality of being that

Joe ambivalently desires.[45] Pregnant, she is another vessel, another urn. Traveling across the country in wagon after wagon, she is "like something moving forever and without progress across an urn" (7). She is two-in-one, the mother before there was separation, and she seems to incarnate what Joe has alternately fled and desired all his life—the lost first other of the identificatory stage. And, although Joe has no direct contact with her, his ambivalent feelings toward the identificatory imago she represents are reflected by the acts of his "partner" (113), Joe Brown (alias Lucas Burch), who makes love to Lena, fathering her child, and deserts her.[46]

By abandoning Lena, Joe Brown reenacts the passage from the imaginary to the symbolic, in accordance with the Law of the Father. Byron Bunch, by contrast, violates this law: he falls in love, "contrary to all the tradition of his austere and jealous country raising which demands in the object physical inviolability" (49). Lena is violable: she is pregnable and pregnant. She transgresses boundaries, climbing out the window of her elder brother's house to fornicate with Lucas Burch. She is not a seamless urn but a cracked urn, seeping and flowing, obscuring distinctions between self and other.

Like Joe Christmas and Joe Brown, Byron's attitude toward Lena, the mother who is not yet other, is also ambivalent. While Byron loves Lena, he also yearns for the qualities that characterize the symbolic order—consciousness, language, and subjectivity. For example, when he runs into the room where she is giving birth, he expects and hopes to see her "placid, unchanged, timeless" (399) and "completely aware of him" (399). Instead "she did not even seem to be aware that the door had opened, that there was anyone or anything in the room save herself and whatever it was that she had spoken to with that wailing cry in a tongue unknown to man" (399). As she gives birth, Lena is unaware, unconscious. She speaks not with the symbolic order's empty signifiers but rather in a preverbal, unmeaningful, unorganized flow— what Kristeva calls "the semiotic." In these critical moments, Lena is not a conscious speaking subject; rather, she embodies the loss of subjectivity of the imaginary: "she lay raised on her propped arms on the cot, looking down at the shape of her body beneath the sheet with wailing and hopeless terror" (398). Because the imaginary is now ascendant, Lena, like the dietitian, Joanna, and others, evokes images of the pit and the Medusa: "Her hair was loose and her eyes looked like two holes" (399). Like the mythic representation of the preoedipal mother, the Medusa who turns men to stone, Lena now "stop[s]" Byron "dead as a wall" (398).

Byron's response to this psychic image of incorporation approximates Joe Christmas's and Joe Brown's. Like them, he is pulled by a strong drive to separate—to reenact the splitting that gives rise to subjectivity. As he watches Lena giving birth to her child, Byron reflects: " 'If I had known then. If it had got through then.' He thought this quietly, in aghast despair, regret. 'Yes. I would have turned my back and rode the other way. Beyond the knowing and memory of man forever and ever I reckon I would have rode.' But he did not" (400). Threatened by a return to the formlessness of an unmediated connection with the mother and the world, Byron desires alienation. But, unlike Christmas and Burch/Brown, he does not reenact the oedipal act of exclusion. Instead, he surrenders control to Lena; he follows her aimless wandering.

This is the situation as the final chapter of the novel opens, and, to describe it, Faulkner deliberately turns the narration over to a new voice. For twenty chapters of *Light in August,* an omniscient, third-person narrator has controlled the story, but in chapter twenty-one Faulkner introduces a new narrator—a nameless furniture repairer and dealer. As Christopher LaLonde says, this is "a stunningly crafty and craftful move on Faulkner's part," as "the salesman's voice allows Faulkner the luxury of sidestepping what he found most difficult to write about."[47] The closing chapter of the novel poses a dilemma for Faulkner because it portrays what patriarchal culture forbids: the ascendancy of an imaginary relation to the mother. Because language and meaning depend on the renunciation of the connection with the (m)other, Faulkner is at a loss to evoke this resurgence of a preoedipal imaginary unity in any way other than with denunciation. Faced with no option but censure, Faulkner divorces himself from the narrative voice and puts this censure in the mouth of an unreliable narrator. As LaLonde persuasively argues, the furniture-dealer narrator is a familiar character out of a humorous oral tradition in the United States: the traveling salesman. He is an archetype of patriarchal culture, outspokenly masculinist, phallocentric, and sexist. Clearly his perspective is biased and suspect. By turning over to this figure the narration of Byron's capitulation to Lena, Faulkner successfully delegitimizes and disavows the only perspective available to him.[48]

Even the circumstances of the nameless furniture dealer's narration undermine his point of view: he lies in bed with his wife, and he tells Byron and Lena's story as a diversion after and possibly before sexual intercourse. As, in his voice, the story emerges, he predictably condemns Byron for following Lena's lead: "And I says to myself, 'Well, old fellow, I reckon it aint only since she has been riding on the seat of my truck while you rode with your feet hanging out the back end of it that she has travelled out in front on this trip' " (501). The furniture dealer is pleased to discover, however, that Byron plans to assert himself by attempting to initiate sexual relations with Lena. As the narrator describes Byron sneaking into the truck where mother and child sleep, this spokesman for patriarchal culture is "pulling for the little cuss" (502). Patriarchal culture cheers Byron on because his sexual overture constitutes the oedipal moment, the founding act of law, language, and culture. Prior to Byron's entry into the truck, Lena and her baby exist in the preoedipal or imaginary plane. Lena's infant lives in symbiotic relation with the maternal body, with no defined center of self. When a male presence intrudes on this dyad, he introduces sexual difference, signified by the phallus, the mark of the father's difference from the mother. In this light, Lena's remark, "Why, Mr Bunch. Aint you ashamed. You might have woke the baby, too" (503), takes on new meaning: Byron might have awakened the baby to subjectivity and language. His appearance would trigger a train of events: it would establish difference and separate mother and child; under the threat of castration, Lena's child would repress his desire for the mother, opening up the unconscious.

When Lena firmly ejects Byron by picking him up bodily and removing him from the truck, she rejects a representative of the marker of difference, symbolized by the phallus. She prolongs the original dyadic unity and delays her child's entry into the symbolic. She is the phallic or preoedipal mother, the whole ("The 'whole,' " writes Jane Gallop, "is the pre-Oedipal mother, apparently omnipotent and omniscient, until the 'discovery of her castration' ");[49] and she refuses to permit the split that would create a subject in language. In other words, in this instance, the tables are turned. This time it is not the maternal body but a figure of male difference that is banished. From the perspective of the furniture salesman, this dismissal is an intolerable humiliation for Byron and for all male-gendered human beings: "Well, I was downright ashamed to look at him, to let him know that any human man had seen and heard what happened. I be dog if I didn't want to find the hole and crawl into it with him" (503–4). Metaphorically, the narrator's rural expressions register the victory of the imaginary or preoedipal over the symbolic. "I be dog" implies a loss of self-awareness, a return to brute existence; similarly, the colorful phrase "find the hole and crawl into it," like all the pit, abyss, and womb images in the novel, evokes yet again the original state of being contained in the whole.

Byron responds to this blow to father-power as one might expect. He flees the mother-child dyad. But Byron's flight is short-lived. After a brief absence, a final vacillation, he returns to join Lena and her infant, resolved that the dyadic structure between mother and child must give way to a triadic one: " 'I done come too far now,' he says, 'I be dog if I'm going to quit now' " (506). For her part, Lena acknowledges that inevitably Byron, or some other representative of the paternal metaphor, must disrupt the mother-child dyad. Eventually her child must be socialized and take his place in a community that "is defined by sexual difference, by exclusion (it cannot be its parent's lover) and by absence (it must relinquish its earlier bonds to the mother's body)."[50] Her response to Byron, "Aint nobody never said for you to quit" (506), signifies her willingness eventually to submit to the Law of the Father and to accept the necessity of sexual difference. As the furniture dealer astutely intuits, Lena is merely trying to prolong the preoedipal phase: there will be time enough later for absence and exclusion:

He laughs, lying in the bed, laughing, "Yes, sir. You cant beat a woman. Because do you know what I think? I think she was just travelling. I dont think she had any idea of finding whoever it was she was following. I dont think she had ever aimed to, only she hadn't told him yet. I reckon this was the first time she had ever been further away from home than she could walk back before sundown in her life. And that she had got along all right this far, with folks taking good care of her. And so I think she had just made up her mind to travel a little further and see as much as she could, since I reckon she knew that when she settled down this time, it would likely be for the rest of her life. That's what I think. Sitting back there in that truck, with him by her now and the baby that hadn't never stopped eating, that had been eating breakfast now for about ten miles, like one of those dining cars on the train, and her looking out and watching the telephone poles and the fences passing like it was a circus parade." (506–7)

Eventually Lena will be "settled down for the rest of her life"; that is, eventually she will be suppressed by patriarchal culture. It is the mother's inevitable fate to be associated with the repressed referent, because, as James M. Mellard explains, "human subjectivity (identity) begins to emerge because of a process of covering over (psychoanalytically, the repression) of a dyadic first object (mother, infant)."[51] But, for now, Lena would delay that fate. For now, she incarnates the phallic or preoedipal mother.

The novel closes with a scene that images the temporary triumph of the imaginary register: Lena nurses her infant in the back of a moving truck. Mother and child are a whole—the dyad that precedes identity, gender difference, and language. The nameless nursing baby is fused with the mother-body, unaware of difference or separation. Together, this unit is, in the words of the furniture dealer, "just travelling." Similarly, Lena describes this mother-child motion with the phrase, "A body does get around" (507). Lena's phrase is suggestive. She refers to mother + child, not as two separate individuals but as one body, a body getting around in the world, moving to the pull of the earth's forces, like a planet in orbit. In other words, mother + child represent the state of being contained in the whole. This is the imaginary, "an unbroken union between inner and outer, a perfect control that assures immediate satisfaction of desire."[52] By ending with this image, the novel comes full circle; it ends as it began, with the origin, the source—mother + child in motion. The novel's end is the mirror image of its beginning: an image of mirror-stage identification.

CHAPTER 4

Reading for the Repressed: *Absalom, Absalom!*

Absalom, Absalom! is a disturbing text largely because the novel's narrators seem not to know the tale they tell. I use the negative here advisedly. The narrators are not only partially informed or misinformed; they do not know. For example, Miss Rosa gives no sign of knowing what Mr. Compson knows—that Charles Bon has an octoroon wife and a child by her. Mr. Compson, in turn, apparently does not recognize what Quentin and Shreve eventually acknowledge—that Bon is Sutpen's son. And it is not until the final pages of the novel that Quentin and Shreve make known that Bon is Sutpen's black son. Miss Rosa, Mr. Compson, and even Quentin and Shreve, who only belatedly do know, seem to represent the antithesis of the traditional omniscient narrator. Why, we might well ask, does Faulkner have narrators who appear not to know their story?[1] The answer to this question is that Miss Rosa, Mr. Compson, Quentin, and Shreve do not know because they are forbidden to know: because Charles Bon represents a forbidden libidinal relation with the m(other), they repress Charles Bon's meaning.

The desire of the Other, so central to Lacan's theory of language, is central also to Faulkner's *Absalom, Absalom!* It supplies an answer to the provoking mystery at the novel's core: Why do Miss Rosa and Mr. Compson never recognize Charles Bon's complete identity; and why does Quentin, with Shreve, withhold that identity until the very last pages of the novel? Charles Bon's identity is repressed, must be repressed, because his complete identity *is* complete identity; that is, the completeness of being that is forbidden to the lacking subject under the law of castration. What Charles Bon represents is both the object of desire and what cannot be named, because Bon is the son who will not renounce the mother, who will not accept symbolic castration, who

95

will not accept the child's subordinated role in the mother-father-child triad. Renunciation of the maternal body, according to Lacanian theory, is demanded by the Law of the Father as the price of admission to the symbolic order, but Charles Bon will not renounce. He will not renounce Judith, the sister-surrogate for the mother; nor will he renounce the octoroon wife, the mother of his child. Charles Bon is a meaning that comes attached to others, and, specifically, to the first other, the mother. Because he represents a merging of child and mother, of black and white, Bon appears to be the subject who is not alienated, for whom there is no distance between signified and signifier; he figures the fullness of being that the lacking subject desires, but must repress, because the Law of the Father prohibits the representing of the missing signifier; thus the Law of the Father, under the threat of castration, prohibits the return of Charles Bon.

For this reason, then, because Charles Bon seems to possess the missing signifier that could restore an original plenitude, Charles Bon, Charles the Good, is endlessly shut out in Faulkner's novel. Sutpen refuses to identify Bon, refuses to give him "a sign" (256), and Henry kills Bon to keep him out. More than this, at another level, at the level of narration, Bon is also excluded. Miss Rosa and Mr. Compson and, for a time, Quentin and Shreve, narratively reenact the repression of Bon. They also conspire to murder Bon by refusing to read his meaning: his meaning must be erased from their texts because Bon threatens to fill the gap that makes difference and meaning possible. Thus, Bon must be repressed for the sake of what Miss Rosa calls "the devious intricate channels of decorous ordering" (112), or what Lacan calls the symbolic order. Bon's death, his absence, opens up the space that allows the sign to mean, for a sign signifies what is missing. But, and this is the crucial point, withheld meanings always return—"repressed, it reappears," Lacan writes—and these returned meanings threaten the fragile order constituted by their absence.[2] Repression is never complete and irreversible; there is always spillage, and this spillage marks the narrations of Miss Rosa, Mr. Compson, and Quentin and Shreve. In Miss Rosa's and Mr. Compson's narrations, the repressed meaning—Bon's identity—returns in disguised forms, slipping past conscious censors unrecognized. It is not until the end of the novel, in the Quentin and Shreve section, that the repressed, Bon's complete identity, is fully and consciously acknowledged. Quentin and Shreve finally represence what is only covertly alluded to in the two preceding narrations, that Bon is both black other and brother; that, in other words, Bon effaces the difference that makes meaning possible. To use the novel's ceaselessly repeated metaphor, Quentin and Shreve "overpass" the doors—symbols of psychic interdiction—that stop Miss Rosa and Mr. Compson. This overpassing, however, is achieved at a cost. It is accomplished only at the very end of the novel by means of a reversion, a return. Quentin and Shreve begin their narration as submissive sons who withhold in obedience to the Law, who accept symbolic castration. Then, in the course of their narration, gradually there occurs a change.[3]

"NOTHING HAPPENS: JUST THE WORDS"

Readers of *Absalom, Absalom!* may sometimes feel frustrated by the versions of the Sutpen legend produced by Miss Rosa and Mr. Compson.[4] Whereas Shreve and Quentin eventually tender an answer to the central mystery—why did Henry Sutpen kill Charles Bon?—Miss Rosa seems to offer only fulminations and Mr. Compson garrulous bewilderment. Certainly by comparison to Quentin and Shreve, Miss Rosa and Mr. Compson seem baffled. However, their blindness is not blindness so much as it is interdiction. In their narrations they are *stopped*, a word that frequently surfaces in the narrative, stopped by what Freud calls the superego, and what Lacan calls the Law of the Father. The doors that shut them out, doors that Quentin and Shreve eventually "overpass," are an outward symbol for an internal censoring. The repressed is represenced, however, not only at the novel's conclusion by Quentin and Shreve; rather, traces of repressed meanings erupt also throughout the narratives of Miss Rosa and Mr. Compson. Forbidden meanings slip unrecognized into the discourses of Miss Rosa and Mr. Compson. The repressed always returns, but it returns in a disguised form that permits nonrecognition. Like Charles Bon, who may enter Sutpen's house as long as his identity is unknown, repressed desire may surface so long as it is not consciously recognized.

Mr. Compson never acknowledges what Quentin and Shreve finally unveil—that Bon fills the gap between self and other, that Bon is both Sutpen and black other. Yet Mr. Compson's version of the Sutpen story is a fuller accounting than Miss Rosa's and has more near-approximations of meanings. Perhaps because Miss Rosa is personally involved in the story she tells and Mr. Compson is a bystander, he represses less fiercely than Miss Rosa. For example, Mr. Compson gives a sign of knowing what Miss Rosa never admits. In his narration, the existence of another child of Thomas Sutpen is fleetingly glimpsed. Alluding to Sutpen's children, Mr. Compson repeats with a difference the same phrase. As he waits with Quentin on the porch, before Quentin and Miss Rosa leave for the old Sutpen place, Mr. Compson says, "He named them all himself" (48), and shortly thereafter repeats, "Yes. He named Clytie as he named them all, the one before Clytie and Henry and Judith even, with that same robust and sardonic temerity, naming with his own mouth his own ironic fecundity of dragon's teeth" (48). "The one before Clytie" is the slippage, the spilling over into his discourse of a forbidden meaning. For the identity of this other Sutpen child, however, we will have to wait for the joint Quentin-Shreve narration, where Quentin repeats Mr. Compson's phrase again, this time with yet another variation: " 'He chose the name himself, Grandfather believed, just as he named them all—the Charles Goods and the Clytemnestras and Henry and Judith and all of them—that entire fecundity of dragons' teeth as father called it. And Father said—' " (214). Significantly, this other Sutpen child is named, not in Mr. Compson's telling but in Quentin and Shreve's, where Father's knowledge of Bon's identity is, in a passage added in revision, very carefully attributed to Quentin. It is Quentin who gives the Sutpen child a name, a sign; in Mr. Compson's version, the child may appear only as "the one before"; that is, genderless, nameless, completely unidentified. Thus, Mr. Compson can no more recognize that Charles Bon is Sutpen's son than Thomas Sutpen can.

Mr. Compson never consciously acknowledges that Bon is both Sutpen and black other, for to do so is to restore the missing signifier and fill the gap between self and m(other). And yet, while Mr. Compson consciously clings to the Law of alienation, his subtext speaks a forbidden meaning by identifying Bon as a figure who threatens fusion. For example, Mr. Compson's narration harps, almost obsessively, on the marriage ceremony that unites Bon and the octoroon wife. In fact, Mr. Compson attributes the whole Sutpen tragedy to attachment; that is, to Bon's refusal to renounce either his quasi wife, the octoroon, or Judith. Since both the octoroon, as the mother of Bon's child, and Judith, as the sister-substitute for the mother, are mother-figures, this is a veiled way of identifying Bon with the fantasy of completion in the imaginary. Compson's hidden meaning is that Bon is the oedipal son who refuses to relinquish the maternal body. The attachment that Bon refuses to renounce symbolizes the imaginary identification with the mother of the mirror stage and before. In Mr. Compson's subtext, then, Bon is the son who rejects castration and acts on his desire to be the phallus that is the desire of the mother and the Other.

This veiled identification of Bon with the forbidden phallus goes far toward explaining Mr. Compson's repeated ascription to Bon of feminine qualities. For example, when Mr. Compson offers a mental picture of Bon, he imagines Bon "reclining in a flowered, almost feminised gown, in a sunny window in his chambers" (76); and later he repeats this feminine attribution, observing Bon's "almost feminine garments" (76). In Mr. Compson's imagining, Bon seems both male and female. In other words, he seems to transcend gender difference, which, like all difference, is created at the moment of primal divison, the "event" or moment of symbolic interdiction. Thus Mr. Compson's image, in a concealed way, pictures a transgression of the Law. His portrait of Bon is an image out of the unconscious; it leaks a meaning that Freud's superego and Lacan's Law of the Father prohibits: that, unlike the rest of us, Bon is not a fractured sexual subject; that, instead, Bon possesses the lost object, the phallus, and occupies the undifferentiated space of the mother.

This submerged attribution to Bon of the imaginary object that satisfies all possible desire accounts for the powerful attraction Bon exerts on Judith, Henry, Rosa, and, in Mr. Compson's narration, even Mr. Compson. It would also explain—since the phallus represents the illusion of human fulfillment—why Mr. Compson's portrait of Bon stresses so repeatedly "surfeit" (76) and "satiety" (76). But Mr. Compson cannot speak Bon's claim of the lost object of desire: because the Law forbids this claim. To dissolve the oedipal complex, to move past the oedipal stage, the phallus must be surrendered. In this process, as Jonathan Scott Lee explains, "the phallus as a signifier [is] repressed (or "veiled") and replaced by the name of the father."[5] Acordingly, Mr. Compson speaks in teasing riddles; in his reading, Bon is a figure of mythic power, but this power is shrouded in mystery. For example, Mr. Compson tells us that Bon "appeared, not only to Henry but to the entire undergraduate body of that rural new provincial college, as a source not of envy, . . . but of despair," because envy is reserved only for "what you believe . . . you will someday possess" (76). Mr. Compson's use of the word "what" here is telling. What is it that Bon possesses? What is it that his classmates despair of possessing? Mr.

Compson must leave a gap here, covering it over with the concealing "what," because what Bon possesses can no more be spoken by Mr. Compson than it can be possessed by Bon's college acquaintances. Mr. Compson can supply no word, no sign, for this unspoken "what" because the Law ordains the hidden signifer remain hidden.

In Mr. Compson's subtext, then, Bon represents the missing phallus; he is presumed to possess all that the child surrenders at the constitution of subjectivity. This forbidden meaning slips past conscious censors in yet another of Mr. Compson's prolix descriptions of Bon. Bon, he says, is "an impenetrable and shadowy character. Yes, shadowy: a myth, a phantom: something which they engendered and created whole themselves; some effluvium of Sutpen blood and character, as though as a man he did not exist at all" (82). Covert meanings reside in one cryptic phrase. Bon, Mr. Compson proclaims, is "something which they engendered and created whole themselves." Mr. Compson's phrasing here makes possible two different readings. At the surface level, Mr. Compson appears to mean that the Sutpens wholly created Bon—that they created him, as it were, of whole cloth. But, alternatively, another meaning slips through: what Mr. Compson says might mean that Charles is something that created *them* whole. This second, easily overlooked reading is a secret, unconscious way of identifying Charles with the missing phallus, the lost object, which, the Sutpens imagine, if restored, would endow them with complete identity. Once we fill in the blank and restore the forbidden signifier, the other puzzle pieces fall into place. Bon is the creation of the Sutpens—"shadowy, a myth, a phantom"—because he incarnates the phallus, the imaginary object of desire, which does not exist. The phallus is only a symbol of the father's authority, only another sign to cover over a loss. The speaking subject, deprived and dispossessed as a condition of existence, imagines a position of empowerment, and attributes it to the sign of the father, the phallus. In precisely this way, the Sutpens "engendered" the "shadowy" Bon and attribute to him their desire. He is their wish-fulfillment fantasy; their creation; he, too, is a slip, seepage; he is the shape of their unconscious desire that has slipped out, disguised.

While Bon's existence, his presence among the Sutpens, is the central preoccupation of Mr. Compson's voluble ruminations, he also ponders at length, seemingly aimlessly, a related mystery: Charles Bon's substitution of a photograph of his octoroon wife and child for the photograph Judith gave him of herself. This picture-substitution is Mr.

Compson's contribution to the Sutpen legend. According to Mr. Compson, Judith finds on Charles's dead body the metal case that she had given him containing her photograph, but which now holds a picture of the octoroon mother and child. Oddly, this information, perhaps Mr. Compson's most significant contribution to the story, is absent from Miss Rosa's account. Miss Rosa speaks of Judith's picture, but she betrays no knowedge of an exchange. In her telling, she recalls running up the stairs to the second floor of the Sutpen house and finding Judith standing outside a closed bedroom door, "holding something in one hanging hand" (114). A few sentences later Miss Rosa revisits the scene outside the door, and this time she identifies what is at first only "something": "And now I saw that what she held in that lax and negligent hand was the photograph, the picture of herself in its metal case which she had given him, held casual and forgotten against her flank as any interrupted pastime book" (114). In Mr. Compson's version, the picture of the other woman and child takes the place of Judith's picture; in Miss Rosa's rendering, Judith's photograph is not displaced. What are we to make of this discrepancy?

Miss Rosa does not see that the photographs have been switched because she must not. In other words, the picture-substitution is repressed in her telling. She can no more admit the traded photographs into her discourse than she can pass through that closed bedroom door. The closed door represents interdiction, the Law of the Father. It marks a boundary that may not be crossed, and this precisely is the point, because that boundary has been transgressed. The photograph of the mother and child that replaces Judith's picture emerges from behind that closed door; it is a message from that forbidden space—a message from Charles Bon. Miss Rosa's censors forbid recognition to this meaning: thus Miss Rosa must not know that Bon replaced one photograph with another. Mr. Compson, on the other hand, represses less intensely: in his discourse this disguised, subliminal image slips out, its forbidden content unrecognized.

What does Charles Bon mean by switching the photographs? Certainly this question has generated wide-ranging conjecture, both within the novel and outside of it. For Mr. Compson, the matter is a simple one. By removing Judith's picture and replacing it with the photograph of the other woman and child, Bon proves himself to be "at least an intending bigamist even if not an out and out blackguard" (71). In other words, Bon's act convicts him of infamy and is reason for Judith to spurn him. Mr. Compson penetrates no further. Later, in the course of his joint narration with Quentin, Shreve revises Mr. Compson's harsh estimation. Shreve speculates that Bon displaced Judith's photograph in favor of the photograph of the octoroon wife and child so as to earn Judith's contempt and thereby to release her: "It was because he said to himself, 'If Henry dont mean what he said, it will be all right; I can take it out and destroy it. But if he does mean what he said, it will be the only way I will have to say to her, *I was no good; do not grieve for me*' " (287).

A different, but again sensitive, reading of the puzzling picture-switch comes from outside the novel. Elisabeth Muhlenfeld looks for the meaning that Bon's picture-substitution portends for Judith. Since Judith takes the photograph from the room, she seems to read it as a message to her from Charles Bon. What is that message? The answer, Muhlenfeld argues, is implicit in Judith's attempts, following Bon's death, to open the Sutpen home to this other woman and Bon's son: Judith invites them to Sutpen's Hundred to mourn at Bon's grave, and later, when Bon's son is orphaned, she brings him to live with her and Clytie. These acts of inclusion, Muhlenfeld declares, are driven by the image of the octoroon and the child. Judith reads this image as a sign of Bon's acknowledgement of his wife and son, and because he recognizes them she attempts to follow his example.

Faulkner's large text accommodates all of these readings, and more, for yet another meaning attaches to the photograph found on Bon's dead body. Mr. Compson alludes to this meaning, without consciously recognizing it, in his second reference to the photograph: "[Judith] did not know what happened in the library that night. I dont think she ever suspected, until that afternoon four years later when she saw them again, when they brought Bon's body into the house and she found in his coat the photograph which was not her face, not her child" (73). In my reading, forbidden meanings turn on the phrase "the photograph which was not her face, not her child." Mr. Compson's phrase is a classic example of what Freud calls "the recognition of the unconscious on the part of the ego . . . expressed in a negative formula." In his essay "Negation," Freud explains that a repressed image or idea can make its way into consciousness if it is negated: "Negation is a way of taking cognizance of what is repressed; indeed it is already a lifting of repression, though not, of course, an acceptance of what is repressed."[6] In other words, we can utter a prohibited meaning so long as we simultaneously disavow it by negating it. Accordingly, when Mr. Compson says "not her face, not her child," he is negating the meaning that must be repressed; that is, that the photograph of Bon's wife and child *is* a photograph of Judith; that Bon substitutes one photo for another to imply an equation, an identification. Bon exchanges the photos because Judith, the octoroon, and the child are all interchangeable: they all signify the unravelling of identity in the preoedipal stage. The octoroon mother and child, for example, symbolize the original dyadic unity that preceded the splitting that gives rise to consciousness and separate identity. Similarly, Judith, as sister, a displaced figure for the mother, also recalls the preoedipal relation with the mother. This is the concealed meaning of Mr. Compson's repeated pronouncements that Judith is "too much like" (82) Henry and Thomas Sutpen. This likeness is "almost unbearable" (139) because it reflects a former unmediated connection to the maternal body.[7] Thus, Judith, the octoroon wife, and Bon's son are all figures for the identificatory imago of the mirror stage; and, by substituting one photograph for the other as if they were interchangeable, Bon signifies a forbidden leveling of difference. He signs not only that there is no difference between the pictures, but, more than this, he signs an original undifferentiated stage before the emergence of subjectivity and difference.

Toward the end of Mr. Compson's narration, there appears a passage that the reader may find disconcerting. The passage amounts to an apology: Mr. Compson seems almost to dismiss his own elaborately constructed theory of the Sutpen tragedy. After all that reasoning and rhetoric, all that wordplay, all those invented scenes, in the end, he admits that his account "just does not explain." His feeling of failure, of being unable to make sense of the Sutpen story, can be traced to repression. Mr. Compson is father become Father. He represents the law of castration; necessarily, then, his narration is truncated. Of course, he never consciously admits to censoring his narration; however, as he laments the shortcomings of his account, he alludes to a series of disguised images for repression. He begins by professing utter bewilderment—"It's just incredible. It just does not explain"—but he quickly revises this assessment and suggests not incomprehensibility but prohibition: "Or perhaps that's it: they don't explain and we are not supposed to know" (80). Mr. Compson's phrase covertly insinuates the law of alienation. The "few old mouth-to-mouth tales" "don't explain" because the Law of the Father ordains interdiction; because "we are not supposed to know."

As Mr. Compson continues to contemplate the seeming inexplicability of the Sutpen saga, he identifies a lack, a lacuna, in his narration:

> Yes, Judith, Bon, Henry, Sutpen: all of them. They are there, yet something is missing: they are like a chemical formula exhumed along with the letters from that forgotten chest, carefully, the paper old and faded and falling to pieces, the writing faded, almost indecipherable, yet meaningful, familiar in shape and sense, the name and presence of volatile and sentient forces; you bring them together in the proportions called for, but nothing happens; you re-read, tedious and intent, poring, making sure that you have forgotten nothing, made no miscalculation; you bring them together again and again nothing happens: just the words, the symbols, the shapes themselves, shadowy, inscrutable and serene, against that turgid background of a horrible and bloody mischancing of human affairs. (80)

Mr. Compson's use of the analogy of a chemical formula to illustrate his failure is telling. He brings together the parts "in the proportions called for" and "nothing happens." His finding, then, is "nothing." However, Mr. Compson's bewilderment and regret to the contrary, this finding does not signify failure; rather, he has correctly named the foundation of the Law—"nothing." "Nothing," a vacuum, is what the Law is based upon. His expression, "the proportions called for" is a veiled allusion to the law of castration. For there to be difference and meaning, there has to be a gap, an absence—"nothing." In other words, while, on the surface, Mr. Compson expresses puzzled regret at his narration's failure to explain, beneath the surface, he accurately describes the way the Law functions to create language, identity, and meaning. Mr. Compson's finding, "nothing," is the necessary ingredient for language. Words represent absence. They are the empty symbols to mark a vacancy, a void. Thus, "nothing" produces language, as Mr. Compson lets slip when he says: "nothing happens: just the words, the symbols, the shapes themselves, shadowy, inscrutable and serene."

Mr. Compson's narration is a bewildering play of meanings offered and withheld. It is no wonder that Gerald Langford, surveying these conflicting signals, concludes that Faulkner sometimes means for

Mr. Compson to know Bon's identity and, at other times, wills Mr. Compson oblivious. But these alternating pulls and counterpulls are not the traces of a dizzily indecisive author; rather, they mark the tension between the conscious mind and the unconscious. Language works by mirroring the original prohibition, by censoring. At the same time, however, this censoring is never complete. Try as we will to assign single, stable meanings to signs, this single sense is always disrupted, deconstructed; the turbulent activity of the unconscious always inserts itself. Bubbling beneath the surface of Mr. Compson's narration is a repressed desire of the Other, and this desire makes its way to the surface disguised as Charles Bon. For a full represencing of the repressed, the reader must wait for the long-deferred climax of the Quentin-Shreve account, but, if we read for the meaning that adheres between the meanings, traces of the repressed can be detected in Mr. Compson's narration.

"A BREATHING INDICTMENT . . . OF THE ENTIRE MALE PRINCIPLE"

Rosa Coldfield's account of the Sutpen tragedy appears to explain little. Her telling seems to amount to little more than the acrimonious outrage of a woman scorned, as Faulkner apparently indicates by placing the fifth chapter of the novel in italics, the continuation of Miss Rosa's telling, as if italics were the typeset equivalent of her overwrought emotional state.[8] But, like Mr. Compson's puzzled garrulity, Miss Rosa's vituperations let pass meanings that consciousness prohibits. In fact, her rage is itself an outward manifestation of a psychic wound. On the surface, her furious indignation is provoked by Sutpen's crude sexual proposition, which demeans her and their prospective sexual union. But Sutpen's insult so profoundly offends Miss Rosa because it reenacts an ancient, archetypal indignity, an affront that she herself cannot consciously recall, the injury incurred as the price of consciousness.

To explain, we must return to the beginning. Miss Rosa is silent about her origin, but Mr. Compson tells us that, for Miss Rosa, life began with loss: she "was born, at the price of her mother's life and was never to be permitted to forget it" (46). This bereavement at birth is an analogue for the symbolic castration that attends the coming into being of the subject. For the separate subject to exist, there must be a loss, a renunciation of an original imaginary fullness of being. Rosa's mother's death in childbirth is yet another image—like the injury Sutpen suffered when he was turned away from the front door of the planter's mansion—for this primal blow. If we read Rosa's mother's death in this symbolic context, it becomes clear why Miss Rosa never "forgave her father for [her mother's death]" (46). Her father is accountable as father become Name-of-the-Father. Because of the father's sexual difference from the mother, he stands for difference, for the opening up of a gap, for the introduction of loss. And, like her father, Thomas Sutpen is yet another figure of the almighty Father, the phallic Other, who decrees loss. Sutpen revisits the primal injury at least two times in Miss Rosa's life: when he shames her with his sexual proposition and, before that, when he repeats her father's offense by robbing her of the sister-surrogate for the mother. According to Mr. Compson, from earliest childhood Miss Rosa was taught by her aunt to think of her older sister "as a woman who had vanished, not only out of the family and the house but out of life too, into an edifice like Bluebeard's and there transmogrified into a mask looking back with passive and hopeless grief upon the irrevocable world" (47). Like her mother, her older sister is taken from her, seemingly abducted by a Hades-figure to a deathly underworld.[9] This erasure of her sister restages the original loss of an imaginary dyadic unity, and thus it establishes Sutpen as a representative of the supposedly mighty phallus that takes the place left by the absence of the mother.

For Miss Rosa, then, as for so many others, Sutpen is a figure of the phallic Other.[10] As the paternal representative who dwells in the house with the mother—in Miss Rosa's words, he "*removed*" Ellen to his "*grim ogre-bourne*" (135)—he appears to possess the missing object, the copula that could restore an imaginary completeness of being. Miss Rosa's anger, then, is really directed at the phallus, an imaginary condition of authority and invincibility, which seems to be signified by Sutpen and her father. But the phallus, the hidden signifier, must remain hidden, repressed. Its relinquishment is the price of identity. Accordingly, the object of desire, the missing signifier, can make its way into Miss Rosa's and Mr. Compson's narrative only in veiled forms. For instance, Mr. Compson covertly alludes to the hidden referent when he describes Rosa as "not only a living and walking reproach to her father, but a breathing indictment, ubiquitous and even transferable of the entire male principle" (46–47). Although men do not, of course, possess the complete fulfillment identified with the phallus, they are endowed with the penis, which, because it marks the father's difference from the mother, is a symbol for the phallus. This symbolism explains the ease with which Miss Rosa transfers her rage to "the entire male principle": the male principle is a code word for the real target of her anger, the phallus, the object of desire that, she imagines, could fill her emptiness, but instead decrees loss.

Mr. Compson again gives a hidden form to the forbidden signifier when he invokes Miss Rosa's lifelong rage as "disapprobation regarding any and every thing which could penetrate the walls of that house through the agency of any man, particularly her father" (47). What is the object of Miss Rosa's "disapprobation"? What is this male, fatherly "thing" that penetrates walls? The hidden referent appears to be the phallus. The phallus is the copula that supposedly can reconnect us with the mother—the copula that, the child imagines, the father possesses. While the phallus or Law of the Father decrees that the child respect walls between self and m(other), the all-powerful phallus is presumed to possess the mother, to be within the walls, within the womb-house that the child is forbidden to enter. Thus Miss Rosa's hatred is aimed at the phallus and its representatives that decree her lack, while signifying a completeness that is denied to her. In other words, Miss Rosa's hate is rooted in desire. Like every speaking subject, she yearns for the missing part. She would not hate so intensely if she did not desire the object of her hate.

This reading would explain Miss Rosa's seemingly inexplicably sudden capitulation to the "*ogre*" (135) of her childhood. After all those long years of hating Sutpen, Miss Rosa abruptly, impossibly reverses herself: when he returns from the war and proposes marriage to her, she accepts. This acceptance of Sutpen's marriage proposal betokens yet another concealed acknowledgement of the forbidden signifier. She yields not so much to Sutpen as to her own unconscious desire. In agreeing to marry Sutpen, she is yielding to a desire of the Other. But, while the phallus represents the imaginary object that can satisfy the mother's and the Other's desire, the father, or phallus, forbids that satisfaction, that fullness of being, to the child. This moment of prohibition is replayed in the novel when Sutpen makes the proposal that so outrages Rosa that she cannot name it. By proposing that they attempt to conceive a child out of wedlock and marry only if she produces a viable male heir, Sutpen wounds her, and this psychic wounding reenacts another, the symbolic castration that brought the subject into being. In effect, he is banishing her, just as her mother and older sister were banished before her, and this time Miss Rosa never recovers from her outrage.

Rosa Coldfield's narration, however, is more than an account of the subject's origin in loss recast in terms of the cliché of the woman scorned. As she blazes at Sutpen, the agent of the phallic signifier that has crippled her life, her tirade contains a prohibited meaning from the unconscious. Like all such meanings, it is disguised and scarcely recognizable; certainly it is not consciously recognized by Rosa. Nevertheless, this covert message is her revenge. In the margins of her discourse, she insinuates that Sutpen, the representative of the phallic signifier that stands for the separation of the mother-child dyad, is driven by a desire to return to the origin and restore an unmediated connection with the mother.

This covert meaning lies behind, for example, the title that Rosa affixes to Sutpen: demon. Shreve also fastens on this nickname—impelled by much the same drive as Rosa—but it is with Rosa that the term originates. It emerges from her unconscious, carrying a subliminal message, and she applies it relentlessly to Sutpen: it is a way of naming the forbidden desire to restore a former imaginary relation with the mother. Freud held that people who appear to be possessed by demons are actually exhibiting the repetition compulsion: "in normal persons, [the repetition compulsion] gives the impression of a pursuing fate, a daemonic trait in their destiny." Rosa's "demon" thus carries heavy freight. It is a code word for the repetition compulsion, which, Freud claims, is an expression of the unconscious: in the grip of the repetition compulsion, we are "obliged to repeat as current experience what is repressed."[11] Thus, by demonizing Sutpen, Miss Rosa covertly uncovers his darkest secret. Without conscious awareness, she reveals that he is driven endlessly to reenact a return to an imaginary unity.[12]

This unmasking of Sutpen's desire, however, is implied in Miss Rosa's text not only by her introduction of the term *demon* for Sutpen. She also produces an illustration of Sutpen's desire of the m(other) that, when read for its subtext, exposes a hidden agenda. I refer to Miss Rosa's narration of the savage fights among and with his slaves that Sutpen stages in his barn as entertainments. These contests, which Sutpen rehearses compulsively—they had been going on, Miss Rosa tells us, "ever since he drove the last nail in the house" (20) and they continue on a regular basis long after Supen's marriage to Ellen—are one manifestation of Sutpen's repetition compulsion. But exactly what is Sutpen driven to repeat with this combat? At one level, the conscious level, Sutpen is making a bid for mastery; he is trying to establish his right to accede to the place of the all-powerful Other, as Miss Rosa acknowledges when she explains that on certain occasions Sutpen himself would fight with one of the slaves "perhaps as a matter of sheer deadly forethought toward the retention of supremacy, domination" (21). But the ritualistic fights are also driven by an unconscious motive. Unknown to Sutpen, he is impelled to repeat the brutal fighting because it gives a disguised shape to his desire for a narcissistic return to the first who was made other. As Richard King observes, Sutpen's hand-to-hand combat with his slave adversary is cast in sexual terms; it takes the form of a primal scene, the scene of parental copulation interpreted by the child as a violent struggle.[13] Nearly naked, "panting and bloody," Sutpen grapples with the slave, who plays the subordinate, feminine role; they fight without "rules or weapons," with the two antagonists viciously "gouging at one another's eyes" (20), simulating a violent sexual penetration. In other words, this deadly struggle gives a veiled outward form to a forbidden desire for merger. Like Freud's classic example of the repetition compulsion, the *fort-da* game, which dramatizes both mastery of the mother and her repossession, Sutpen's "games" ritualize both a desire to accede to the place of the symbolic Other and a desire to return.

The desire of the m(other), writes Elizabeth Wright, is the desire to "satisfy the mother's lack" by "becoming the 'phallus' for the mother, all that would complete her desire."[14] This desire is never wholly repressed. It drives Sutpen to fight with the slave, and it drives Miss Rosa to narrate the slave fight. Her narration, no less than his physical participation, allows the repressed to slip by conscious censors. Like her use of the term *demon* for Sutpen, her description of the scene in the barn gives an unrecognized form to a repressed desire to re-fuse with the forbidden other. In Miss Rosa's discourse, this repressed desire erupts in the form of a parapraxis—Freud's slip of the tongue. The slip occurs as she describes Sutpen's participation in the evening event: "It seems that on certain occasions, perhaps at the end of the evening, the spectacle, as a grand finale or perhaps as a matter of sheer deadly forethought toward the retention of supremacy, domination, he would enter the ring with one of the negroes himself" (21). Reflect for a moment on the syntax of Miss Rosa's statement. She does not say, "he himself would enter the ring with one of the negroes." Rather, by saying, "he would enter the ring with one of the negroes himself," Miss Rosa seems to misplace *himself.* Listen again carefully: when Miss Rosa says, "with one of the negroes himself," beneath the surface, she seems to identify Sutpen as one of the negroes. This seemingly negligent word-slip carries weighty, hidden implications. Without conscious recognition, Miss Rosa lets pass the same meaning that is implicit, though veiled, in Sutpen's savage conquest of his slave; she insinuates a merging of white Sutpen and black other.[15] Read for its hidden meaning, her slip of the tongue dismantles the binary oppositions upon which subjectivity, language, and culture rest. Like Sutpen's fight with his slave, Miss Rosa's verbal misplacing fills the gap and fuses slave and master, black and white, self and other. It gives a disguised outward sign to a desire to return.

"YES. MAYBE WE ARE BOTH FATHER"

Quentin and Shreve penetrate where Mr. Compson and Miss Rosa are stopped.[16] Indeed the text of the two young men seems to supercede the two previous accounts; their joint interpretation conjures meanings that are only covertly insinuated in the preceding narratives. And yet, if their reading overshadows the two earlier versions, Quentin seems not to know it, since throughout much of his narrative, he speaks not in his own voice but only as a conduit for Father or Grandfather, a practice that seems to jar dissonantly with the claim of priority in narration. Even Shreve remarks this discordance: in a passage Faulkner added in revision, Shreve interrupts as Quentin appears to make Father the author of the revelation of their section—that Charles Bon is Sutpen's son:

> "He chose the name himself, Grandfather believed, just as he named them all—the Charles Goods and the Clytemnestras and Henry and Judith and all of them—that entire fecundity of dragons' teeth as Father called it. And Father said—"
> "Your father," Shreve said. "He seems to have got an awful lot of delayed information awful quick, after having waited forty-five years. If he knew all this, what was his reason for telling you that the trouble between Henry and Bon was the octoroon woman?"

"He didn't know it then. Grandfather didn't tell him all of it either, like Sutpen never told Grandfather quite all of it."

"Then who did tell him?"

"I did." Quentin did not move, did not look up while Shreve watched him. "The day after we—after that night when we—"

"Oh," Shreve said. "After you and the old aunt. I see. Go on. And Father said—" (214)

Shreve's bewilderment is legitimate, and we may well share it. On the one hand, Quentin's manner of narrating, his habit of prefacing every statement with "Father said" seems to give priority to his father's reading of events; on the other hand, under Shreve's questioning, he admits that he is the authority—that Mr. Compson owes his knowledge of Bon's identity to Quentin. What are we to make of these contrary signals? John T. Irwin cites this passage and picks up on one signal. Noting Quentin's admission of authorship, Irwin argues that Quentin has bested Father in an oedipal contest: "Quentin's act of narration in *Absalom* is an attempt to seize his father's authority by gaining temporal priority. In the struggle with his father, Quentin will prove that he is a better man by being a better narrator—he will assume the authority of an author because his father does not know the whole story, does not know the true reason for Bon's murder; whereas Quentin does. Instead of listening passively while his father talks, Quentin will assume the active role and his father will listen while Quentin talks."[17] Irwin's reading is persuasive, but it overlooks Quentin's practice of echoing his father. If, as Irwin proposes, Quentin is establishing himself as the teller of the tale, why does he obsequiously defer to Father? And Irwin's provocative analysis raises another question: If, as Irwin rightly remarks, Quentin knows "the whole story," "the true reason for Bon's murder," why is that story and that reason withheld until the last pages of the novel?

The answer to both these questions is that, like Sutpen, Grandfather, Mr. Compson, and Miss Rosa, Quentin also doesn't "tell . . . quite all of it." Like them, he obeys the Law of castration that ordains absence. When Quentin cites Father as his authority, he is signaling his acceptance of his subordinated position in the father-mother-child triad. Similarly, when Quentin censors his narration, he is also obeying the Law of the Father: as the obedient son who renounces an illusory wholeness, Quentin cannot speak the completeness of being that Bon represents. Eventually, as Irwin astutely observes, Quentin will mount a challenge to the Father; he will seek to fill the gap and restore the lost object; but that process takes place gradually and is not complete until the final pages of the novel. For now, Quentin effaces his own voice in favor of the rule of the father become Father.

While Quentin narratively represses, he can never wholly restrain the irrepressible unconscious that ceaselessly challenges identity and conscious meanings.[18] In *The Sound and the Fury*, for example, where Quentin's section is also marked by the ubiquitous "Father said," Quentin's suicide simultaneously signals repression and return. On the one hand, suicide reenacts the primary repression of being that constitutes subjectivity; on the other hand, by drowning himself, Quentin signifies a return to a former fused state. In the earlier novel, then, Quentin's desire to overcome lack culminates ultimately in suicide; in *Absalom,* this desire for completeness erupts again and takes a new form.

Gradually, almost imperceptibly, there occurs a change in the Quentin-Shreve narration. This change is signaled by two outward signs: first, somewhere, unobtrusively, Quentin's catchphrase—"Father said"—drops from the narration; and second, the voices of Quentin and Shreve begin to sound alike. This second change cannot go unnoticed: it upsets our readerly expectations. At some indeterminate point in their joint narration, their voices merge; we can no longer distinguish Quentin's voice from Shreve's or Father's. More to the point, we can no longer distinguish the teller of the tale.

This breakdown of distinctions among speakers is flagged in the text. Listening to Shreve's voice, Quentin reflects, "*He sounds just like Father*" (147). And later, Shreve remarks the uncanny likeness of Quentin's dense rhetoric to Father's: "Dont say it's just me that sounds like your old man" (210). Immediately following Shreve's comment, the narrative is interrupted as Quentin seems to lose himself in thought, in a long, labyrinthine revery. This revery did not appear in the manuscript version of the novel;[19] Faulkner added it when revising, and he italicizes it as if to underscore its importance. For my purposes, the passage is crucial: it articulates the unraveling of identity and meaning that accounts for the evolving narrative form of Quentin's and Shreve's telling:

Yes. Maybe we are both Father. Maybe nothing ever happens once and is finished. Maybe happen is never once but like ripples maybe on water after the pebble sinks, the ripples moving on, spreading, the pool attached by a narrow umbilical water-cord to the next pool which the first pool feeds, has fed, did feed, let this second pool contain a different temperature of water, a different molecularity of having seen, felt, remembered, reflect in a different tone the infinite unchanging sky, it doesn't matter: that pebble's watery echo whose fall it did not even see moves across its surface too at the original ripple-space, to the old ineradicable rhythm thinking Yes, we are both Father. Or maybe Father and I are both Shreve, maybe it took Father and me both to make Shreve or Shreve and me both to make Father or maybe Thomas Sutpen to make all of us. (210; italics removed)

Covertly, Quentin's revery represences the repressed. His pool-and-pebble metaphor conceals as it reveals the loss of difference that is the unconscious. It moves from a disquisition on connecting pools to the seemingly unwarranted and unreasonable claim that "maybe we are both Father." But Quentin's identity-dismantling claim makes a kind of sense in context if we apprehend his tacit analogy between identity and watery bodies. Implicitly, Quentin compares identity to attaching pools that flow freely into one another. There is no separate Shreve, Quentin, or Father, because there is no difference; or, as Quentin puts it, what difference there might be—in the pool's "different temperature" or "different molecularity"—"doesn't matter," for such differences are subsumed by an overarching sameness: over every pool flows the same "original ripple-space, to the old ineradicable rhythm." Here Quentin's meaning becomes even more difficult to unpack. What is the symbolic meaning of the "original ripple-space" and "the old ineradicable rhythm?" The hidden referent is implied in another image, Quentin's reference to a "narrow umbilical water-cord" that attaches one watery body to another. This umbilicus image is the key that unlocks the meaning not only of this passage but also of the fusing voices in the Quentin-Shreve narration. The umbilicus connects the child to the maternal body; it recalls the original symbiotic unity, the condition of existence before the appearance of the sign of difference, before the opening up of loss, difference, and consciousness. According to Freud's *Beyond the Pleasure Principle,* all existence is driven by a desire "for the reinstatement of an earlier situation" (74). If we read Quentin's revery as a poeticizing of Freud's text, Quentin's image of "the old ineradicable rhythm" of the "original ripple-space" represents the desire to return, to flow back to the beginning, to restore the stillness before the awakening of motion, before the pebble fell. Similarly, this desire for a return—Freud's theory of the regressive nature of the instincts—helps explain the merging of voices in the Quentin-Shreve narration. Driven by this desire to return, to restore an imaginary unity symbolized by the umbilicus, Quentin and Shreve are reverting to an earlier stage of development, a stage that precedes the oedipal: together, they are revisiting the mirror stage of development.

Quentin's obligatory "Father said" disappears from the narration; the voices become indistinguishable; the sentences become longer and longer, a seemingly endless series of connected clauses, because together Quentin and Shreve are regressing to a stage of development that preceded the appearance of the Law, a stage in which the child still experienced psychic fusion and corporal identification. This mirror phase of development is an intermediary stage between the imaginary and the symbolic. James M. Mellard cogently explains:

> Since there is no subject as such in the beginning (that is, in the pre-mirror phase), the onset of a real subject occurs in the child's passage through the mirror phase, for from that pregnant moment both consciousness-as-consciousness and an unconscious built on repression are born. Even so, the mirror phase does not produce a fully realized subject. Although this moment initiates the subject into the *function* of the Symbolic order, the *rule* of the Symbolic is not yet formalized or internalized. Instead, for a time the subject's use of symbolism is marked by the dualities of the Imaginary order such as one finds in Lacan's conception of neurosis in later life.[20]

In the mirror phase, the child still has glimpses of the evanescent, totalizing images of the imaginary: there are still only two, the Father has not yet appeared, and the child has not yet internalized the Law. But the mirror phase *is* an intermediary phase. Thus, at the same time as the child still has, as it were, one foot in the imaginary, he or she also begins to have an incipient sense of self. This budding self-awareness differs dramatically from the consciousness built on repression that will characterize the postoedipal subject. Rather, this self-image derives from dependency and identification. The child finds itself within the gaze of the mother: when the child looks at the mother, the child identifies with this image. Thus, in this phase, identity is based in identification. In Lacan's words, "We have only to understand the mirror stage *as an identification,* in the full sense that analysis gives to the term: namely the transformation that takes place in the subject when it assumes an image."[21] Again Mellard offers a lucid explanation:

> The structural foundation of speech—though speech is not actualized in it—emerges in that function Lacan calls the mirror stage. . . . One of the most frequently discussed references to Freud occurs in Lacan's effort to explain the onset of the capability (the logical "moment") of speech in the infant. That enabling moment rests on the infant's assumption or introjection of a unified body image found not in itself, but in its other, the mother. We may say that the subject finds itself in the other, the mother who signifies for the child a totality introjected by the child, who before this moment was a congeries of parts that remained unsignified and perforce unthought as such. Thus for Lacan the *infans*-subject is brought into being precisely by a signifier, the other found in the mirror-phase identification.[22]

The mirror stage, then, is an identificatory phase. In strong contrast with the oedipal or phallic phase, which is characterized by absence, in the mirror phase it is through identification that there is being. This disquisition on the mirror stage is relevant to *Absalom, Absalom!,* because the dependency and identification of the mirror stage characterize the later narration of Quentin and Shreve. The two young men are finally able to penetrate further than Miss Rosa and Mr. Compson because of a regression to the mirror stage. Because in the mirror stage the child still has fleeting visions of the plenitude of the early imaginary, Quentin and Shreve are able to "overpass," to fill the gap, to represence the totality—the total meaning of the Sutpen story.

This reversion to the mirror stage occurs gradually in the joint narration. In the early stages of their telling, Quentin observes the Law that decrees absence, and his telling signs this loss: he is "brooding, almost sullen" (177); he speaks in a "curious repressed calm voice" (177); and he frequently stops his narration, only to be prodded back into speech by Shreve.[23] But even as Quentin resists the completeness

115

of being that is Charles Bon, there appear in the text hints of the coming mirror-stage fusion. For example, the rarely heard omniscient narrator now intervenes to harp on the sameness of the two seemingly different young men:

> both young, both born within the same year: the one in Alberta, the other in Mississippi; born half a continent apart yet joined, connected after a fashion in a sort of geographical transubstantiation by that Continental Trough, that River which runs not only through the physical land of which it is the geologic umbilical, not only runs through the spiritual lives of the beings within its scope, but is very Environment itself which laughs at degrees of latitude and temperature, though some of these beings, like Shreve, have never seen it—the two of them who four months ago had never laid eyes on one another yet who since had slept in the same room and eaten side by side of the same food and used the same books from which to prepare and to recite in the same freshman courses, facing one another across the lamplit table. (208)

The striking propinquity of the two roommates makes them likely candidates for identification. For four months their existence has been "the same." This sameness presages the coming infant-identificatory stage: in the mirror phase, the child finds itself in the other and perceives itself and its other as the same. And this mirror stage fusion makes possible the "transubstantiation" that is about to take place: the crossing over of Quentin and Shreve to Henry and Bon. Because of a mirror-stage apprehension of relatedness, because they are not separate but the same, part and parcel of "Environment itself," they are able to merge with Henry and Bon.

This regression to an early, infant developmental phase is also signaled by Shreve's rather singular appearance. He is, in fact, naked to the waist, but, seated behind a table, he appears to be totally nude: "(from the waist down the table concealed him; anyone entering the room would have taken him to be stark naked)" (177). At one level, Shreve's apparent nakedness signals that he is exposed; that he conceals nothing, unlike, for example, Thomas Sutpen who, according to Miss Rosa, seems to hide behind his beard and swaggering manner. At another, related, level, Shreve's naked appearance recalls the nakedness of infancy. Indeed, the narrator specifically calls attention to this baby-likeness: "Shreve leaning forward into the lamp, his naked torso pink-gleaming and baby smooth, cherubic, almost hairless" (147). Such references point to Shreve's reversion to an infant identificatory stage. Shreve, who looks like a baby, is beginning to assume the ego-identity of an infant, an ego based in the identificatory other.

Perhaps the most telling outward signs of this reversion, however, are the insistent references to Shreve's spectacles. The glinting spectacles function like a mirror. When Quentin looks at Shreve, he looks into a reflecting surface, the "glinting spectacles," and locates his specular (mirror) image in the other; in this instance, Shreve. Moreover, not only the considerable number of references to Shreve's spectacles, but also the rather peculiar way they are described point to a reversion to an earlier phase of development. Most typically, the spectacles are imaged as "twin moons . . . glinting against his moonlike rubicund face" (147). The "twin moons" register the duality characteristic of the early phase when there are only two; as well, the emphasis here on round images, "twin moons," "moonlike," and "rubicund," suggests Jung's image of the round, or mandala, a primordial image for a pre-conscious unity.

Quentin has entered the mirror phase with Shreve as the imaginary other. As we recall, in this early phase prior to the oedipus complex and symbolic castration, the separate subject does not exist. Rather, in this transitional phase, existence is dependent on the other: the incipient subject finds itself in the identificatory imago. For Quentin and Shreve, this means that they each call the other into being; they each find an image of the self reflected in the other. Given this dependency, it is no wonder that Quentin and Shreve should exchange long, searching, penetrating looks. Because each occupies for the other the place of alterity, because each plays for the other the role of phallic mother, the gaze of the other confers an imaginary unity. It follows, then, that the text should take for its subject focal moments—moments when Quentin and Shreve look at one another: "They stared at one another—glared rather—their quiet regular breathing vaporising faintly and steadily in the now tomblike air. There was something curious in the way they looked at one another, curious and quiet and profoundly intent, not at all as two young men might look at each other but almost as a youth and a very young girl might out of virginity itself—a sort of hushed and naked searching" (240). Because the look that passes between the young men speaks desire, critics, puzzled and unable to to explain this desire in any other way, have sometimes tentatively ascribed homosexual feelings to Quentin and Shreve.[24] But, while desire is played out in this reciprocal gaze, it is not the homosexual desire that is defined after the oedipus complex and the assumption of the Law of the Father. Rather, it is desire of the m/other, desire for a return to the profound physical and psychic intimacy of the mother-child relation, the desire for introjection, incorporation.[25] This meaning is implied in the image of the young heterosexual couple. The "youth" and "very young girl," to whom Quentin and Shreve are compared, are veiled figures for the child and the mother. The "virginity" that characterizes their gaze makes them—and, by analogy, Quentin and Shreve also—signifiers for the mother-child dyad, because the mother-child relationship is the only truly virginal relationship: it is preceded by no other.

Through this mirror-stage fusion, Quentin and Shreve "overpass"; they defy boundaries; they flow freely into Henry and Bon; and, ultimately, Quentin is able to reveal the hidden contents of Sutpen's dark house. This long-deferred revelation is the climactic conclusion of the novel. It is withheld from us even though, at some level, Quentin knows what is hidden in the house—has known ever since the evening of 9 September 1909, when he and Miss Rosa broke into Sutpen's house. But Quentin cannot speak this revelation until the very close of his narration with Shreve, for to name the contents of the house is to fill the gap and to restore an imaginary unity: to do that, Quentin must wait until he has achieved complete mirror-stage identification with Shreve as other.

I have said that the long-deferred represencing of the missing signifier occurs as the climactic conclusion of the novel: for Quentin, this climax seems literally a sexual one. When Quentin finally admits to a desire for incorporation, this admission is accompanied by signs of sexual orgasm. Just after Quentin and Shreve psychically fuse with Henry and Bon to recreate the moment during the Civil War when Bon, for the first time, is named as both brother and black other, Quentin, back in his dormitory room at Cambridge, exhibits surprising but unmistakable physical sensations. He lies in bed

> feeling the warming blood driving through his veins, his arms and legs. And now, although he was warm and though while he had

sat in the cold room he merely shook faintly and steadily, now he began to jerk all over, violently and uncontrollably until he could even hear the bed, until even Shreve felt it and turned, raising himself (by the sound) onto his elbow to look, though Quentin himself felt perfectly all right. He felt fine even, lying there and waiting in peaceful curiosity for the next violent unharbingered jerk to come. (288–89)

The blood pulsing through his limbs metaphorically suggests another blood-suffused member—a blood-engorged penis. Likewise, the involuntary spasms that shake him are the outward signs of sexual orgasm. Clearly, as John N. Duvall observes, Quentin appears to be in the climactic throes of sexual excitation. But what does this orgasmic sexual response signify?[26]

Quentin is experiencing what Lacan calls *jouissance;* that is, ultimate sexual enjoyment or bliss (the French *jouissance* literally means orgasm). *Jouissance* is the satisfaction of the sexual drive that Lacan, following Freud, defines as a drive toward completion, toward self-completion through the other. *Jouissance* is an always-momentary rapture experienced when we satisfy our desire to become one again with the lost other, when we restore the missing signifier, the phallus, that can reconnect us with the mother. Lacan uses the sexual term *jouissance* for this ecstatic union because sexual intercourse also enacts our desire to recapture a lost unity: in the act of intercourse, the man attempts to have the phallus for the woman; the woman attempts to be the phallus for the man.[27] All such attempts to restore the phallus are, of course, prohibited by the Law. In fact, Lacan writes that the Law is the Law against *jouissance:* "But we must insist that *jouissance* is forbidden to him who speaks as such, although it can only be said between the lines for whoever is subject of the Law, since the Law is grounded in this very prohibition."[28] *Jouissance,* then, is the forbidden pleasure that comes from the violation of interdiction—from the restoring of the missing signifier. Quentin experiences *jouissance* at this particular moment in the text because he, at long last, has represented the repressed. He has introduced into the text Charles's complete identity, which *is* complete identity; that is, he has recognized Bon's identity as the missing copula between self and other.

Quentin is not alone in experiencing *jouissance.* Miss Rosa and Henry, respectively, also exhibit signs of a rapturous sexual consummation. For example, when Miss Rosa urges Quentin to penetrate the walls of the old Sutpen place with the hatchet she has given him, they figuratively are restoring the forbidden signifier and returning to the womb. Accordingly, as she enters the house, Miss Rosa pants, trembles, moans, and more—as Quentin helps her up the steps of the house: "he could feel something fierce and implacable and dynamic driving down the thin rigid arms and into his palms and up his own arms; lying in the Massachusetts bed he remembered how he thought, knew, said suddenly to himself, 'Why, she's not afraid at all. It's something. But she's not afraid' " (293). The something "fierce and implacable and dynamic" that Quentin feels coursing through Miss Rosa's limbs is the life force—what Dylan Thomas calls "the force that through the green fuse drives the flower" and Addie Bundren calls "the terrible blood, the red bitter flood boiling through the land" (*AILD*, 161). This pulsing blood marks a return of the lost object; it marks completion of being and fulfillment of desire in a momentary *jouissance*.

Henry also experiences *jouissance* at the climactic moment of the Civil War scene that Quentin and Shreve conjure by fusing with Henry and Shreve. The moment of forbidden fulfillment occurs when Henry grasps Charles's pistol:

> Now it is Bon who watches Henry; he can see the whites of Henry's eyes again as he sits looking at Henry with that expression which might be called smiling. His hand vanishes beneath the blanket and reappears, holding his pistol by the barrel, the butt extended toward Henry.
> —Then do it now, he says.
> Henry looks at the pistol; now he is not only panting, he is trembling; when he speaks now his voice is not even the exhalation, it is the suffused and suffocating inbreath itself:
> —You are my brother.
> —No I'm not. I'm the nigger that's going to sleep with your sister. Unless you stop me, Henry.
> Suddenly Henry grasps the pistol, jerks it free of Bon's hand and stands so, the pistol in his hand, panting and panting: again Bon can see the whites of his inrolled eyes while he sits on the log and watches Henry with that faint expression about the eyes and mouth which might be smiling. (285–86; italics removed)

When Henry takes the pistol, symbolically he is reclaiming the missing signifier. Like Miss Rosa and Quentin, he is restoring the copula that was renounced at the constitution of subjectivity. He is proclaiming himself the father become Name-of-the-Father who presumably possesses authority over the mother and the world; and this claim is heralded by signs of sexual arousal: he trembles and pants; his voice is suffocated, and his eyes in-rolled. The passage further contains another, concealed, reference to Henry's sexually heightened state. One sentence is crucial; it describes the moment when Henry takes the pistol from Charles: "Henry grasps the pistol, jerks it free of Bon's hand and stands so, the pistol in his hand." The phrase "and stands so, the pistol in his hand"—like a phrase from *The Wild Palms,* "and now it did stand to his hand" (324)—is a covert allusion to a penile erection, the outward sign of Henry's phallic *jouissance.*

Quentin, Miss Rosa, and Henry, then, all momentarily overcome lack and achieve self-completion, as marked by *jouissance.* This completeness of being, however, does not confer the power and authority that the subject fantasizes exists in the phallic Other. Quentin, Shreve, Miss Rosa, and Henry have restored the life force, but, as Freud tells us, the life force, ultimately, is a drive toward death. In *Beyond the Pleasure Principle,* Freud contends that the desire for pleasure, for what Lacan calls *jouissance,* masks a more fundamental desire for a return to an original, inanimate state. *Jouissance* heralds, then, not an accession to a fantasized place of power identified with the Father as symbolic Other; rather, *jouissance* is the rapture that precedes a narcissistic merging with the lost other. Indeed, the signs of *jouissance,* which mark sexual exaltation, are simultaneously signs of death. For example, Miss Rosa's and Quentin's "rigid" (292, 293, 298) limbs figure not only an erect penis, the symbol for phallic power; this rigidity is also and equally an image for rigor mortis. As the French seem to recognize when they refer to sexual orgasm as a *petit mort* and as the Elizabethans similarly intimate when they use the phrase *to die* as a metaphor for orgasm, the sex drive is allied to the death instinct. *Jouissance,* Lacan says, is "*de trop*";[29] it is too much; it is the last gasp of the subject as it dissolves into an imaginary relation with the other.[30]

Jouissance, then, the death rattle of the merging subject, immediately precedes the ultimate moment of overpassing in the text, the novel's long-deferred climax. Just after Quentin exhibits signs of sexual bliss, he, at long last, reveals what is hidden in Sutpen's house. We must not underestimate the importance of this long-delayed denouement. When

Quentin and Miss Rosa break into Sutpen's house, they are passing where others were stopped. They pass where Tom Sutpen, a young boy at the front door of the planter's house, was turned away. They pass the phallic gateposts where Henry killed Charles Bon to keep him out. What, then, is the symbolic signficance of this passage that has been thwarted so many times before in the novel and is only now, in the concluding pages, accomplished? At one level, Quentin and Miss Rosa are storming the place of the father become Father, and within that place they expect to find the phallic Other, who rules the mother and the world. At another level—because, as Freud teaches, the house is a symbol for the self—by searching out the forbidden upper reaches of the house, Quentin and Miss Rosa are trespassing the boundary between conscious and unconscious. They are throwing open the door to the unconscious mind.

All of the narrations of *Absalom, Absalom!*, like all narration, are driven by a desire of the Other. In language, we move from one empty signifier to another, endlessly seeking what Lacan calls the "supreme signifier," the ultimate reference point that gives meaning to all other referents. Another way to state this is to say that all of the narrators of *Absalom* are searching for the symbolic father, for "that one ambiguous eluded dark fatherhead" (240).[31] "Every narration," Roland Barthes writes, "is a staging of the (absent, hidden, or hypostatized) father."[32] Within the Sutpen house, Miss Rosa and Quentin expect to find the elusive fatherhead. They break into the house, they accede to the place of the Other, and they find what has so long been concealed—they find that the father is the dead father. As Lacan puts it, "the symbolic Father is, in so far as he signifies this Law, the dead Father."[33] Within the house is Henry, who, like them, stormed the place of the Father. When Henry killed his elder brother, a father-figure, and burst through the bedroom door of his sister, a mother-figure, he claimed the hidden phallus, the imaginary object of the Other's and mother's desire. He, then, as they do now, rejected lack and claimed the father's privileged place with the mother within the house. But within the house there is no privileged father reigning supreme over the mother and the world. The house, as Freud tells us, is not only a symbol for the self; because it contains us, it is also a symbol for the womb. Within the womb-house, Quentin and Miss Rosa find completeness of being, but it is not the complete identity they imagined: it is the plenitude of the imaginary, the fullness of being of a preconscious existence absorbed in the preoedipal mother.

Let me repeat, *Absalom, Absalom!*, like our lives, is driven by a desire for completeness of being. Within the upper chamber of Sutpen's house, Quentin, Shreve, and Miss Rosa finally find that long-desired completeness. They have restored the hidden signifier, the missing part—Quentin and Shreve by revisiting a mirror-stage fusion, Quentin and Miss Rosa by trespassing on the forbidden space. Driven by their desire of the Other, they have filled the gap and fused with the forbidden m(other). And within the house they find the image of this fusion— the corpse-like Henry. How is Henry, lying on his deathbed, an image for fullness of being? Henry has come full circle. In the end, he returns to the beginning, the origin. We find him in the house of his birth, enclosed in a small, dark room, nursed (mothered) by his elder sister, Clytie. His desire to overcome lack has carried him back to an original dependency, to an original mother-child unity before the appearance of difference, before the sundering that gives rise to identity.

All of *Absalom, Absalom!* moves inexorably toward one moment, the moment when Quentin overpasses the last barrier, and is finally face-to-face with Henry Sutpen. In this confrontation, Quentin looks into the face of his alter ego, and sees reflected the image of his own unconscious—a life-in-death image. Hidden in the upper chamber of Sutpen's house, Quentin finds a living corpse—a living being that seems to be blending into his inanimate surroundings: "the bed, the yellow sheets and pillow, the wasted yellow face with closed almost transparent eyelids on the pillow, the wasted hands crossed on the breast as if he were already a corpse" (298). Henry incarnates being-toward-death. He is a portrait of Freud's definition of life as a mere temporary perturbation that interrupts the quiescence that precedes and follows it. And when Henry and Quentin speak, their verbal exchange is the syntactical equivalent of Freud's death instinct:

> And you are——?
> Henry Sutpen.
> And you have been here——?
> Four years.
> And you came home——?
> To die. Yes.
> To die?

Yes. To die.
And you have been here——?
Four years.
And you are——?
Henry Sutpen. (298; italics removed)

In a novel filled with echoes, from its title to its last words, *"I dont hate it! I dont hate it!,"* this passage is perhaps the most striking example of repetition. The dialogue very nearly forms a palindrome: it reads almost the same forward and back. Peter Brooks calls this verbal play "an unprogressive, reversible plot," and laments that it "generates no light, no revelation."[34] Like many readers, Brooks feels cheated. We have waited so long for this moment, and when it arrives, the dialogue seems to go nowhere, or, more precisely, it moves in a circle, retracing its steps, ending where it began.[35] But the revelation that we seek is at hand: the revelation is the very redundancy, the circularity. This circularity mirrors Freud's schema of life. In *Beyond the Pleasure Principle,* Freud writes:

> It would be counter to the conservative nature of instinct if the goal of life were a state never hitherto reached. It must rather be an ancient starting point, which the living being left long ago, and to which it harks back again by all the circuitous paths of development. If we may assume as an experience admitting of no exception that everything living dies from causes within itself, and returns to the inorganic, we can only say *'The goal of all life is death,'* and, casting back, *'The inanimate was there before the animate'.*[36]

Like life, which, according to Freud, doubles back upon itself, seeking "to return to lifelessness,"[37] a palindrome objectifies a desire to retrieve what was before; in this case, the repetitive form is an analogue for Henry's return home and for his dissolution into the environment. Along with these other signs, it is a formulation of the repressed. The meaning, then, that has so long eluded us is at last before us. What is repressed in the unconscious? Inside the dark house, Quentin, Shreve, and Miss Rosa find the desire to return to the origin, to restore a former inertia; they find a death wish.[38]

At the end of *Absalom, Absalom!* Sutpen's mansion, Clytie, and

Henry are consumed in flames. As Shreve notes, it is as if every trace—but one—of the Sutpens has been erased. In his final exchange with Quentin, which, given its terminal position, reads like a summation of the entire Sutpen tragedy, Shreve alludes seemingly flippantly to this incineration as a failed attempt to clear the Sutpen "ledger"; the attempt fails because it leaves behind one trace. Ultimately, Shreve says, you can never wipe the slate clean because there is always a residue; there is always Jim Bond: "the house collapsed and roared away, and there was only the sound of the idiot negro left" (301). Jim Bond is the irreducible residue of the Sutpen debacle. He is there in the end because he is the end that is also the beginning. Our clue to Jim Bond's role in the novel appears in the form of a double negative. When Quentin looks into the "saddle-colored slack-mouthed idiot face," he sees "no nothing" (296). The conscious, separate subject is created out of nothing; the self is called into being by virtue of repression, by creating a void; but the idiot grandson of Charles Bon knows "no nothing"; that is, he knows no absence, no gap. He incarnates a preconscious, fused existence before the onset of alienation and the opening up of the unconscious. Jim Bond is Henry's countrapuntal image: whereas Henry is dying back into the universe, Jim Bond has never known a difference between self and universe. Together, they form a matched set: identical origin and end.[39]

In revising the novel, Faulkner expanded the role of Jim Bond,[40] adding, for example, the closing passage that contains racist language, Shreve's derogatory reference to Jim Bond as the "one nigger Sutpen left" (302). Shreve's use of this racial slur seems unaccountable and indefensible,[41] until we realize that Shreve is deliberately echoing Charles Bon, who uses the same epithet a few pages earlier in the climactic scene that follows Henry's interview with his father in Colonel Willow's tent. After that meeting, Henry-Quentin and Charles-Shreve confront one another, and Charles Bon's identity is finally spoken:

—You are my brother.
—No I'm not. I'm the nigger that's going to sleep with your sister. Unless you stop me, Henry. (286; italics removed)

Charles Bon uses the inadmissible word here precisely because it is inadmissible: he uses it to underscore otherness. Similarly, Shreve uses the contemptuous racist term to foreground Jim Bond's role as the scorned, subordinated other, and then he elides this other with Sutpen. This fusion represents the effacing of the bar of difference and the re-presencing of the repressed. Shreve's term "nigger Sutpen" unleashes the repressed because only repression, only the opening up of a space, separates Jim Bond from Sutpen, and Shreve's elision fills that space. Thomas Sutpen is separated from Jim Bond only by virtue of the vacuum that opens up when the subject is constituted of lack. Before that renunciation of being, before Tom Sutpen was turned away from the front door of the planter's house, he was Jim Bond.[42] The barefoot boy who walked up the drive to the planter's big white house "knew neither where he had come from nor where he was nor why" (184); like Jim Bond, he was unaware of self. It is only repression, the bar at the door, that creates a difference. The full measure of Shreve's elision, his collapsing of difference, can be taken by Miss Rosa's equal and opposite insistence on difference. Miss Rosa insists on keeping a space between white and black, high and low, master and slave, Thomas Sutpen and Jim Bond. Even after having gone out to the old Sutpen place and having seen Henry, she refuses to know what Quentin, Shreve, and even Mr. Compson know—that Jim Bond is related to Sutpen. As she leaves the Sutpen house escorted by Jim Bond, walking in the rutted road, she falls, and as Quentin hurries forward to help her, he overhears her saying to Bond, "You aint any Sutpen. You dont have to leave me lying in the dirt" (297). Miss Rosa insists on the negation, the cancellation, of Jim Bond's meaning, for denial—repression—is all that separates Jim Bond from Thomas Sutpen.

The negation of his meaning separates not only Bond from Sutpen; negation is also all that stands between Jim Bond and us. Bond rep-resents a repressed desire for completeness of being. His howling gives voice to the unconscious, wordlessly wailing for recognition. We carry Bond—repressed—within us, and, for this reason, his howling is con-stant and inescapable. The citizens of Jefferson are bewildered by this trace of his presence: "They could hear him; he didn't seem to ever get any further away but they couldn't get any nearer and maybe in time they could not even locate the direction of the howling anymore" (300–301). The howling gets no nearer or further away because it moves with them and with us. In a novel filled with forbidden, unrecognized images out of the unconscious, Jim Bond is the last one. He is yet another formulation of our desire to return, both to return the repressed and to return to the origin. Endlessly we re-repress this forbidden desire, and endlessly it returns—like Bond, who lurks about the chimneys of the gutted mansion, is driven away, and then reappears again. We can only temporarily drive Bond away; we can never erase him permanently, because the unconscious never ceases to challenge conscious meanings.

CHAPTER 5

Renouncing the Phallus in
Go Down, Moses

Go Down, Moses is structured around two narrative reversals, two plot developments that run counter to our readerly expectations. On two closely related occasions, Ike McCaslin surprises us. Seemingly abruptly, he shifts course and alters the direction of his life. The first of these shifts occurs when he refuses to slay Old Ben; the second when he repudiates the patrimony that descends to him from Old Carothers. These two jarring narrative twists constitute the focal point, the nexus, of Ike's life and of the novel.

Ike's paralysis at the moment of crisis, the moment during the hunt when Old Ben turns at bay, constitutes a startling narrative reversal. The whole of "The Bear" chronicles the hunt for Old Ben and moves unerringly toward one climax—the slaying of the seemingly indomitable old bear. The reader, along with the hunters, fully expects that Ike McCaslin, the promising fledgling hunter and the novel's central protagonist, will be the one to bring down the old bear. But in the ultimate moment, Ike fails: he refuses to act.

Throughout the text, the pursuit of the legendary old bear is cast in terms of an oedipal conflict, a rivalry between father and son. The bear, an "old Priam"-figure (186), who is "the head bear," "the man" (190), and "r[uns]" the wilderness (201), functions in the text as a kind of elusive fatherhead. The hunters are the sons who harbor the not-so-secret desire to kill this father-representative and assume his position as the master of the wilderness. Chief among these son-figures is "the boy," Ike McCaslin, for whom the hunt is an initiation into manhood. To become a man, he must ritually enact the oedipal drama. He must kill the symbolic father, the bear, and lay claim to his domain, the wilderness; and, as the hunt proceeds, it appears to move undeviatingly toward this conclusion. For example, General Compson, the most senior hunter, surrenders his place to Ike in a representation of genera-tional change—what Freud calls the oedipal conflict. McCaslin pre-sumes that General Compson, the oldest of the hunters, will assume the privileged position, will ride the one-eyed mule that will stand even in the wild, bloody conflict. But, saying he is "too old" and has "had [his] chance" (227), General Compson declines the mule and decrees that the youngest among them, the boy, Ike, should be seated on the mule. Old General Compson's abdication of the privileged position in Ike's favor prefigures a passing of the mantle of power that is to be ritually enacted by the killing of the bear. When the old general elects Ike to take his place, he predicts that Ike will kill the bear and assume the place of power.

But, contrary to expectation, Ike does not kill the bear. At the critical juncture, when Lion holds Old Ben at bay, Ike stands as if paralyzed. Although he holds his gun leveled with both hammers drawn back, he does not shoot. He merely watches, a spectator rather than a partici-pant, as the drama unfolds before him, and Boon Hogganbeck kills Old Ben. This is a startling narrative upset. Of all the hunters, Boon seemed least likely to take the life of the old wild bear. In fact, Ike, who had earlier reflected to himself that "it would not be Boon" (225), had specifically ruled out Boon as a potential slayer of old Ben. But Ike is wrong: it is Boon—Boon, the "plebeian" (213), who "has the mind of a child" (218), who "had never hit anything bigger than a squirrel that anybody ever knew" (225)—this Boon passes the test of manhood and takes the place that Ike was elected to—the place he declined.

Ike's refusal to kill the bear represents a disruption of an expected order. This same tampering with the customary order occurs when Ike refuses to accept his patrimony. Once again the normal sequence of succession is overturned. In both instances—when Ike refuses to kill Old Ben and when he repudiates his patrimony—Ike is rejecting the place that has been set aside for him: he is renouncing the role of father. In Freudian terms, when Ike refuses to kill the bear, who functions as a father in the wilderness, Ike is refusing to be the oedipal son who kills the father and claims the father's favored, empowered status. Similarly, when Ike repudiates his paternal inheritance, he is once again disclaim-ing the paternal signifier: he is refusing to accede to a place of power and authority identified with the father and with fatherly repression, as exemplified by the killing of the bear or by Old Carother's dehuman-ized treatment of his black family.

Ike's rejection of the role of father can be interpreted in terms of both Freudian and Lacanian theory. From a Freudian perspective, Ike is rejecting the oedipal conflict. Read in terms of Lacan, Ike is refusing to lay claim to the phallus, a concept that requires some explanation. According to Lacan, we come into existence as speaking subjects by means of a rupture, a split from the imaginary dyadic unity with the mother. The void that occurs at this rupture creates difference, the basis for language, meaning, and culture, but following this rupture there remains in us a *béance*, a gap. In Eliot's terms, we are all "hollow men," and we desire a completeness of being, a condition of invincibility and inviolability. That state—which we identify with the constitution of the self and with the father become Father—Lacan calls the phallus. Jonathan Scott Lee explains: "The phallus . . . serves to signify . . . that fullness of being, that complete identity, the lack of which is the fact of our ineluctabale want-of-being."[1] In other words, the phallus represents the all-powerful state that all symbols of power, among them the penis, promise. Since this condition of empowerment is nominally the father's in Freudian theory, Lacan's phallus is roughly equivalent to Freud's father. But, and this is the crucial point, this empowered, fully-constituted self, identified with the phallus, does not exist. While it is the signifier of supremacy, the phallus is still only an empty signifier, a representation of desire that fills the space left by the absence of the mother. In Lacanian terms, then, when Ike refuses to kill the bear and again when he rejects his patrimony, he is refusing the desire to have the (always-)mythical phallus.

Ike chooses to reject the father's position because it is the father's place to represent castration and loss to the child. In both the Freudian and Lacanian models, the father, or phallus, is identified with the child's castration. In Freud's oedipal conflict, the child performs a symbolic self-castration to escape the father's punishment—castration. Seeing the mother's genitals, the child believes that the father is responsible for the mother's lack of a penis, that he has castrated her, and further that the same fate will befall the child unless he surrenders his desire to take the father's place with the mother. Prompted by this threat, the child attempts to preserve the genital organ at the cost of paralyzing it, by promising not to use it to restore union. In Freud's words, the child "has removed its function."[2]

In Lacan's formulation of this same moment of division, once again the father, or phallus, signifies repression. For Lacan, the "father is a function and refers to a law"[3] that ordains loss. Lacan refers to the father alternately as the phallus or the paternal signifier, but, however named, the paternal function always signifies lack. Lacan writes that "the phallus forbids the child satisfaction of his or her own desire, which is the desire to be the exclusive desire of the mother."[4] Jacqueline Rose even more explicitly identifies the phallus with loss when she writes: "In Lacan's account, the phallus stands for the moment of rupture."[5] Although the phallus, or paternal metaphor, signifies completeness of being, it is a completeness that the subject lacks; thus, paradoxically the phallus is both the supreme signifer and the signifier that designates our lack, the lack of the phallus.

In both the Freudian and Lacanian paradigms, then, the father represents the threat of castration. It is the paternal role to enforce loss, the rift that creates identity by creating an other. To be father become Father is to represent the paternal metaphor by prohibiting merger and standing for absence. In *Go Down, Moses* this paternal role is endlessly reenacted. When Boon kills the bear, when Major DeSpain sells the Big Bottom to the logging company, when Old Carothers uses his black family as slaves, all are acts of fatherly repression; each instance reenacts the rule of the empty signifer over the signified, or what Juliet Mitchell describes as "the symbolic threat [of castration] to which one is inevitably subjected as the price of being human."[6] What the paternal signifier stands for and what Ike is eschewing by refusing the place of the Father is most strikingly illustrated by one singular paternal representation—the Indian chief, Doom, whose name aptly describes the rule of the paternal metaphor. True to his name and to the role of the father, Doom sells into slavery Sam Fathers—his unacknowledged son—and Sam's mulatto mother. This selling into slavery is comparable to the role of the Law of the Father in the emergence of the subject: the father ushers the child into subjectivity metaphorically enslaved—powerless and dispossessed.

Doom's enslaving of his son and his son's mulatto mother analogizes the condition of the subject, created by lack; in addition, Sam's response to his enslaved state also has a wider meaning. As McCaslin explains to Ike, Sam does not hold his father responsible for his captivity. Rather, Sam feels "betrayed" by his mulatto mother: "Not betrayed by the black blood and not wilfully betrayed by his mother, but betrayed by her all the same, who had bequeathed him not only the blood of slaves but even a little of the very blood which had enslaved it; himself his own battleground, the scene of his own vanquishment and the mausoleum of his defeat" (162). Sam's mother's mixed blood metaphorically represents fusion; it figures the undifferentiated state before the advent of the father and the sign of difference. It is this preconscious existence that Sam identifies with loss. Thus, it is his mother, not his father—despite the paternal role in the creation of lack—that Sam associates with a loss of autonomy.

Sam's blaming his mother is indicative of a pervasive cultural tendency to hold women responsible for phallic lack. Because women, as mothers, are identified with a preoedipal unity before the emergence of identity, women are blamed for the subject's fragmentation. In this way, by projecting loss on women, patriarchal culture seeks to repudiate loss. Both Jane Gallop and Jacqueline Rose discuss this projection. Gallop writes that, paradoxically, because woman is imaged as the "whole," she comes to be viewed as a "hole";[7] and Rose states: Woman "is the place onto which lack is projected, and through which it is simultaneously disavowed."[8]

However, even while patriarchal culture contrives to identify the father with the constitution of the self and the mother with the annihilation of the identity, still the paternal role in the wounding of the separate subject should be self-evident. The Law of the Father, or phallus, prohibits merging and decrees a rupture, under the threat of castration. Thus, the father become Father ordains loss: the father's threat prompts repression, the subject's psychic castration.

Because the phallus is the place of prohibition and loss identified with the father, then, Ike refuses to aspire to the place of the phallic Other. At first glance, Ike would seem to have found a resolution to the endless conflict between fathers and sons. However, Ike's choice is problematic. Specifically, the problem is that the only alternative to the role of castrating father is the role of the self-castrated child. For example, if we read Ike's relinquishment of the phallus in terms of Freud's oedipal complex, Ike is refusing to seek to take the father's place and chooses instead the only other option: to remain forever the son: by surrendering the use of the penis at the father's command, he performs a metaphorical self-castration. This same fate awaits Ike if we assess his choice to renounce the paternal metaphor through Lacan. For example, Rose explains that "for Lacan the subject can only operate within language by constantly repeating the moment of fundamental and irreducible division";[9] that is, by endlessly reenacting the primary repression that constitutes identity. This Ike refuses to do. Instead, he figuratively regresses to a former stage of development: he recreates with a mother-substitute—the wilderness—a former libidinal relation with the mother.

Ike chooses, then, to renounce the phallus. In obedience to the Law of the Father, Ike relinquishes a proedipal unmediated relation with his biological mother, creates the self as lack, and thereafter seeks to cover over the void with a substitute, the wilderness. Lacan explains that we spend our lives seeking substitutes for the lost mother: wives, for example, are disguised mother-figures.[10] For Ike, however, the woods are the all-satisfying mother-surrogate. He declares that someday he will marry "but still the woods would be his mistress and wife" (311). Whereas wives and mothers are repressed in the text (Ike's wife, for instance, is denied a name), the wilderness, a veiled avatar of the mother, is foregrounded. For example, the woods are the only mother Ike acknowledges: they are, Ike says, "the mother who had shaped him if any had toward the man he almost was" (311); his biological mother, on the other hand, he seeks to efface.[11] When forced to allude to his mother, he uses this curious construction, "his Uncle Hubert's sister" (295), a tortuous circumlocution that subordinates her to the male, his uncle, and conceals his own relation to her. And, indeed, as Philip M. Weinstein has noted, even to imagine Miss Sophonsiba as Ike's mother is difficult.[12]

With Sam Fathers as guide and mentor, Ike learns a way of communion with the wilderness as maternal-substitute. As a disguised figure for the lost mother, the wilderness must be re-repressed when the veil is lifted and this representation is discovered. However, as long as this meaning is concealed, Ike and Sam can relinquish to the boundless wilderness, and simulate a return to a register before the advent of the father and difference. For this reason, when Ike first makes his trip into the pristine wilderness, his passage is described with an unmistakable sexual symbology: he seems to be returning to the womb. He "enter[s]" (187) the Big Bottom, a name that itself has a womb-connotation, through "a very tiny orifice" (170), an image for the vaginal opening. Ike negotiates this passage "with Sam beside him, the two of them wrapped in the damp, warm, negro-rank quilt while the wilderness closed behind his entrance as it had opened momentarily to accept him" (187). Wrapped together in a quilt, like infants, Sam and Ike, in the wagon, assume a fetal position as they pass through the woods, progressing by means of a "channel," symbolizing the birth canal. As Ike and Sam advance, they seem to drift like the fetus in the womb: "the wagon progressing not by its own volition but by attrition of their intact yet fluid circumambience, drowsing, earless, almost lightless" (187).

It is no wonder, as Ike is first admitted into this "drowsing" world, that he feels as if "he was witnessing his own birth" (187). Ike is reenacting a return to the imaginary with a substitute mother, the wilderness; and when, at the age of ten, he kills his first deer, a symbol of the wilderness, he ritually dramatizes the advent of the father, or phallus; he recreates the splitting that gives rise to the empty subject. Ike's slaying of the deer marks a turning point; with this slaying Ike becomes a man, as Sam outwardly signs by anointing him with the blood of the slain deer. This tacit cultural identification of manhood with hunting is put into words by Sam Fathers, who says to Ike, "You'll be a hunter. You'll be a man" (170). Manhood, perhaps not surprisingly, is equated with the gun, symbol for the phallus, and with the subordination of the signified to the signifier. To be a man, then, is to represent the phallus. In the wilderness, the hunters represent the phallus by figuring the birth of the self-alienated subject: they figure both a return and a disruption of the imaginary. For this reason, General Compson and Major DeSpain both celebrate their birthdays in the woods each June "although the one had been born in September and the other in the depth of winter" (196). In the woods, they celebrate their coming of age; they celebrate manhood; they celebrate the phallus.[13]

It is the desire of the phallus, the desire to accede to the place of the symbolic Other and to become fully constituted, that Ike, taught by Sam Fathers and Old Ben, learns to relinquish. At first, however, Ike is driven by a desire for the phallic Other, and this desire manifests itself as an obsession with Old Ben. To Ike and the other hunters, Old Ben appears to have achieved the satisfaction and completeness of being that is identified with the phallus. The old bear, "the epitome and apotheosis of the old wild life" (185), has attained the relationship with the wilderness (the displaced mother figure) that all seek: he is one with the wilderness at the same time as he is its master, "the head bear," "the man" (190). Thus, in secret, or so Ike thinks, he hunts the bear. Each morning before sun-up Ike leaves camp on his secret mission. But the old bear eludes him: day after day, Ike fails to find the bear's tracks. On the evening of the third day, Sam Fathers, who has divined the object of Ike's quest, shows him the way of relinquishment: "It's the gun," Sam said. . . . "You will have to choose" (197–98). Ike does choose, and his choice shapes the rest of his life. He chooses to divest himself of the gun. We must not underestimate the enormity of this relinquishment. The gun symbolizes the phallus, the object of the mother's and the Other's desire. By disarming himself, Ike is symbolically surrendering the means to be father; he is representing his willingness to relinquish the father's place, the mythical place of the fully constituted phallic Other. Paradoxically, then, Ike can only glimpse the power that he desires by rendering himself powerless. He can only find the phallus by renouncing the phallus. According to Jane Gallop, this paradox is the crux of Lacanian theory. "The ultimate Lacanian goal," she writes, "is for the subject to assume his/her castration."[14]

Ike comes to the bear not as hunter, not as rival, but as supplicant, voluntarily disabling himself in obedience to the Law of the Father: "He had left the gun; by his own will and relinquishment he had accepted not a gambit, not a choice, but a condition in which not only the bear's heretofore inviolable anonymity but all the ancient rules and balances of hunter and hunted had been abrogated" (198). Yet, despite this relinquishment, nine hours later, Ike, without his gun, is "farther into the new and alien country than he had ever been" (199), and he still has found no trace of the bear. Ike has renounced the gun, symbol of the phallus, but his renunciation, as he comes to realize, is incomplete. He is "still tainted" (199). He still relies on instruments of repression: the watch and compass. With watch and compass, patriarchal culture attempts to govern, divide, and categorize that which is essentially chaotic, undifferentiated, and one. To see the bear, Ike must give up all such attempts to create difference and meaning. He must abandon all efforts to assert the supremacy of the empty signifier over the signified. Only when he "relinquishe[s] completely to it," only when he becomes "a child, alien and lost in the green and soaring gloom of the markless wilderness" (199), only then is he vouchsafed a vision of the absolute.

Once Ike has made this final renunciation, stripping himself also of the watch and compass, his state of helplessness in the wilderness simulates the original imaginary dyadic unity in which there is no self and no other before the advent of the paternal signifier. What ensues is a reenactment of the constitution of subjectivity. Ike is saved from annihilation by a signifier, by the mark of the old bear. Utterly helpless and lost, Ike sees the paw print of Old Ben. These "paw prints" are the pa's prints—the sign of the Father. In other words, into the "markless" wilderness there comes a mark, a sign. These hollow, "dissolv[ing]" (200) traces represent the sign of difference: "Even as he looked up he saw the next one, and, moving, the one beyond it; moving, not hurrying, running, but merely keeping pace with them as they appeared before him, as though they were being shaped out of thin air just one constant pace short of where he would lose them forever and be lost forever himself" (200). The prints, these evanescent, empty signs, "shaped out of thin air," are the fragile chain of signifiers that lead Ike to identity and meaning in the symbolic order. The empty traces of the old bear lead Ike back to the watch, the compass, the stick, to a world of conceptual difference. Without the chain of empty signifiers, Ike would be "lost forever," forever absorbed into a primordial unity to which he voluntarily relinquished himself.

Old Ben, then, is the representation of the symbolic Other, the place of the constitution of the self. And, as the locus of the self, Old Ben is a "phantom" (185), an absence. Like the empty traces that lead finally to him, Old Ben is a space to fill a lack. In his investigation of absent centers in Faulkner's fiction, John T. Matthews argues convincingly that the old bear is "a derived presence, created by language." As Matthews perceptively notes, from the onset the old bear is known to Ike as a word-name, descending to him from the words of others: "the bear which had run in his listening and loomed in his dreams since before he could remember" (192). Moreover, as Matthews demonstrates, Old Ben's climactic appearance in the text—the moment when the old bear finally reveals himself to Ike—is preceded by a number of scenes that "establish Old Ben more strictly as an absence than a presence."[15] For example, on the first occasion that the old bear approaches Ike's stand, Ike identifies the old bear with "nothing": "[The hounds were] leaving even then in the air that echo of thin and almost human hysteria, abject, almost humanly grieving, with this time *nothing ahead of it, no sense of a fleeing unseen smoke-colored shape.* He could hear Sam breathing at his shoulder. He saw the arched curve of the old man's inhaling nostrils. 'It's Old Ben!' he cried, whispering" (189; emphasis added). This immateriality persists during Ike's next encounter with the bear, when again Old Ben does not appear. As before, Ike merely senses the bear. He "knew that the bear was looking at him. He never saw it. . . . Then it was gone" (194).

In the climactic appearance, when the old bear's traces lead Ike back to selfhood and to the bear, once again Old Ben appears not as a living creature of the world of motion and sound but as an image of desire, shaped by Ike's dreams and fantasies:

> Then he saw the bear. It did not emerge, appear: it was just there, immobile, fixed in the green and windless noon's hot dappling, not as big as he had dreamed it but as big as he had expected, bigger, dimensionless against the dappled obscurity, looking at him. . . . Then it was gone. It didn't walk into the woods. It faded, sank back into the wilderness without motion as he had watched a fish, a huge old bass, sink back into the dark depths of its pool and vanish without even any movement of its fins. (200–201)

What Ike has witnessed is not an appearance but an apparition. The old bear seems spectral, ghostly, emerging and vanishing "without motion"; and in the moment of this apparition what Ike sees is a static image: "immobile, fixed in the green and windless noon's hot dappling." This substanceless representation aptly figures what Lacan calls the phallus or symbolic Other, the place of the constitution of the self, to which we turn for the fulfillment of all desire and which does not exist in the Real. Like Ike's vision of the bear, any appearance of a phallic Other is, Lacan insists, always an "apparition," a ghost, what Lacan calls "a phallophany."[16] This ghostly representational nature of the Other occurs precisely because the Other is the moment when the self was created out of lack, or, in Lacan's words, because the other "is not being, but the place of speech where the ensemble of systems of signifiers rests, that is, language."[17]

Ike is vouchsafed a glimpse of the imaginary object of desire, and he attains this vision, not by attempting to have the phallus, as do the hunters, but by relinquishing the phallus and symbolically castrating the self. It is this experience, in conjunction with the instruction and example of Sam Fathers, that indoctrinates Ike, or, as Ike puts it: "If Sam Fathers had been his mentor and the backyard rabbits and squirrels his kindergarten, then the wilderness the old bear ran was his college and the old male bear itself so long unwifed and childless as to have become its own ungendered progenitor, was his alma mater" (201–2). Having relinquished utterly to the wilderness and having observed Sam's abdication of the world, Ike has learned an alternative to the hunt, to chasing the imaginary object of desire. He has learned to immolate the self by surrendering the use of the phallus in submission to the Law of the Father. For the rest of his life, Ike remains committed to relinquishment of the phallic signifier. When, for example, Ike stands helplessly by, his gun useless in his hand, as Lion holds Old Ben at bay, Ike is reenacting the moment in the wilderness when he voluntarily accepted self-immolation and surrendered his gun.

Similarly, Ike's renunciation of his patrimony is another form of denial of self. Once again, Ike is stripping himself of all symbols of power and authority, outwardly signing his willingness to relinquish the I. Like the gun that Ike lays down in the wilderness, the house and land he forfeits would also mark him as father or phallus. While these symbols function similarly in this context, we should note that the symbolic meaning of the house and land is quite different from the gun symbol. Specifically, whereas the gun symbolizes the phallus that Ike is renouncing, the house and land represent the mother that Ike is refusing to master. This land-house-mother analogy has been well documented both by feminist critics and by Freud. Annette Kolodny, for example, has extensively analyzed American literature, identifying metaphors equating mother with land. Similarly, Freud maintains that all-containing images, like houses, are disguised representations of the womb, the original containing whole.[18] The house that surrounds and contains us is a symbol for the state of being contained in the whole. Given this symbolism, when Ike forfeits ownership of the big house and its surrounding acres, he is renouncing all title to the mother. Since it is the father who possesses the house and dwells in it—or, in Lacanian terms, since the phallus is the privileged signifier that appears to "hold all signifieds in thrall"[19]—when Ike surrenders claim to the house and farmland, he is once again abdicating the place of power identified with the father as symbolic Other.

BOON HOGGANBECK AND THE DESIRE OF THE OTHER

Ike's choice to divest himself of the phallus symbolically unmans him; however, had Ike chosen the other alternative, had he attempted to be the phallus that can re-fuse with the mother, he just as surely would have met with the same powerless, dispossessed fate.[20] Either choice would doom him. This no-win situation Faulkner dramatizes by means of a double, Ike's rival, or foil. This foil character is Ike's reverse mirror image: whereas Ike is the submissive son who strips himself of all signs of power, this other figure lays claim to the place of the symbolic Other. This other figure, Ike's opposite number, is Boon Hogganbeck, who kills the old bear that Ike will not kill.[21]

To make the point that Boon is Laertes to Ike's Hamlet,[22] I would like to examine at some length a pivotal moment in the novel—the moment when Ike defaults and Boon takes his place and kills Old Ben. I have already argued that the hunters' pursuit of Old Ben conjures the oedipal encounter. Building on that argument, I propose now to show that the crowning moment of the hunt, the slaying of Old Ben, is rendered in terms of a childhood fantasy, an image out of the unconscious that depicts the child's oedipal desire and related castration anxiety. This childhood sexual fantasy Freud calls the primal scene.

The primal scene is a wish-fulfillment fantasy: it pictures the satisfaction of the child's every desire. Specifically, the child experiences dual desires for the mother: he or she desires a blissful sexual merging with the mother; simultaneously, the child wishes to master the mother on whom the child is so dependent. The primal scene images the satisfaction of both these desires, but, pointedly, it is not the child but the father who experiences the fulfillment of the child's yearning for the mother. In the primal scene, before the watchful gaze of the child, the father and mother copulate. Observing this copulation, the child reads into it the satisfaction of both yearnings for the mother. In the child's eyes, the father appears to be forcing the mother to submit to his will, disempowering and even castrating her (thus explaining the mother's lack of a penis). Paradoxically, at the same time, the child imagines that the father is satisfying the mother's desire and his own desire for the mother. The primal scene, then, is a wish-fulfillment fantasy in which the child attributes to the father a relationship with the mother that is completely gratifying. In Lacanian language, the father of the primal scene appears to be satisfying the desire of the Other; that is, the primal desire that arises at the moment of symbolization to possess the missing signifier that is the mother's desire. Elizabeth Wright explains that the desire of the mother is the desire to "become all that would satisfy the mother's lack, in psychological terms, becoming the 'phallus' for the mother, all that would complete her desire."[23]

Significantly, however, from that ardently desired consummation, the child is always excluded. In the primal scene, the child is always the excluded observer, who can only watch, enviously, passively. It is because the child is always the onlooker that the primal scene takes its name. The primal scene is an observed tableau, a "scene" that is performed before an audience, the child-spectator, who is forbidden to become a participant in the drama. The child may never assume the father's role, may never satisfy the dual desire for the mother, because the father prohibits the merging of mother and child under the threat of castration. And however the child responds to that threat—whether one complies with or defies the father's prohibition against merger—the child will suffer the same fate: castration. For example, if one elects to separate from the mother and renounce the use of the phallus to rejoin with her, one is essentially performing a self-castration. On the other hand, if one acts on the desire to usurp the father's place and merge with the mother, one will suffer the father's punishment: castration.[24]

It should be clear, then, that the primal scene is a formulation of the child's oedipal desires. The child longs to assume the father's role with the mother. The primal scene, one might say, is the oedipal complex from the child's perspective, a perspective that reveals the child's sense of frustration and powerlessness. The child watches the desired consummation helplessly; the child is barred from the satisfaction of desire under the threat of castration; and, ultimately, the child's response to this threat will lead to a form of castration.[25]

As the primal scene is played out in *Go Down, Moses,* it also discloses that the choice the child is faced with is no choice; that, however the child responds to the father's prohibition, the child will experience castration. In the novel, the two alternative responses to the father's threat are tested by Ike McCaslin and Boon Hogganbeck, and both these son-figures experience only loss.

To uncover the analogy between the slaying of Old Ben and the archetypal scene of parental intercourse, we first need to identify the principal protagonists. The father's role is played by Old Ben. The mother's part belongs to the wilderness, the hunters' mother-surrogate. However, because the wilderness is an amorphous presence, in this reprise of the archetypal drama, the wilderness is represented by the wild dog, Lion. In particular, Lion functions as Boon Hogganbeck's surrogate for the lost mother. Boon feeds and nurses and sleeps with the dog. He kneels beside the dog, "feeling the bones and muscles, the power." He loves Lion "as if Lion were a woman—or perhaps Boon was the woman" (211). In other words, Lion is a displaced representation—Lacan's *objet petit a*—of the imaginary double who is first the mother.[26] Boon may express his desire as long as this desire is veiled. It is in this capacity, as the representative of a lost dyadic unity, that Lion functions as the mother in this version of the primal scene.

The son-figures in the primal scene's reenactment are the hunters, who each year hunt Old Ben in a "pageant-rite of the old bear's furious immortality" (186); that is, the hunt plays out the son's desire for the place of power presumed to be the father's. Chief among these son-figures is, of course, Ike McCaslin, who is designated by them to kill Old Ben. On the surface, Ike assumes the role of child in this ritual reenactment of the primal scene, but, as the drama unfolds, it becomes apparent that the role of child-spectator is also played by Ike's dark double, Boon, who acts on Ike's repressed desire to accede to the place of power.

The scene of parental intercourse is enacted in *Go Down, Moses* when, before the watching gaze of the child, a coupling takes place; that is, as Ike watches, Lion and Old Ben cling to one another in a death grip. In the primal scene, there is always a merging of sex and death: the child interprets parental intercourse as simultaneously a sexual act and a life-and-death struggle. This same blurring of murderous violence and sexual gratification obtains in Faulkner's replay of the primal scene as the dog and the bear lock in a fatal embrace. The dog leaps onto the bear, and the bear clasps the dog to him with both arms, "almost lover-like," and then "they both went down" (230). The two bodies lock, and the moment of ultimate crisis is reached; before the watchful gaze of Ike McCaslin, penetration occurs as the fully erect bear disembowels the dog: "he could see Lion still clinging to the bear's throat and he saw the bear, half erect, strike one of the hounds with one paw and hurl it five or six feet and then, rising and rising as though it would never stop, stand erect again and begin to rake at Lion's belly with its forepaws" (230). Faulkner's version of the observed scene of parental intercourse sheds light on the hidden content of the child's fantasy. The primal scene is a demonstration of phallic power: it images the phallic power that the child desires and, at the same time, forever bars the child from wielding such power, because this performance piece depicts the fate that will be that of the child who dares to defy the father's prohibition and restore union with the mother. On the mother's body, the father inflicts the punishment that the child will suffer if he or she attempts to use the phallus. The primal scene is both a lesson and a threat, and the child-observer can respond to this threat either with submission or defiance. In *Go Down, Moses,* both of these alternative responses to the father's prohibition are tested.

As this pageant-rite is rehearsed, the reader sees it through the eyes of Ike McCaslin, the excluded son-figure. However, at the moment of penetration—the moment that the bear tears open the belly of the dog—Ike recognizes another son-observer, Boon Hogganbeck, who, at this critical juncture, enters the scene: "Then Boon was running" (230), Ike says. Boon's active participation contrasts starkly with Ike's helpless, inert stance. Ike watches the spectacle with his gun leveled, with both hammers of the gun drawn back. But Ike does not, will not, fire the gun. Fearing the father's punishment, Ike performs a symbolic self-castration and renounces the use of his tool. Ike, who renounces the phallus, will be forever a "boy" (232, 233), "uncle to half a county and father to no one" (3).

Whereas Ike is always the excluded child-spectator, Boon rejects the role of the son who can only watch helplessly the object of his desire: he attempts to take the place of the father with the mother. He mounts the bear and assumes the role of the father; similarly, he raises his knife, an act that signs his desire to have the phallus and to restore a lost connection with the m/other.

But Boon's action and Ike's inaction culminate in the same fate—castration and death. Boon, who seizes phallic power, no more achieves his dream of omnipotence than Ike, who voluntarily renounces the phallus. In making his bid for father-power, Boon is violating the father's prohibition against merger; he is using the phallus to restore union with the m(other) and filling the *béance,* the gap that the Law of the Father decrees. But it is by means of absence that language, meaning, and identity are constructed. For there to be meaning there has to be difference, a difference between self and other or self and (m)other. This difference is established by splitting the imaginary dyad. Boon's act, however, has filled the gap and restored a forbidden unity. Accordingly, in the death scene that ensues, there is no difference. With the fall of Old Ben, the representative of the phallus, the sign of difference, all difference collapses. Death merges with sex as Boon straddles the bear and rides him in an orgiastic, ritualistic slaughter: "Astride the bear" with "his legs locked around the bear's belly, his left arm under the bear's throat," Boon kills by "working and probing the buried blade" (230–31). In this love-death, all difference disappears among the three participants. Lion, Old Ben, and Boon merge. Locked together, they are one whole, one "piece of statuary," and the single figure that surges and falls is denoted now by a singular pronoun: "It didn't collapse, crumble. It fell all of a piece, as a tree falls" (231).

The goal of the hunt has always been to achieve complete self-identity by defying the father's prohibition to have the forbidden phallus. When Ike refuses to kill the bear, he represses this desire and accepts lack; in terms of the primal scene, he accepts the role of the excluded, helpless child-spectator. Boon Hogganbeck, on the other hand, rejects the role of passive observer and seeks to attain the completeness of being identified with the phallus. He is the oedipal son who seeks to kill the father and take his place with the mother. But what Faulkner's rendition of the primal drama makes startlingly clear is that neither course of action will empower the subject. Killing the symbolic Father does not confer on Boon the completeness of being that he identified with the father become Father. Having killed Old Ben, the representative of the phallic Other, Boon does not put on his power and authority. He has only struck at an illusion, the fragile illusion of identity, created out of absence, and unleashed chaotic indeterminacy.

That Boon has not achieved the fulfillment he seeks, that he still burns with unsatisfied desire for the phallus after having killed the bear, is the hidden meaning of the somewhat puzzling episode that closes "The Bear." In this sequence, Faulkner focuses once again on the pursuit of the missing phallus, and he invokes images of masturbation and castration to describe the futility of the quest for authority and transcendence.

The final sequence of Faulkner's hunt story takes place the summer after the deaths of Old Ben, Lion, and Sam Fathers. Ike, who is hunting squirrels, has arranged to meet Boon at a large gum tree in the middle of a clearing. As Ike nears the meeting place, he hears "a queerly hysterical beating of metal upon metal" (315). When Ike reaches the edge of the clearing, he locates the source of the banging. Beneath a tree "alive with frantic squirrels," Boon Hogganbeck sits, his back against the trunk, "hammering furiously at something on his lap" (315). "What he hammered with was the barrel of his dismembered gun, what he hammered at was the breech of it" (315). Without looking up to see who approaches and without stopping his maniacal hammering, Boon shouts in "a hoarse strangled voice," " 'Get out of here! Dont touch them! Dont touch a one of them! They're mine' " (315).[27]

143

At one level, this odd closing scene reiterates Ike's alienation. Ike, who refused to kill the bear, who has relinquished his claim to mastery of the m(other), is an intruder, an outsider, and Boon's cry, "Get out of here," articulates once again that Ike is the excluded child-spectator.[28] But this curious coda tells us more than this. It tells us also of Boon's own sense of dispossession. Having killed Old Ben, Boon, by right, should take the old bear's place, and his cry, "They're mine," invokes his claim to proprietorship and authority. But Boon has not acceded to the place of power. His evident frustration, rage, and greed attest that he still burns with unsatisfied desire to be father become Father. His tool lies useless in his lap. He is still the dispossessed, excluded son.

Boon's unsatisfied desire to be the phallus is the substance of this scene, and to render visually that desire Faulkner invokes a masturbatory image. Boon, who is "hammering furiously at something on his lap" (315), resembles a man engaged in masturbation. Because the phallus represents the consummation of all desire, a blissful satiation that Boon urgently and furiously lusts after, the desire for the phallus is imaged as masturbation: the phallus is the orgiastic climax that Boon is laboring feverishly to reach.

But Boon does not simply desire the phallus. His attitude toward the phallus is complex and even contradictory: it comprehends as well the opposite of desire—repudiation, flight, even abhorrence. For Boon not only yearns to occupy the place of power; he also would violently suppress the desire to take the father's place. Both of these competing urges are reflected in the image of Boon, hunched over, hammering furiously at part of his dismembered gun in his lap—a picture that simultaneously symbolizes masturbation, self-flagellation, and even self-castration. As the slayer of Old Ben, Boon is the oedipal son whose consuming desire to be the phallus has led him to kill the symbolic Father; and, like Oedipus who suffers remorse and performs a metaphorical self-castration by blinding himself, Boon similarly executes a ritual self-castration. In a fury of self-loathing, Boon signals a willingness to emasculate himself by dismantling his gun and savagely beating the dismembered pieces. In effect, Boon is representing his readiness to accept the father's punishment of the child who has violated the Law of the Father.

"The Bear" ends, then, with an image that simultaneously invokes masturbation and castration. With this image, Faulkner pictures the quest for the missing phallus: between two forms of self-abuse, masturbation and castration, human beings endlessly vacillate, in a ceaseless swing of the pendulum. But whether we choose the one or the other, whether we choose to unleash our desire for the lost object—masturbation—or we choose to relinquish the phallus—castration—our fate will be the same. The pursuit of the object of our desire does not lead to a blissful consummation; instead it culminates in the same fate that relinquishment would incur. As Boon Hogganbeck's bid for father-power clearly illustrates, killing the seemingly deathless father does not confer immortality: it only rends the veil and unmasks what Lacan calls "the great secret of psychoanalysis";[29] that the fulfilment the child imagines in the primal scene does not exist and that the father, too—the father to whom we turn for identity—is castrated.

THE DEATH OF SAM FATHERS

"Castration" is our "human lot," writes Jane Gallop.[30] Because this fate is altogether intolerable, most of the characters in *Go Down, Moses,* particularly the male characters, spend their lives in denial. There are, however, exceptions to this general adherence to repudiation. One such exception is Sam Fathers. Sam Fathers embraces death: he chooses to live in the wilderness among "the old people," the spirits of his dead ancestors. While Ike also chooses to repudiate patriarchal culture in favor of life in the wilderness, Ike's renunciation differs significantly from Sam's. Whereas Ike believes that renunciation will buy him freedom from death—"Sam Fathers set me free" (286), Ike says—Sam knows that there is no escape from death. He recognizes that the subject is hopelessly characterized by lack and that renunciation of the phallus is just another form of castration and death. Once we understand Sam's clear-eyed recognition that we exist as insubstantial wraiths, poised on the edge of an abyss, we are in a position to interpret his hermit-like withdrawal to the Big Bottom and, perhaps what is even more puzzling, the manner and meaning of his death.

Just as the final section of "The Bear" closes cryptically, with an image of Boon Hogganbeck hammering at pieces of his dismantled gun, so also section three, which narrates the slaying of Old Ben, concludes enigmatically. Section three ends with Sam's sudden and unexpected death and with an accusation: McCaslin accuses Boon of killing Sam at Sam's request. This closing scene seems to trail off, open-ended, leaving questions unanswered: Did Boon kill Sam, as McCaslin suspects, and, if so, why would Sam wish to die in this way?

The answers to these questions are to be found in the text. For example, the first question—Did Boon kill Sam in compliance with Sam's wish?—is posed directly to Boon, and Boon twice answers "No"; however, even as Boon utters his denial, his actions betray him: "He turned, he moved like he was still drunk and then for a moment blind too, one hand out as he blundered toward the big tree" (243). Boon walks like a blind man, or perhaps more accurately like a blinded man, like Oedipus who blinds himself when confronted with the knowledge that he has killed the father and taken the father's place with the mother. This oedipal imagery convicts Boon of the crime he would conceal even from himself. Boon, the slayer of Old Ben, has also slain Sam Fathers, who, as the rightful (albeit unacknowledged) heir of Doom, Boon's tribal chief, is, in a sense, Boon's chief, or father.

But if, as I contend, Boon killed Sam, he did so at Sam's request. A mystery still remains: Why does Sam ask Boon to take his life? Why does Sam desire this odd intermarriage of murder and suicide?

The manner of Sam's death is the logical extension of his life. Like Ike, who models his life after Sam's, Sam is the son who submits to the father's authority and voluntarily relinquishes the phallus in obedience to the Law of the Father. That Sam responds to the father's prohibition submissively is acted out in the novel when Sam is confronted with the lesson of the primal scene; because Sam Fathers, as well as Ike and Boon, is an observer as Old Ben tears open Lion's belly. As the primal scene is rehearsed, Sam is another son-spectator who witnesses the fate of the child who defies the father's prohibition. Sam's response to this threat is instructive. After the drama is played out, Sam is found lying face down in the mud, unconscious. This prostrate position signifies Sam's utter submission to the Law. Sam is the son who accepts symbolic castration.

As his submissive posture symbolizes, Sam has lived a life of self-abasement before the father. At the same time, however, he has also found this abject, enslaved existence intolerable, and has sought to retire from existence in the living world by choosing to live in the Big Bottom, among the spirits of the dead. In effect, he chooses a living death. Sam, then, like Quentin Compson, who "loved death above all, who loved only death,"[31] has always desired death. Sam is a figure comparable to Sophocles' Antigone, who, according to Lacan, embodies "a pure and simple desire for death."[32] But—and this is the crucial point—the death he desires is forbidden by the Law of the Father. Sam's desire for death is ultimately a desire for the m(other), a desire to restore an imaginary unity before the advent of the father and difference. The Law of the Father forbids such merger. Thus Sam's desire for death conflicts with his lifelong compliance with the Law of the Father.

The peculiar manner of Sam's death is an attempt to resolve this conflict. He finds a way to return to a preoedipal existence—he becomes "a blanket-wrapped bundle" (241)—while at the same time signifying his submission to the Law of the Father. Sam balances these contrary demands by asking Boon to kill him. Boon, who has slain Old Ben, now, in Sam's eyes, takes the old bear's place: Boon represents the Name-of-the-Father. Thus when Sam asks Boon to kill him he is choosing to die at the hand of the symbolic Father. His death, then, is concordant with his lifelong subservience to the law of alienation. In death, Sam once again prostrates himself before the father become Father. At the same time, however, as his death signifies his total abjectness before the paternal metaphor, this death also satisfies his lifelong desire for reincorporation. In other words, Sam orchestrates his death so that it is the father's punishment that restores him to the fused state that preceded the rise of identity and consciousness.

THE SNAKE IN THE GARDEN

Sam Fathers lives and dies recognizing the sovereignty of death. In this respect, in his lifelong acknowledgement of death, he differs significantly from Ike McCaslin. Whereas Sam is unillusioned, Ike clings to a dream of escape. In fact, Ike believes that Sam, who has taught him to relinquish himself to the wilderness, has shown him the way to freedom. Taking his cue from his fateful experience in the wilderness—when he stripped himself of gun, compass, and watch and relinquished himself utterly—Ike believes that if he only lives his life in accordance with the lesson of self-abandonment he will find an escape from death. Sam, on the other hand, knows better; Sam knows that relinquishment is just another form of death.

Ike's dream of immunity within the wilderness is most fully expressed in the closing section of "The Bear." Just before Ike finds Boon hammering away at his dismembered gun beneath a tree full of squirrels, he visits the final resting place of Sam Fathers and Lion. As Ike makes his way to this remote wilderness site, he gives himself over to a reverie devoted to celebrating the wilderness as a sanctuary from death and loss. Read closely, this reverie discloses that Ike's belief in a deathless existence within the woods rests on two closely related aspects of the natural world, aspects that Ike calls the wilderness's "immutable progression" (313) and "concordant generality" (313). By "immutable progression," Ike refers to the cyclical rhythms of nature—nature's ceaseless seasonal cycle of death and rebirth. This endless cycle of renewal, Ike believes, constitutes a form of immortality. Thus Ike describes the seasons—"summer, and fall, and snow, and wet and saprife spring in their ordered immortal sequence"—as "the deathless and immemorial phases of the mother who had shaped him if any had toward the man he almost was" (311). Here Ike is expressing his faith in a primitive belief—what Mircea Eliade calls the myth of the "eternal return." As Eliade explains, primitive peoples held that time's cyclical direction "annuls its irreversibility" and "reveals an ontology uncontaminated by time and becoming."[33]

But more than this, Ike further believes that the fluidity and chaotic indeterminacy of the original wilderness, its "concordant generality," vitiates death. Death does not exist in the wilderness, Ike holds, because the wilderness knows no distinctions, no I and no you, and, therefore, no death. In the world of Ike's chosen mother, there is no representation, no sign to represent what is lost, because nothing is lost, nothing is absent. Ike can discern, for example, no sign of the graves of Sam and Lion: "After two winters' blanketings of leaves and the floodwater of two springs, there was no trace of the two graves anymore at all" (312). And when the markers of civilization do appear—as, for example, the four concrete markers designating the plot reserved out of the sale of the land to the lumber company—they look "lifeless and shockingly alien" (312). Here, nothing is held back; all is assimilated into one vast, seething existence, like the gift of candy that Ike leaves at Sam Fathers's grave and that immediately is "gone too, almost before he had turned his back, not vanished but merely translated into the myriad life" (313). All is presence—what Jung terms the state of being contained in the whole and Lacan calls the imaginary; and within this fullness of being, Ike contends, death, too, is absorbed, and, because absorbed, abolished. This is the "true wilderness" (187) Ike speaks of, a "place where dissolution itself was a seething turmoil of ejaculation tumescence conception and birth, and death did not even exist" (312). Thus, leaving the gravesite, Ike calls it "no abode of the dead because there was no death." Sam and Lion, he protests, are not dead, "not held fast in earth but free in earth and not in earth but of earth, myriad yet undiffused of every myriad part" (313). They are not dead, but only returned, restored to the great deathless mother.

But even as Ike is extolling the wilderness—as he exclaims that in the woods nothing is lost and therefore Old Ben's paw, which had been removed by the hunters in a ritual castration, would be restored to him—even in the midst of this declaration, Ike is stopped dead. "Froze[n], immobile," "not breathing," he is like a dead man or, more precisely, like a man glimpsing the reality of death, "feeling again and as always the sharp shocking inrush from when Isaac McCaslin long yet was not" (313). Ike is stopped, paralyzed, by the sudden sighting of a snake: "the old one, the ancient and accursed about the earth, fatal and solitary and he could smell it now: the thin sick smell of rotting cucumbers and something else which had no name, evocative of all knowledge and an old weariness and of pariah-hood and of death" (314). As the appearance of the snake makes palpably evident, Ike's wilderness retreat contains death. The snake, ancient symbol for death, is "concordant too with the wilderness it crawled and lurked" (314). Death is not, as Ike so hopefully professes, abolished in the wilderness's myriad oneness; rather, that myriad oneness is the death of the subject. To explain, the pristine forest simulates the preoedipal stage before the appearance of the father, who represents difference. In that original undifferentiated state, the speaking subject does not exist. Where there is no difference, there can be no separate subject. Ike's wilderness refuge, as Sam Fathers always knew, is not a retreat from death but a retreat to death.

This revelation should come as no surprise. Even if Ike fails to realize that his chosen lifestyle represents an acceptance of death, the reader should know better. The turning point in Ike's life occurred when, as a young boy in the wilderness, he surrendered his gun, watch, and compass, and voluntarily rendered himself completely lost and helpless. On that day, Ike gave himself over to the wilderness; he permitted all boundaries between self and other to collapse; he willingly accepted self-extinction. His condition then—helplessly lost in the woods—ritually reenacts a return to a preoedipal relation with the first to become other. That experience has determined the rest of Ike's life. All of his subsequent actions—his repudiation of his patrimony, his refusal of ownership, his rejection of patriarchal culture, his passionate attachment to the wilderness—can be traced back to that boyhood experience: all of these subsequent acts reenact that first relinquishment to the wilderness, which, in turn, reenacts a return to a former imaginary relation with the mother. All his life, Ike has chosen to relinquish the I; whether he is consciously aware of it or not, Ike has chosen death.

At least once in his life, when he is confronted with "the old one," Ike acknowledges that death is his long-time familiar. The snake's abrupt appearance seems to shock Ike into an instinctive admission of mortality.[34] Confronted with this death's head, Ike responds by repeating a gesture he had seen Sam Fathers make, years earlier, when Fathers had saluted a huge buck as an avatar of "the old people," his dead ancestors: "he put the other foot down at last and didn't know it, standing with his hand raised as Sam had stood that afternoon six years ago when Sam had led him into the wilderness and showed him and he ceased to be a child, speaking the old tongue which Sam had spoken that day without premeditation either: 'Chief,' he said: 'Grandfather' " (314). Ike's salute is spontaneous. It is not articulated by the brain or will; it comes directly from the body. He signs what the body knows: that dissolution is his destiny. Like Shakespeare's Prospero, who, at the conclusion of *The Tempest,* acknowledges Caliban, saying, "This thing of darkness is my own," so Ike, too, owns death.

In the instant of the snake's sudden, shocking appearance, Ike apprehends death and instinctively identifies this death symbol as "Chief" and "Grandfather." This naming inevitably draws an analogy to another grandfather, Old Carothers, and Ike's lifelong project of dissociating himself from that old patriarch. By means of this grandfather-snake analogy, Ike reveals what really lies behind his efforts to sever the line of succession from father to son. As McCaslin accuses and Ike concedes, he repudiates his inheritance from his grandfather to "escape" (271) death, to "repudiat[e] immolation" (270) at the father's hand. But now, for once, confronted with this representation of death, Ike acknowledges kinship: he admits that death is the primal father and that there is no escaping this father's bequest.

Thus, when Ike salutes the snake, an avatar of death, as "Grandfather," he is breaking the taboo of culture and recognizing his being-in-the-world, which is being-toward-death. Ike's admission echoes Freud, who in *Beyond the Pleasure Principle* writes: "the goal of all life is death."[35] In effect, Ike is owning what Freud calls "the death instinct." Rewriting Freud, Lacan formulates the death instinct this way: "So when we wish to attain in the subject what was before the serial articulation of speech, and what is primordial to the birth of symbols, we find it in death, from which his existence takes on all the meaning it has."[36] Death is "primordial," or, as Ike says, death is "Chief," "Grandfather."

IKE'S WIFE AND THE DESIRE OF THE MOTHER

Thus far, my narrative of Ike's self-dispossession has made no mention of Ike's wife. In omitting reference to her, I follow a critical precedent: critics of *Go Down, Moses* often overlook her.[37] There is of course reason for this neglect. *Go Down, Moses* explores a patriarchal culture, and, in this culture, women, along with blacks, are subordinated. Thus Ike's wife is unnamed, and she appears only once, in a scene of fewer than four pages that appears to interrupt the central unfolding narrative of the hunt. Despite its brevity and apparent tangentiality, this often over-looked episode is signally important. This importance Faulkner marks by his placement of the brief aside dealing with Ike's wife. Her momentary visibility in the text occurs as the climactic ending of section four. By this positioning, Faulkner ranks this scene along with two others, the conclusions of sections three and five, which narrate respectively the death of Sam Fathers and Ike's visit to the grave and subsequent encounter with Boon Hogganbeck, hammering his gun at the foot of a tree.

The scene itself depicts a seduction. Ike's wife, full of desire for the house and land he has forfeited, attempts to persuade him to accept ownership. As an incentive, she uses her body. She, "the chaste woman, the wife" (298), who had never before permitted her husband to see her naked, now offers him sex with her naked body in exchange for a promise that he will acknowledge ownership of the farm. When Ike remains steadfast to his commitment to renounce, Ike's wife announces that this sacrifice will entail another: if he will not accept the farm, she will no longer permit sexual relations.

Only when we understand that Ike is refusing to act the role of the Name-of-the-Father can we fairly assess Ike's wife's decision to discontinue conjugal relations. Simply put, Ike has rejected the phallus that is his wife's desire; which is, in fact, according to Freudian and Lacanian theory, the desire of all men and women. As Juliet Mitchell explains, a girl's oedipal complex consists in transferring her object love to her father, who seems to have the phallus, while identifying with her mother, who, to the girl's fury, does not have it: "Henceforth, the girl will desire to have the phallus and the boy will struggle to represent it."[38] Since what the father has that the mother does not have is the penis, it is important to distinguish between the penis and the phallus. As explained in the introduction, whereas the phallus represents a state of total empowerment and completeness of being, the penis is one of many representations for this empowered state. But what is significant about the penis is that it is a representation that women lack. On this point, Lacan is uncharacteristically clear. He explains that what the son "may have that corresponds to the phallus is worth no more than what he does not [that is, the phallus]"—but what signifies is that "the mother does not have it."[39] Lacan is of course speaking of the penis. This physical organ, which only symbolizes the phallus (itself another signifier), in fact does not endow the power that we seek from the symbolic Other; however, because the woman does not possess this symbol, she appears to be marked by lack.

It is in these terms that we should read Ike's wife. She is a desiring subject. Her "dark eyes and passionate heart-shaped face" (297) bespeak her desire of the Other, for which the phallus is the signifier. Where Ike has chosen dispossession and disempowerment, his wife hungers for possession, authority; she yearns to accede to the place of power.

In refusing to represent the phallus, then, Ike is rejecting his wife's desire. It is, in fact, precisely for this reason—to satisfy the mother's desire—that the son desires the phallus. Lacan explains, "If the desire of the mother is the phallus, the child wishes to be the phallus in order to satisfy that desire." Indeed, Lacan continues, the "demand for love requires that he be the phallus."[40] Thus, when Ike refuses to play the role of the symbolic Other, or phallus, he is rejecting this demand for love.

Even more than this, however, by renouncing the phallus, Ike is surrendering the copula by means of which he could claim his wife. In other words, he is rejecting not only his wife's desire, he is rejecting his wife. Here the analogy between mother and house is instructive. The house is, in Jungian terms, a womb-symbol, a symbol for the original state of being contained in the whole. When Ike refuses ownership of the big house, he is, in effect, rejecting the desire to possess the mother.

Since, as previously noted, it is the father who dwells in the house and masters the mother, Ike has forfeited the role of father. He chooses to play the part of the son, who may neither enter the house nor merge with the mother.

Thus, when Ike surrenders title to the house and land, he symbolizes his willingness to forfeit all claim to the mother. Ike's own references to his wife, especially his sexual relationship with her, in terms of land imagery—his marriage to her is "the new country" (297); his wife's body after their sexual union is "the insatiate immemorial beach" (300)—suggest an unconscious awareness that the land he will not own is somehow intimately connected with his wife's body.

Ike's wife's seduction of Ike needs to be read in these terms. On the surface, when Ike's wife for the first time allows him sex with her naked body at the same time as she begs him to promise to accept his patrimony, she appears to be using her body to extort a promise from him. Certainly this is one way of reading this temptation scene. But I would modify this harsh reading somewhat. If we bear in mind the numerous land = woman metaphors in *Go Down, Moses*, then, when Ike disinherits himself, it is, in a sense, his wife he has disowned; and when she tempts him with sex with her naked body, she is attempting to move him to assume his identity as a desiring being. She is allowing him, one might say, the opportunity to make an informed renunciation: she is permitting him to taste the body that belongs to the father, to which Ike refuses to aspire.

As the scene of their naked sexual coupling unfolds, it is chiefly distinguished by Ike's passivity and inexperience. Ike comes to his wife, not as master or father but as uninitiated boy, as a son-figure. Ike's wife is in control: she controls his movements. She draws him to her and holds him with a "steady and invincible hand" (300). Gazing at her in wonderment, Ike recognizes that she is experienced, knowledgeable, where he is innocent, ignorant—a mere boy: "She already knows more than I with all the man-listening in camps where there was nothing to read ever even heard of. They are born already bored with what a boy approaches only at fourteen and fifteen with blundering and aghast trembling" (300; italics removed). Were we to read the scene of this sexual consummation out of context, without prior knowledge of the characters, we might well imagine that we were witnessing a sexual encounter between an older woman and a much younger boy, who had never before tasted the pleasures of adult sexuality. And, in a sense, we are, because Ike's refusal to pass through the phallic phase keeps him forever a boy.

Not surprisingly, even as his wife offers him her naked body, he reiterates his relinquishment, repeating, "No, I tell you. I wont. I cant. Never" (300). Ike will not seek the place of the father become Father. He will not attempt to have the phallus with which he could reconnect with her; and, as if to drive home this point, there appears in the text an image of Ike's renunciation of the phallus. The image occurs as a seemingly irrelevant metaphor describing Ike's wife's hand and arm. His wife grasps him and draws him to her, we are told, "as though arm and hand were a piece of wire cable with one looped end" (300). Ike's wife's arm acts as a cable connecting him to her, but the cable is looped, connected, only at one end—at her end. At Ike's end, the cable trails off connected to nothing, symbolizing his self-castration. When he voluntarily surrendered the use of the phallus, Ike sundered the copula by means of which he might restore the connection with the lost m/other.

After their intercourse, Ike's wife likewise severs the connection she has made—"and again with a movement one time more older than man she turned and freed herself" (300). Laughing hysterically, she announces that she will not again join what he has loosed: "And that's all. That's all from me. If this dont get you that son you talk about, it wont be mine" (300–301). As she speaks, she lies on her side, "her back to the empty rented room, laughing and laughing" (301). The empty rented room symbolizes the dispossession Ike has chosen;[41] her turned back signifies her equal resistance to this passive self-eviction.

Reading this scene, one finds it easy to judge Ike's wife harshly, to fault her for withholding conjugal relations and refusing to give Ike the son he dreams of. But before we condemn his wife, we should note that Ike himself does not blame her for their childless state. Instead, he holds himself responsible. In "Delta Autumn," as an old man in his seventies, he reflects on his barren marriage, and acknowledges that he lost his son as a direct consequence of his choice to repudiate his patrimony—ironically, a choice made for the purpose of saving his son. Looking back on his life-choice, Ike retraces the steps—all well-meaning—that led to this loss:

if he couldn't cure the wrong and eradicate the shame, . . . at least he could repudiate the wrong and shame, at least in principle, and at least the land itself in fact, for his son at least: and did, thought

154

he had: then (married then) in a rented cubicle in a back-street stock-traders' boarding-house, the first and last time he ever saw her naked body, himself and his wife juxtaposed in their turn against that same land, that same wrong and shame from whose regret and grief he would at least save and free his son and, saving and freeing his son, lost him. (334–35)

Ike has attempted to free his son from the sins of the father by not passing on that sin; that is, by not repeating it. But the problem is that this repetition is precisely the father's role. It is the function of the Law of the Father to represent prohibition and loss. This role Ike refuses: he will not be the father that dooms his son. Thus Ike's wife has not prevented Ike from being a father; because, before she ever could do so, he had already refused to represent the paternal signifier and effectively rendered himself ineligible for fatherhood. The only sin Ike's wife is guilty of is the desire for the supreme signifier, and Ike, who knows his wife well, knows well her desire and does not fault her for wanting and hoping where he has long ceased to want and hope: "But women hope for so much. They never live too long to still believe that anything within the scope of their passionate wanting is likewise within the range of their passionate hope" (335).

SLAIN DOES AND BANISHED MOTHERS: "DELTA AUTUMN"

Faulkner's three sections—"The Old People," "The Bear," and "Delta Autumn"—form a trilogy: they chart three successive stages in the career of Ike McCaslin. "The Old People" narrates Ike's initiation into manhood—or the desire of the phallic Other—by killing his first deer; "The Bear" records Ike's subsequent repudiation of the pursuit of the always-missing phallus—his refusal to kill the bear; and "Delta Autumn," which depicts the final phase, chronicles decline, attrition, and phallic lack. In "Delta Autumn," Ike, an old man nearing death, seems to preside over the depletion of his beloved wilderness. As Ike recognizes, the wilderness is besieged, "being conquered, destroyed" (326); it retreats ever southward in an "inverted apex" that is pictured in the text with an image that unmistakably resembles a woman's pudenda: a "v-shaped section of earth" (326). This wilderness = woman comparison is reiterated insistently throughout "Delta Autumn." Roth Edmonds's rejected mistress, for example, is repeatedly referred to as a doe (321), and the analogy signals a similar ravagement: as is the land, women and children are under attack. Women, particularly black women and mothers, and children seem to figure an imaginary unity that must be displaced to establish the supremacy of the empty signifier of difference.

"Delta Autumn" opens with talk of a former profligacy. In the old days the hunters used up the woods as if there were limitless resources. In those days—a time depicted in "The Old People" and "The Bear"—men killed wild turkey merely to test their marksmanship, "feeding all but the breast to the dogs" (319); moreover, they even "shot does" (329). Given the proximity of this last remark to Legate's representation of Roth's mistress as a doe "that walks on two legs" (321), this profligacy with does extends to include the abuse of women and children. By implication, the shooting of does becomes a generic metaphor for the relation of signifier to signified, a relation that Lacan characterizes with the term *castration*. Clarifying his use of this term, Lacan writes that the signified "disappears" under the being of the signifier.[42] This disappearance is represented in "Delta Autumn" by the vanishing wilderness. Likewise Old Carothers's "boundless conceiving" (251)—that is, his unrestrained begetting of a child on his own child—also figures the domination of the empty signifier.[43] By fathering a child on his unacknowledged child, the old patriarch reenacts the role of the hunters who seek communion with the wilderness even as they violate it. Like the hunters, Old Carothers also represents the law of castration: he is the father become Father who banishes the child even as he calls the child into existence.

Since the moment in the woods when Ike relinquished utterly, he has refused to represent the paternal function; that is, he has refused to represent prohibition and loss. Instead Ike has sought to remain true to a vision of integral unity and presence experienced in the wilderness. But in "Delta Autumn," Ike turns his back on that dream, or at least he fails to see that mothers and children are representative of the same "concordant generality" (313) that he cherishes in the "myriad" (313) wilderness. If Ike is overlooking this correspondence, it is a particularly striking blindness, given that he himself uses does and fawns and women and children interchangeably, as, for example, when he paraphrases Roth: "He said on the way here this morning that does and fawns—I believe he said women and children—are two things this world aint ever lacked" (331).

In this final phase of his life, Ike, who has always shunned the alienating role of the father become Father, now reverses himself and plays that role. He represents the absent father—Roth—and banishes Roth's common-law wife and child. Since the unnamed woman is descended from Old Carothers, Ike, who has spent his life trying to distance himself from his evil and unregenerate old ancestor, now reenacts the old man's crime. Many years before, Old Carothers had refused to acknowledge his black daughter, Tomasina, or his son by that daughter, Terrel; now Ike turns away another mother and child, the descendants of Tomey's Turl. Giving the lie to his dream of an all-inclusive unity and presence in the pristine wilderness, Ike now assumes the paternal function and decrees alienation. In a voice "thin not loud and grieving," he expels her: " 'Get out of here! I can do nothing for you! Cant nobody do nothing for you!' " (344). Ike's repeated use of "nothing" and the double negative is charged with meaning. Nothing is what she must become. This is the moment of symbolization, the displacement of being.

Throughout the interchange with Roth's unacknowledged wife, Ike unfailingly represents the paternal metaphor that ordains alienation.[44] He counsels her to respect patriarchal culture's boundaries: marry "a man in your own race" (346), he tells her; and, more, he instructs her in the way of the Law, the way of repression: "forget all this," he says, "forget it ever happened, that he ever existed—" (346). To this, the unnamed woman replies scathingly by reminding Ike that love dismantles all of patriarchal culture's divisions and that love is not ruled by the empty signifier: " 'Old man,' she said, 'have you lived so long and forgotten so much that you dont remember anything you ever knew or felt or even heard about love?' " (346). Indeed, Ike seems to have forgotten. He has forgotten the blissful surrendering of the self to the m(other) in the wilderness. He has forgotten his dream of resplendent unity and fullness of being, of a world without difference. Ike has forgotten to such an extent that he, who has devoted his life to refusing to represent the sign of difference, now presents the child with a hunting horn, yet another representation of the missing phallus.

In one sense, the horn is a fitting gift. The horn, which Ike represents as a gift from Roth, from the absent father, emblemizes the role Ike is playing by proxy, the role of the Name-of-the-Father, or Law. Its introduction into the mother-child dyad ends the original preoedipal unity. By giving the child the hunting horn, Ike symbolizes the induction into the symbolic order, the opening up of a gap, a *béance,* that the child will forever seek to fill by pursuing the phallus that takes the place left by the absence of the mother. In a way, the horn forecasts the child's future, a life devoted to chasing a dream of power.

In another sense, however, Ike's gift of the hunting horn is deeply ironic. The hunting horn symbolizes the desire of the Other, precisely the desire that Ike McCaslin years before, a boy lost in the wilderness, renounced. Thus, by giving the horn to Roth's unacknowledged son, Ike is contradicting his former choice to renounce: he is summoning the child to the very oedipal conflict he declined and encouraging the child to desire the mythical phallus he refused. More ironic still, Ike refused the desire of the phallic Other specifically to "save and free his son" (335); in other words, to avoid the role of father who introduces the child to loss. Yet now Ike is playing exactly this role: the horn represents a displacement of being and an induction of the subject to a lifelong search for a complete identity.

This gift of the hunting horn is significant for another reason, too: the gift is a lie that opens upon another lie—the false representation of paternal power. When Ike presents the child with the horn, he falsely states that this symbol of the phallus, the supposedly all-powerful signifier, is owned by the infant's father: "It's his. Take it" (346), Ike says. But the horn does not belong to Roth; it was a bequest to Ike from General Compson. This lie marks another, the lie that phallic power exists and that the father possesses it. The horn symbolizes a condition of complete autonomy and total fulfillment identified with the place of the symbolic Father, but the horn is not owned by Roth Edmonds, the child's father; similarly, the power that the horn promises does not belong to the father. That empowered state belongs to no one. "The phallus," Lacan explains, "is bound to nothing: it always slips through your fingers."[45]

"Delta Autumn" does not end with the gift of the hunting horn: there follows a seemingly anticlimactic scene. After the woman and child leave, Ike huddles down into his blankets, "trembling, panting" (347), when suddenly one of the hunters, Legate, bursts into the tent. Legate moves quickly about, rummaging hurriedly among Roth's bedclothes for Roth's knife. He answers Ike's questions shortly and impatiently. "We got a deer on the ground," he tells Ike. Sensing his kinsman killed the deer, Ike asks, "Who killed it? . . . Was it Roth?"; and Legate, as he raises the tent flap to leave, briefly replies, "Yes."

Then Ike stops the hunter: "Wait," McCaslin said. . . . "What was it?" Pausing, his back to Ike, Legate answers: "Just a deer, Uncle Ike, . . . Nothing extra" (347–48). The scene ends with Ike answering his own question. He lies back down on his narrow cot, folds his hands on his breast, and says aloud, "It was a doe" (348). Given the repeated identification of Roth's common-law wife with a doe, this killing metaphorically reenacts Roth's refusal to acknowledge the mother of his child. The slain doe and the banished mother and child represent the being, the myriad life, that is sacrificed to assert the sign of difference.

But this brief exchange tells us even more. Legate's succinctly worded reply—"Just a deer, Uncle Ike, . . . Nothing extra"—addresses the nature of sexual difference. For example, from these words Ike infers that the deer is a doe; that is, he interprets Legate to mean that the deer has not the "extra" that marks the male as different from the female. The doe is marked by lack, by "nothing." The female does not possess "the extra," in this case, the buck's antlers, that the male cherishes as the sign of his difference.[46] Legate's words expose the contempt of the hunters for the female who is marked by "nothing," and the hunters' veneration of the "extra" that symbolizes the phallus. But this veneration is misplaced, and this is the subtext of Legate's succinct phrase "Nothing extra." The hunters pursue a potency identified with the phallus. But the phallus they turn to for a fully constituted self cannot confer completeness of being; the phallus is just another signifier: it is only a marker to represent an absence. In other words, try as patriarchal culture will to project nothingness on women, it is the phallus that is a space to fill a lack. The phallus, then, the "extra" that the hunters so ardently desire, is, in actuality, "nothing."[47]

BRINGING DEATH HOME: "GO DOWN, MOSES"

Go Down, Moses closes with a deceptively simple narrative that can be encapsulated in a sentence: Mollie Beauchamp, with the help of Miss Worsham, Gavin Stevens, and others in Jefferson, brings home and buries her dead grandson, who has been executed for the murder of a policeman.[48] On the surface, this story of Mollie Beauchamp and her dead grandchild seems to relate only indirectly to the central focus of the novel; for example, with the singular exception of Mollie, all of the other characters are introduced for the first time in this closing episode. Yet on this seemingly simple and even inapposite section, Faulkner con-

159

fers titular significance, naming the novel *Go Down, Moses* after this closing sequence. As both the conclusion of the novel and the title story, the section "Go Down, Moses" must be relevant to the other sections of the novel. This relevance, however, has not so much to do with an unfolding plot or character development as with a continuous line of questioning. "Go Down, Moses" addresses the central preoccupation of the novel: the desire of a male patriarchal order to deny death.

"Go Down, Moses" contrasts two responses to death. Gavin Stevens personifies the patriarchal order's repudiation of death; Mollie and Miss Worsham, on the other hand, represent an "old, timeless, female affinity for blood and grief" (358). From the moment Stevens learns of Butch Beauchamp's imminent execution, Stevens's every instinct is to prevent this death from being known or uttered. When Miss Worsham comes to see Stevens on Mollie's behalf, he is ready with an elaborate scheme. They will not tell Mollie about her grandchild's death until two or three months later, long after "he is dead and buried somewhere in the North. . . ." As he says this, Miss Worsham stops him with a look, saying simply: "She will want to bring him back home with her." Stevens responds with incomprehension: " 'Him?' Stevens said. 'The body?' " (358). To Stevens, the dead boy is an object to be disposed of. Now that he is *was,* he represents nonexistence that must be consigned to oblivion, "buried somewhere in the North." Stevens would disown death; but Miss Worsham, speaking for Mollie, is determined on an exactly opposite course of action. "He must come home," Miss Worsham says, and Stevens repeats, "He must come home" (358). While he acquiesces and even makes the arrangements, Stevens still does not, cannot, understand this redemption of the dead. Even as he collects money to cover the cost of this homecoming, his language reveals his contempt for the very project he is engaged in: "It's to bring a dead nigger home" (360), he says. For Stevens, death and "niggers" must be other, and his scornful language signals his disavowal.

To help us understand what Stevens finds so alien and unacceptable, Lacan's analysis of *Hamlet,* which he calls a play about the "encounter with death,"[49] may be useful. Possibly inspired by Shakespeare's drama, in this essay Lacan addresses the subject of death with unusual clarity. For example, Lacan writes: "The one unbearable dimension of possible human experience is not the experience of one's own death, which no one has, but the experience of the death of another."[50] The death of another opens up "a hole in the real" for the subject and "sets the signifier in motion" in a search for the all-powerful signifier that will make up for the lost object.[51] But because that signifier is the phallus, the missing signifier, it is always unavailable, and thus the death of another brings home to us the loss of the phallus, or our own castration.

If we apply Lacan's theory about death to "Go Down, Moses," we see the larger meaning of bringing home the dead Butch Beauchamp. Stevens accedes to Mollie's request to restore to her her dead grandson, but he assists her against his every impulse, because the dead boy represents a return to an original inchoateness that threatens the symbolic order. The project Stevens agrees to undertake is nothing less than claiming death, or, alternately stated, engaging in the work of mourning, which entails accepting the loss of the phallus. Since the mythical phallus is, or symbolizes, that extraordinary object that we imagine will fully satisfy all possible desire, accepting the loss of the phallus signifies acknowledging our own castration and mortal condition. "Successful mourning," writes Lee, "mourns not only the object lost but the human condition of castration."[52]

The desire of the phallic Other is the point of contact between "Go Down, Moses" and the other sections of the novel. *Go Down, Moses* narrates the pursuit of the missing phallus, and, in the novel's final sequence, the phallus is still the object of desire, but certain members of the community have resigned themselves to its inevitable and irretrievable loss. Ironically, Butch Beauchamp, whose death is the occasion for acceptance of loss, devoted his life to pursuing the mythical supreme signifier, and this tragic quest cut short his life.

It is precisely to this—that the desire of the Other costs Butch his life—that Mollie cryptically alludes when she repeats her refrain: "Roth Edmonds sold my Benjamin. Sold him in Egypt. Pharaoh got him—" (353).[53] Mollie's biblical allusion sums up Butch's tragic, futile attempt to have the mythical phallus. She blames Roth Edmonds because, as the acknowledged heir of Old Carothers and the owner of the land they farm, Edmonds is the father-figure, the representative of the paternal metaphor that Butch pursued at the price of his life.[54] To explain: like all of us, Butch is a subject created by lack: his fall into being is represented in the text by his mother's death and his father's desertion; thereafter, he devotes his life to seeking from the symbolic Other the fully constituted self. When, for example, as a young boy, he breaks into Roth's commissary store, Butch's act bespeaks the desire of the

Other. The commissary store, a storehouse of the plantation owner's wealth, symbolizes the completeness of being identified with the Name-of-the-Father. By breaking into the store, Butch is attempting to raid the father's plenty—to find the missing phallus. Roth punishes the son's desire to be the symbolic Father or Other by expelling him; and this expulsion reenacts the original loss that constitutes subjectivity and dooms Butch to a lifelong search to fill the gap that is the self. Accordingly, all of Butch's subsequent crimes are crimes against the Law of the Father that ordains lack. In Jefferson, he strikes at a police officer with a piece of iron pipe—a phallic symbol; and in Chicago he is executed for the murder of another officer of the law (the Law).

While Butch Beauchamp chases the imaginary object of desire, seeking immortality and finding only death, his grandmother accepts the loss of the phallus, accepts castration and its symbolic analogue, death. This contrast is marked in the text by the use of ashes as imagery. Ashes are the archetypal symbol of the disintegration of the subject's integrity. Throughout "Go Down, Moses," Mollie, a wizened little woman "with a shrunken, incredibly old face" (353), a death's head, is identified with ashes. When she appears in Stevens's office, she seems "impervious" to the breeze that blows through it "though by appearance she should have owned in that breeze no more of weight and solidity than the intact ash of a scrap of burned paper" (353). This comparison of Mollie to "intact ash" is reinforced later when she sits before the hearth fire "on which even tonight a few ashes smoldered faintly," holding "a reed-stemmed clay pipe . . . the ash dead and white in the stained bowl" (361). By contrast, on the one brief occasion that we glimpse Butch Beauchamp alive, he is characterized by one repeated gesture: even as he awaits his imminent execution, he "snap[s] the ash from the cigarette" (352) away from him.

As Mollie's identification with ashes implies, she represents the alternative to the futile quest to have or be the missing phallus: she accepts that the object of desire is an illusion. Since the phallus would fill our lack, this acceptance signifies an acknowledgement of our constitution through language, through empty signifiers, which cannot compensate us for our mortal condition. In a word, Mollie embraces death; and, indeed, in both sections of *Go Down, Moses* in which she figures, "The Fire and the Hearth" and "Go Down, Moses," she performs the same function; in both, this incredibly old, incredibly tiny black woman, by her example, leads others to abandon all narcissistic desire and to come to terms with their own mortality.[55]

In "The Fire and the Hearth," for example, Mollie turns Lucas away from the hunt for the missing phallus, the imaginary object of desire. In this early section of the novel, the search for the hidden signifier takes the form of Lucas's hunt for buried treasure. The gold that Lucas so obsessively searches for aptly represents the signifier of signifiers. Like the imaginary phallus, which always eludes us and is localized in the place of the father become Father, the treasure is lost and is alleged to be the father's; that is, it is rumored that the buried gold belonged to Old Carothers and was buried by his sons Buck and Buddy. Thus, for Lucas, the unacknowledged grandson of Old Carothers, the lost treasure becomes a symbol for his dispossession. Like his grandson Butch Beauchamp, who breaks into Roth Edmonds's commissary store in search of the father's bounty, Lucas also seeks to lay claim to the riches that are identified with the Name-of-the-Father.[56]

Thus when Lucas surrenders his quest for the buried treasure at Mollie's request, he is giving up the search for a signifier that can guarantee our being and make good our loss. More, he is accepting phallic lack. It is important to distinguish here between Lucas's renunciation of the phallus and Ike McCaslin's. Although both men renounce the search for the absolute, Ike believes that relinquishment will buy him freedom from death. Even as Ike abandons all narcissistic attachments, he nevertheless characterizes himself as "repudiating immolation" (270), because he believes that by surrendering himself to the wilderness he will find everlasting life. Lucas, on the other hand, cherishes no such illusions. In forfeiting his claim to the phallus, the desire of the Other, Lucas knows that he is giving up the pursuit of immortality and acknowledging the inevitability of his own death. Thus, as he hands over to Edmonds the divining rod with which he hoped to attain godlike immunity, Lucas ritually closes the search with a statement of his mortality: "I am near to the end of my three score and ten, and I reckon to find that money aint for me" (127).

Lucas signals the symbolic significance of abandoning his search for the lost treasure with yet another ritual. In a gesture of reconciliation, he presents Mollie with a gift of candy. As he proffers the gift, he speaks baldly of her infirmity: "Here, . . . You aint got no teeth left but you can still gum it" (125). If Lucas's words seem cruel, it is because they address directly the body's cruel fate—dissolution. What signifies here is that Lucas acknowledges bodily decay. In contrast to a patriarchal order determined to deny the maternal body as a reminder of being-in-the-world, Lucas unflinchingly owns that body with a gift of candy. His gift acknowledges his attachment to Mollie even as it recognizes his own being-toward-death.

Whereas, in "The Fire and the Hearth," Lucas, faced with a choice between the phallic rod and his aged wife of forty-five years, chooses Mollie, in "Go Down, Moses," Gavin Stevens, faced with a somewhat similar choice, turns and runs from Mollie, like a man fleeing a night terror. Stevens's flight, the climactic moment of "Go Down, Moses," occurs on the evening of the day Mollie has been told of her grandson's death, as Stevens visits the bereaved grandmother. He finds her in Miss Worsham's bedroom, where she, Miss Worsham, Mollie's brother, and the brother's wife form a grieving human circle before the hearth fire, "the ancient symbol of human coherence and solidarity" (361). Stevens takes a chair and attempts to join them. But death is everywhere in the room and he feels suffocated. Moments after he is seated, he stands and "not wait[ing] for [Miss Worsham] to precede him," he leaves, going "down the hall fast, almost running." All he can think of is making his escape: "Soon I will be outside, . . . Then there will be air, space, breath" (362). The word *space* resounds importantly in this context: Stevens needs to put space between himself and the mourners: he welcomes the space, the gap, that by exclusion creates an other and thereby distinguishes the self. The mourners, on the other hand, cling to no such makeshift barriers. They see past such artifice to the essentially illusory and provisional nature of identity, and they mourn the human condition. "It's our grief" (363), Miss Worsham says simply.

Stevens distances himself from the mourners and from death on this occasion and again later when the funeral procession makes its way out of town to Roth Edmonds's farm, where Butch will be buried. The hearse bearing the dead boy followed by two cars—Mollie, Miss Worsham, and the hired driver in the first, Stevens and the editor in the second—form the funeral cortege that is taking Butch home. The word *home* resonates with meaning in this context.[57] At a literal level, Butch is returning to the home from which Roth Edmonds expelled him so many years before. But that childhood home figures another place: the original inchoate state before the advent of the father and the law that ordains loss, before the rise of the separate subject. Significantly, Mollie and Miss Worsham accompany Butch on this journey back home; Stevens and the editor do not. When the cars reach a metal sign announcing "Jefferson. Corporate Limit," Stevens turns off the ignition; he "cut[s] the switch" (364) and opens up a yawning gap between himself and the hearse and Mollie's car: "the editor's car coasted, slowing as he began to brake it, the hearse and the other car drawing rapidly away now as though in flight, the light and unrained summer dust spurting from beneath the fleeing wheels; soon they were gone" (364). Then Stevens and the editor turn the car toward town. They will not venture beyond the boundaries that by exclusion make possible identity and social orderings; they will go no further than the "Corporate Limit."

Stevens and the editor flee the scene of death because to admit the death of Butch Beauchamp is to admit death, or, alternately stated, is to admit that the integrity of the subject is a fragile web of illusion that soon collapses back into an original anarchy. Mollie and Miss Worsham, too, realize the terrible cost of acknowledgement; they know that, like Antigone who was buried alive for burying her dead brother, they, too, will suffer death-in-life, the knowledge of death in life, for bringing home Butch Beauchamp.[58] But, like Antigone, they pay the price because the alternative is to deny what was. To deny Butch Beauchamp because he is dead, as Stevens would do, is to erase him. Mollie calls for just the opposite of this erasure: she asks the editor of the newspaper to publish the story of her grandson's life and death—"All of hit" (365), she says. With this public notice, Mollie is validating that Butch lived and died; that he was. This request for public testimony has a close counterpart in another novel of Faulkner's. In *Absalom, Absalom!* Judith Sutpen also seeks to commemorate what was.[59] It is for this purpose—to bear witness to what is past and dead—that Judith passes on to Mrs. Compson the letter that Bon wrote to her. As she gives Mrs. Compson the letter, Judith attempts to put into words the critical need for acknowledgement:

> "And so maybe if you could go to someone, the stranger the better, and give them something—a scrap of paper—something, anything, it not to mean anything in itself and them not even to read it or keep it, not even bother to throw it away or destroy it, at least it would be something just because it would have happened, be remembered even if only from passing from one hand to another, one mind to another, and it would be at least a scratch,

something, something that might make a mark on something that *was* once for the reason that it can die someday, while the block of stone cant be *is* because it never can become *was* because it cant ever die or perish." (101)

Judith is asking for a validation of what was. To acknowledge *was* is to accept temporality, mortality. But if we deny *was,* we deny all there is, because there is only *was.* In the very moment of apprehending *is, is* already has become *was.* All existence is in the process of becoming past, becoming dead. All life is a movement toward death. This pre-empting of *is* by *was,* which Freud terms the death instinct, underlies all of Faulkner's novels, but is perhaps addressed most directly by Mr. Compson in *The Sound and Fury,* when he elegizes: "was the saddest word of all there is nothing else in the world its not despair until time its not even time until it was" (178). Mr. Compson encapsulates the human tragedy: there is no being that is not being-toward-death. In almost analogous terms, Lacan also finds that death is irrefutably our own. Lacan writes that life "has only one meaning, that in which desire is borne by death."[60] From the shadow of death, the patriarchal order retreats in denial. Mr. Compson, for example, seeks oblivion in alcoholism that brings on death, and Quentin takes refuge in suicide. Both, seeking to repudiate being-toward-death, cast away life with death. Mollie and Judith represent an alternative to patriarchy's denial. They stand for the represencing of *was;* they acknowledge life as life-in-death; they issue a call to mourning; and they ask us to remember.

EPILOGUE

Lacan, Faulkner, and the Power of the Word

R ecently, during a class discussion, a student said: "My grand-mother calls black people 'niggers,' but she doesn't mean anything by it." Like so many people, this student fails to recognize the determining power of language. She valorizes some notion of "reality" over words. Her assertion that the word *nigger* does not signify runs counter to Lacan's insistence that we exist as creatures in language and that words matter because meaning is constructed through empty word-symbols. Lacan directs us to see the always arbitrary relationship between language and meaning; he reveals that, although language has nothing to do with the Real, which always eludes us, nevertheless, we exist as creatures in a realm of symbols, and these symbols take on a terrible power over that which they signify. Lacan's theory matters because it teaches that men and women make themselves in culture through language.

The language theorist Ferdinand de Saussure was the first to adduce that the word bears no relation to the signified other than that which we arbitrarily assign it.[1] Lacan's theory of subjectivity builds on Saussure's recognition. For Lacan, the importance of language cannot be overstated: he maintains that "the world of words . . . creates the world of things."[2] James M. Mellard explains this generative power of language: "while Lacan—and we after him—may posit a primal real apart from words or signs or even perception itself, there is for Lacan another real, a symbolic Real that comes to have priority over the first because of its being available to apprehension by the subject. That apprehension occurs only through signs and symbols."[3] As noted in the introduction, in Lacan's view, biology, the signified, is dominated by the word-sign, and this relationship Lacan denotes with the formula S/s, with uppercase S standing for the signifier and lowercase s representing the signified. Lacan's revelation is that sense is made by signification, by signing. In "The Insistence of the Letter in the Unconscious," Lacan elucidates the arbitrary and subordinating relationship of the sign to the "thing" it represents. Lacan offers two pictures. The first is a picture of a tree with the word *tree* written beneath. This image illustrates our presumption that there is a one-to-one correspondence between symbol and signified. This correspondence, Lacan stresses, is not the relationship between symbol and thing. Stating Lacan's position, Madan Sarup writes that "there can be no natural, automatic or self-evident transition from signifier to signified, from language to meaning, or from human behaviour to its pyschological significance."[4] The second figure Lacan introduces underscores the arbitrariness of the relationship between the symbol and the thing it represents. The picture is of two identical doors, under one of which is written "Ladies" and under the other "Gentlemen." This figure represents Lacan's version of structural linguistics. Words do not designate meanings already existing. Rather, they arbitrarily assign a meaning to what was, before the advent of the sign, identical. We locate meanings and we locate ourselves as subjects through language. Jane Gallop describes the subject as trapped within language: "There is no place for a 'subject,' no place to be human, to make sense outside of signification, and language always has specific rules which no subject has the power to decree."[5] Indeed, Lacan has even said that whatever being the subject has "whether in effect it is a question of being oneself, being a father, being born, being loved or being dead, how can one not see that the subject, if he is a subject who speaks, can only sustain himself through discourse."[6] The meanings that we assign to things are hollow and arbitrary because signs merely point to other signs in a signifying chain, and there is no supreme signifier, no basis or token to ground these associations. Paraphrasing Lacan, Madan Sarup writes: "[Lacan] argues that the meaning of each linguistic unit can be established only by reference to another. In short, there can be no final guarantee or securing of language."[7]

Faulkner's texts powerfully illustrate the arbitrary relationship between the signifier and the signified. In *Light in August,* Faulkner demonstrates how racial difference is a product of language. Joe Christmas becomes the despised racial other because of a word. Despite all Joe's efforts to elude social constructions of his identity, language constructs Joe's identity, just as, Faulkner implies, it constructs all identity. As

Light in August opens, Joe Christmas is designated as a white man. One instance will illustrate my point. When the sheriff investigating Joanna Burden's murder wants to know who lived in the cabin behind her house, a black man is selected at random—"Get me a nigger" (291), the sheriff says—and beaten until he reveals what he knows. As it turns out, the arbitrarily designated black man knows very little. He cannot name the men; he can only identify their race, and he identifies them as white: " 'It's two white men. . . . I just heard tell about two white men lived there' " (293). These "two white men" are subsequently identified as Joe Christmas and Joe Brown by one of the sheriff's deputies. Thus, at this point in the novel, Joe Christmas, like Joe Brown, is perceived—or constructed—as white, but, shortly hereafter, Joe becomes black, and he becomes black because of a word. Joe Brown, alias Lucas Burch, who was found in the burning house by Hamp Waller and tried to keep Waller from finding Joanna's corpse in the upstairs bedroom, is suspected of murdering Joanna. The evidence against Joe Brown is mounting, but Brown is serene in the knowledge that a word will save him. The word is "nigger":

> Because they said it was like he had been saving what he told them next for just such a time as this. Like he had knowed that if it come to a pinch, this would save him, even if it was almost worse for a white man to admit what he would have to admit than to be accused of the murder itself. 'That's right,' he says. 'Go on. Accuse me. Accuse the white man that's trying to help you with what he knows. Accuse the white man and let the nigger go free. Accuse the white and let the nigger run.' (97)

At this moment, Joe Christmas, formerly a white man, becomes a black man in the eyes of the citizens of Jefferson. Formerly, Joe was alluded to as "that fellow Christmas" (293). Now, however, he is identified as "the nigger"; that is, now he is the anonymous despised racial other.[8] Hereafter, he is insistently and exclusively designated as "the nigger" precisely because he is "nigger" only by virtue of the saying of it. The word *nigger* constructs and enforces racial difference. With Joe Christmas, Faulkner dramatizes how language constructs identity.

I have said that from the moment the word *nigger* is uttered, Joe becomes a black man in the eyes of the citizens of Jefferson. It seems he becomes black in the eyes of readers of the novel, too. Some critics, for example, refer to Joe as a "Negro."[9] But in the novel, his race, and by implication all racial difference, is always a matter of language. Throughout *Light in August,* Faulkner is at pains to demonstrate that Joe's racial otherness, like all otherness, depends on what people say. Joe's racial identity hinges on what Doc Hines says, on what the children in the orphanage say, on what Joe says, on what Brown says, and on what the people of Jefferson say; and inexorably and relentlessly they say "nigger." Like all those who are identified as other, Joe is other by virtue of a word.

By means of Joe's assigned racial identity, Faulkner drives home the point that all identity is culturally assigned. Joe's racial identity is constructed by a chain of signifiers. Joe tells people he is black because he has been told he is black. Joe has no "knowledge" of his racial identity. He tells Joanna that "one of [his parents] was part-nigger," and when she asks, "How do you know that?," he responds: "I dont know it. . . . If I'm not, damned if I haven't wasted a lot of time" (254). Joe's answer is illuminating. This assigned identity has determined his life, but it is nothing more than a shadow, a projection cast by others onto him. The shadow was cast first by Doc Hines. Joe's father, who is never named, tells Milly that he is Mexican, but his word is erased by Hines, who says that Joe's father is black. By what token does Hines know? Byron Bunch speaks to this issue: " 'But he—' again he indicates the old man—'knew somehow that the fellow had nigger blood. Maybe the circus folks told him. I dont know. He aint never said how he found out, like that never made any difference' " (374). Byron exposes the baseless nature of Doc Hines's words. The word-sign has no authority behind it; there are no grounds for our associations; words point only to other words, which are equally arbitrary. Faulkner's novel traces a chain of signification seeking an ultimate authority, a supreme signifier that stands outside the chain and imbues the chain with meaning, but ultimately the chain rests only on more signifiers. In *Light in August,* the chain of signification leads back ultimately to the owner of the circus that Joe's father worked for. Mrs. Hines tells us that after the trial the "circus owner came back and said how [Joe's father] really was a part nigger instead of Mexican, like Eupheus said all the time he was, like the devil had told Eupheus he was a nigger . . . . [A]nd all the folks knowing it and me trying to get Eupheus to let's move away because it was just that circus man that said he was a nigger and maybe he never knew for certain, and besides he was gone too and we likely wouldn't ever see him again" (377–78). It is on this authority, the circus man's word, that most critics and readers base an interpretation of Joe as the racial other. But the circus owner's word is just another empty word-symbol. As Mrs. Hines eloquently puts it, "it was just that circus man that said he was a nigger." In other words, this "authority" is just another signifier in a long chain of signifiers, a word that has no necessary attachment to Joe and that disappears in the absence of saying, as Mrs. Hines intimates when she suggests that they move away. Faulkner's novel illustrates Lacan's brand of structuralist linguistics: it reveals that our identifications and our identities are arbitrarily constructed out of words.

Joe's skin, Faulkner's novel insistently repeats, is "a level dead parchment color" (34). In a novel where Joe's race is at issue, this skin color is significant, since dark skin denotes otherness in a predominantly light-skinned culture. This association, like the assigning of a meaning to a word-sign, is arbitrary. Otherness could as readily be denoted by blue eyes or left-handedness or any other recessive physical characteristic, just as it has been associated over the centuries with various marginalized peoples—Jews, gypsies, Muslims, and so on. Faulkner's choice of parchment-color skin denotes that otherness is not determined by skin color (or any other physical trait) but by what other people project onto physical characteristics. Parchment is a sheet of writing material prepared from the skin of a sheep or a goat, and Joe's parchment-colored skin symbolizes that Joe is a blank slate on which others write, that his identity as racial other is culturally inscribed.

We must not read and dismiss Joe Christmas's case as some impossible fiction. Nor is Joe a one-of-a-kind aberration. On the contrary, from a Lacanian perspective, his case history is representative. He exemplifies the Lacanian tenet that identity is constructed through language. Joe's story calls our attention to what is so common and customary in culture as to be overlooked—to what Lacan calls the rule of the signifier over the signified. Jane Gallop calls this rule "unreasonable" and "disproportionate";[10] and, according to Lacan, this rule so dominates the subject that "the subject disappears under the being of the signifier."[11] In *Light in August,* we see Joe Christmas disappear under the word-sign *nigger.* The novel dramatizes how a symbol denoting ignominy is assigned to Joe Christmas and rules his life. Joe's racial identity, like all identity, was bequeathed to him by others. Joe's grandfather, Doc Hines, first assigns racial otherness to Joe and, before

Joe, to Joe's father. In assigning this identity, Hines's language is instructive. Hines says that he "could see in [Joe's father's] face the black curse of God Almighty" (374). Hines's statement partly reveals and partly conceals that Joe is cursed, not by God, but by Hines, who confuses himself with God, and by a social order into which he is assigned a place even before his birth. The infant, Lacan writes, is inserted into "a symbolic order that pre-exists the infantile subject and in accordance with which he will have to structure himself."[12] Lacan means that we are trapped within representations that exert a terrible power over our lives. Juliet Mitchell eloquently describes this power. She defines the signifier as "the very world into which the human child is born and by which he is named and placed (man does not speak, language speaks him)."[13] Mitchell could be speaking of Joe Christmas, who is articulated through language. And, like Joe, we all exist as subjects alienated in language. "Man speaks," Lacan writes, "but it is because the symbol has made him man."[14] Lacan's stunning realization is that cultural meanings created through language take precedence over any primal real; that is, a real that is apart from signs. Recondite as Lacan's theory of subjectivity appears to be, it nevertheless carries this urgent message: As long as we continue to valorize "reality" over our own inscriptions through language, as long as we ignore the ego-subverting power of the word, as long as we continue to cling to a traditional belief in an essential, unified ego or a "true nature," we will remain trapped within cultural meanings, and we will never begin the important cultural work of reexamining our assumptions and remaking our signs.

Notes

PREFACE

1. Lacan, *Four Fundamental Concepts*, 20.
2. Eagleton, *Literary Theory*, 168.
3. Ibid., 129.
4. Mellard, *Using Lacan*, 10–11.
5. Lacan, *Écrits* (Seuil, 1966), 379.
6. Bowie, *Lacan*, 82.
7. Eagleton, *Literary Theory*, 130.
8. Wright, *Psychoanalytic Criticism*, 114.
9. Lacan, *Four Fundamental Concepts*, 61.
10. Lacan, *Écrits* (Norton), 311.
11. Rose, introduction, 40.
12. See Bowie, *Lacan*, 5. In *Psychoanalysis and Feminism*, Juliet Mitchell disputes the notion that Freud's theory is rooted in biologism. She argues that those who accuse Freud of biologism and essentialism misread and distort Freud's texts. According to Mitchell, for Freud, as for Lacan, man makes himself in culture. For a discussion of Mitchell's interpretation of Freud, see Gallop, *Daughter's Seduction*, 1–14.
13. Irwin, *Doubling*, 3, 2, 2–3.
14. Bowie, *Lacan*, 12.
15. Sarup, *Jacques Lacan*, 80.
16. Lacan, *Écrits* (Norton), 297.
17. Boothby, *Death and Desire*, 21.
18. *FIU*, 77.
19. Zender, "Faulkner at Forty," 301.
20. Rose, introduction, 38.
21. Lacan, *Écrits* (Norton), 297.
22. Felman, "To Open the Question," 5–10.
23. Bleikasten, *Ink of Melancholy*, xii.

INTRODUCTION:
FAULKNER'S "HEART IN CONFLICT"

1. Cowley, *Faulkner-Cowley File*, 126. See also Faulkner, *Selected Letters*, 48, and *Faulkner-Cowley File*, 80.

2. See also Michael Grimwood's *Heart in Conflict: Faulkner's Struggles with Vocation* and Michel Gresset's "Faulkner's Self Portraits," both of which demonstrate that Faulkner's fictional self-representations pervade his fiction. For an examination of Faulknerian posturing in the early poetry, see Judith L. Sensibar, *The Origins of Faulkner's Art.*

3. For example, years after writing *The Sound and the Fury* Faulkner would deny that Quentin harbored incestuous feelings for Caddy (*FIU*, 262–63), and when asked about a historical source for the marshal in *A Fable*, Faulkner inexplicably became angry (Bezzerides, *Life on Paper*, 113).

4. Cohen and Fowler, eds., "Faulkner's Introduction to *The Sound and the Fury*," 271–72.

5. *Selected Letters*, 348.

6. Grimwood, *Heart in Conflict*, 9, 11.

7. Minter, *William Faulkner*, xi.

8. Blotner, *Faulkner* (1974), 1442.

9. *Faulkner-Cowley File*, 14.

10. *SE* 14:154; *Écrits* (Norton), 297.

11. *Faulkner-Cowley File*, 114.

12. *LIG*, 239.

13. Freud, *Beyond the Pleasure Principle*, 22, 18.

14. *FIU*, 268, 147. In *Doubling and Incest/Repetition and Revenge*, John T. Irwin questions Faulkner's claim that he was unfamiliar with Freud's work. Irwin wryly observes that, if Faulkner did not know Freud, his characters in *Mosquitoes*, who discuss Freudian concepts, certainly did. In a provocative and persuasive argument, Irwin advances the notion that Faulkner denied a Freudian influence precisely because Faulkner recognized similarities between his own work and Freud's (5). In other words, Faulkner denied Freud's influence in a fiercely Freudian gesture, as the son denies the father out of a desire to be first, to be father. In the final analysis, however, whether or not Faulkner read Freud is a moot point since, as I have noted, Faulkner openly acknowledged that meanings that can be interpreted through psychoanalytic paradigms enter a writer's work unconsciously.

15. Friedman, ed., *Joyce*, 3.

16. Mellard, *Using Lacan*, 17.

17. Lacan, *L'Éthique*. Séminaire 7, 270.

18. Lacan, *Freud's Papers*, 122.

19. Lacan, *Four Fundamental Concepts*, 197.

20. Mellard, *Using Lacan*, 12.

21. Moi, *Sexual/Textual Politics*, 95.

22. Melanie Klein's theories call attention to the fearful aspect of the imaginary. She finds that at a very early age the infant will harbor murderously

aggressive instincts toward its mother's body and entertain delusions that this body will in turn destroy it. See *Love, Guilt and Reparation.*

23. Boothby, *Death and Desire,* 24.

24. Lacan, *Écrits* (Norton), 2.

25. Ibid., 196.

26. Eagleton, *Literary Theory,* 164–65.

27. Ragland-Sullivan, *Jacques Lacan,* 278.

28. Some critics of Lacan would say that Lacan shifts the emphasis away from the mother and unduly emphasizes the role of the father. But Lacan's writings are subject to interpretation, and different readers read his theory differently. Richard Boothby argues, for example, that the imaginary, associated with the mother, is crucially important to Lacan's theory. Most Lacanians, however, would agree with Jacqueline Rose's assertion that "Lacan argued . . . for a return to the concept of the father" (Rose, introduction, 38).

29. While Lacan makes little distinction between the son's and the daughter's experience in entering the symbolic order, it should be clear that Lacan's narrative of the origin of the subject describes the male experience. Specifically, whereas the son perceives himself as different from the mother, the daughter identifies with the mother. However, as Homans explains in *Bearing the Word,* the male orientation of Lacan's theory doesn't necessarily invalidate it as a description of the daughter's relation to sexuality, because it is a cultural myth that women as well as men have internalized. Modified, so as to account for the daughter's identification with the mother, Homans states that Lacan's account of the origin of the subject also applies to the female experience. Homans cites Nancy Chodorow's work, *The Reproduction of Mothering,* as having revised Lacan's description of the entry into culture so as to account for the significant differences between male and female experience; namely, that the daughter does not share the son's powerful incentives to renounce the mother. More specifically, Chodorow theorizes that because the daughter is like the mother and because the daughter cannot be threatened with castration in the same way that the son can, she does not enter the symbolic order as wholeheartedly or as exclusively as does the son.

30. Eagleton, *Literary Theory,* 165.

31. Lacan, *Les Psychoses.* Séminaire 3, 309.

32. Lacan, *Écrits* (Norton), 289. See also Lacan's essay, "Desire and the Interpretation of Desire in *Hamlet.*" Lacan's Séminaire 6, "Le désir et son interprètation," is composed of seven sessions held between 4 March and 29 April 1959. Although the complete text of the seminar has not yet been published, the text of the sessions can be found in the following issues of *Ornicar?:* sessions 1 and 2 in *Ornicar?* 24 (1981): 5–31; sessions 3 and 4 in *Ornicar?* 25 (1982): 13–36; sessions 5, 6, and 7 in *Ornicar?* 26/27 (1983): 7–44. I cite these sessions by the short title, "Le désir," followed by the session number and the page ref-

erence in *Ornicar?* The last three sessions, translated by James Hulbert, are published in *Yale French Studies* entitled "Desire and the Interpretation of Desire in *Hamlet*." I cite this English translation in my text as "Desire," followed by the session number and the page number.

33. Gallop, *Reading Lacan*, 136.

34. Lacan, *Écrits* (Norton), 285, 287.

35. Mellard, *Using Lacan*, 31.

36. Mitchell, introduction, 24; Gallop, *Daughter's Seduction*, 95–96.

37. Lee, *Jacques Lacan*, 111; Rose, introduction, 32, 38, 32.

38. Eagleton, *Literary Theory*, 166.

39. Lacan, *Freud's Papers*, 155.

40. Clément, *Lives and Legends*, 98.

41. Lacan, *Four Fundamental Concepts*, 62. See also Lacan, *Écrits* (Norton), 103.

42. Rose, introduction, 40; Boothby, *Death and Desire*, 65.

43. Gallop, *Daughter's Seduction*, 19, 96.

44. Mitchell, introduction, 7; Gallop, *Daughter's Seduction*, 96; Rose, introduction, 40; Lee, *Jacques Lacan*, 118.

45. Rose, introduction, 41, 44; Safouan, *La sexualité féminine*, 131.

46. Mellard, *Using Lacan*, 160, 159; Sarup, *Jacques Lacan*, 109, 85. See also Lacan, "Desire and the Intepretation of Desire in *Hamlet*," 6:37–38. In my reading of Lacan's dense prose, I have found a number of his interpreters extremely helpful. James M. Mellard's *Using Lacan, Reading Fiction* contains the most lucid explanation of Lacanian thought I have encountered. His book serves as an excellent model for Lacanian analyses of literary texts. For a particularly eloquent discussion of Lacanian themes, see Robert Con Davis's "Critical Introduction: The Discourse of the Father."

47. Lee, *Jacques Lacan*, 47; Moi, *Sexual/Textual Politics*, 100.

48. Gallop, *Reading Lacan*, 59; Moi, *Sexual/Textual Politics*, 100; Lacan, *Écrits* (Norton), 42.

49. Minter, *William Faulkner*, x.

50. Lee, *Jacques Lacan*, 23.

51. Mellard, *Using Lacan*, 54, 55.

52. All psychoanalytic studies of Faulkner's art owe a debt to Judith Wittenberg's pioneering attempt at psychobiography, *Transfiguration*. See especially Wittenberg's first chapter. See also Jay Martin's essay "'The Whole Burden.'" For the biographical details that follow, I am indebted to Joseph Blotner's massive biography of Faulkner. Blotner's work is an invaluable resource to Faulkner scholarship.

53. Dean Faulkner Wells recalls hearing Faulkner and his mother talking and laughing together behind the closed door of Maud's chamber. According to Mrs. Wells, John Falkner also regularly visited his mother, and his wife, too, was not invited to be there. Mrs. Wells remembers how John would drive up,

park the car in front of the house, and leave his wife sitting outside in the car waiting, while he entered the house and visited with his mother (personal interview, 17 June 1990).

54. See Faulkner, *Thinking of Home: William Faulkner's Letters to His Mother and Father, 1918–1925.*

55. *LIG,* 239. Deborah Clarke's insightful feminist study *Robbing the Mother* was published after I had written this chapter. Clarke argues persuasively that Faulkner's fictional representations of mother-power reveal how precarious is patriarchy's hold on cultural identity.

56. Chodorow, *The Reproduction of Mothering,* 199.

57. Blotner, *Faulkner* (1984), 468.

58. In *No Man's Land: The Place of the Woman Writer in the Twentieth Century,* Sandra M. Gilbert and Susan Gubar cite this passage and others like it to support the charge of misogyny in Faulkner's fiction. While they are right to a degree—such passages do confirm a fear of maternal engulfment—they overlook an equal and opposite desire present in Faulkner's writing, a desire for a lost plenitude identified with the mother.

59. *Faulkner-Cowley File,* 67.

60. Blotner, *Faulkner* (1974), 631.

61. Snell, *Phil Stone of Oxford,* 8.

62. Lacan, *Encore.* Séminaire 20, 156; Rose, introduction, 49.

63. Bezzerides, *Life on Paper,* 67.

64. Ibid., 105.

65. Homans, *Bearing the Word,* 9; Eagleton, *Literary Theory,* 168; Chodorow, *Reproduction of Mothering,* 199.

66. Blotner, *Faulkner* (1974), 152–53; see also Wittenberg, *Transfiguration,* 22–23, 29.

67. Blotner, *Faulkner* (1974), 438.

68. Blotner, *Faulkner* (1984), 361.

69. *Selected Letters,* 94–101.

70. Wilde, "Unpublished Chapter," 453.

71. Williams, personal interview, 5 August 1990.

72. Ibid.

73. Blotner, *Faulkner* (1974), 1746–47; *FIU,* 6.

74. Capote, personal interview, 11 April 1975.

75. Brodsky and Hamblin, ed., *Brodsky Collection,* 258.

76. Rose, introduction, 41.

77. Blotner, *Faulkner* (1974), 10.

78. Ibid., 17.

79. Ibid., 66–68; Blotner, *Faulkner* (1984), 9–10.

80. Lee, *Jacques Lacan,* 118.

81. Blotner, *Faulkner* (1974), 187; Wells, "Dean Swift Faulkner," 47–48.

82. Blotner, *Faulkner* (1974), 10.

83. Ibid., 48–51. For a lively discussion of Faulkner's family history as re-written in *The Unvanquished* and *Light in August,* see David M. Wyatt, *Prodigal Sons,* 94–100. See also Freud's myth of the primal horde in "Totem and Ta-boo," *SE.*

84. Blotner, *Faulkner* (1974), 53–662 passim; Grimwood, *Heart in Conflict,* 62–68.

85. Blotner, *Faulkner* (1974), 154; *LIG,* 7.

86. Blotner, *Faulkner* (1974) 364–66; see Faulkner, *Thinking of Home.*

87. Blotner, *Faulkner* (1974), 178–79.

88. Ibid., 168–248; ibid., 579–80; Blotner, *Faulkner* (1984), 55.

89. Blotner, *Faulkner* (1974), 368–430 passim; ibid., 534–36; *FIU,* 281.

90. Blotner, *Faulkner* (1974), 19–20.

91. Karl, *William Faulkner,* 347; Blotner, *Faulkner* (1974), 720.

92. Karl, *William Faulkner,* 347.

93. *FIU,* 61; Dos Passos, "Faulkner," 11.

94. Blotner, *Faulkner* (1984), 709; Karl, *William Faulkner,* 483, 84; Blotner, *Faulkner* (1974), 1458; ibid., 1772–829.

95. Ibid., 975.

96. Faulkner, "Appendix," *Portable Faulkner,* 710.

I. "THE BEAUTIFUL ONE" IN THE SOUND AND THE FURY

1. See "Faulkner's Introduction to *The Sound and the Fury,*" ed. by Philip Cohen and Doreen Fowler, 266. See also James B. Meriwether, ed., "An In-troduction to *The Sound and the Fury,*" 156–61; and James B. Meriwether, ed., "An Introduction for *The Sound and the Fury,*" 705–10. For an insightful dis-cussion of the aesthetics of desire as articulated in Faulkner's introduction to *The Sound and the Fury,* see Broughton, "Economy of Desire." In discussing the origins of *The Sound and the Fury,* it should be remembered that the novel does not represent a break with Faulkner's earlier writing. In *William Faulkner: The Making of a Novelist,* Martin Kreiswirth convincingly demonstrates that *The Sound and the Fury* emerges from the early work. For an examination of Faulkner's reworking of themes in the novels from 1927 to 1962, see my de-velopmental study, *Faulkner's Changing Vision.*

2. In a provocative feminist reading of Caddy's absence, Minrose C. Gwin eloquently theorizes that Caddy represents Faulkner's attempt to write a female subject. The attempt fails, says Gwin, but, in the failure, Faulkner succeeds importantly: he creates "the enormous bisexual tensions which play themselves out so powerfully within *The Sound and the Fury,* which in fact are essential to

its subversion of the whole idea of a unified subject" (*Feminine and Faulkner,* 37).

3. My interpretation owes much to the insights of other scholars; in particular, I am indebted to John T. Irwin's pioneering Freudian study, *Doubling and Incest/Repetition and Revenge,* which draws attention to the importance of doubling in Faulkner's fiction; John T. Matthews's *The Play of Faulkner's Language* and André Bleikasten's *The Ink of Melancholy,* both of which sensitively consider Caddy's focal role as the absent center of *The Sound and the Fury;* and Gail L. Mortimer's *Faulkner's Rhetoric of Loss: A Study in Perception and Meaning,* which convincingly demonstrates that the perceptual habits of Faulkner's characters and narrators serve to assert control, reinforce boundaries, and deny interrelatedness in a world of flux.

4. John T. Irwin offers a complementary gloss on Caddy's name. Irwin ties Caddy to the biblical Candace, the queen served by the eunuch converted by St. Philip. Irwin explains that, in effect, Quentin is Caddy's eunuch because he is disabled by "the fear of castration that she embodies for him" (*Doubling,* 51).

5. Sarup, *Jacques Lacan,* 98.

6. Eagleton, *Literary Theory,* 164.

7. Gallop, *Daughter's Seduction,* 27.

8. Rose, introduction, 49.

9. Lacan, *Encore.* Séminaire 20, 156.

10. See Lacan's essay, "The Signification of the Phallus," in *Écrits: A Selection.* Freud's notion that the child perceives the mother as castrated is summarized clearly by Mitchell: "The boy discovers the fear of castration through threats . . . , but more importantly at the sight of female genitals—or rather, as it seems to him, at the sight of their absence" (*Psychoanalysis and Feminism,* 96).

11. Rose, introduction, 48.

12. Gallop, *Daughter's Seduction,* 22.

13. In a sensitive and intelligent interpretation, which I read after writing my chapter on *The Sound and the Fury,* Deborah Clarke draws on feminist theory to argue persuasively that the Compson brothers seek to recover Caddy, to control the woman's body, but the maternal semiotic constantly threatens to engulf them. See *Robbing the Mother,* 19–35.

14. Bleikasten, *Ink of Melancholy,* 71.

15. For a discussion of the way enclosures are associated with women in several of Faulkner's short stories, see Myriam Diaz-Diocaretz, "Faulkner's Hen-House," 235–69.

16. Lacan, *Écrits* (Norton), 154.

17. Mitchell, introduction, 7.

18. Lacan, *Écrits* (Norton), 281.

19. Mitchell, introduction, 5.

20. Lacan, *Écrits* (Norton), 289.

21. Of course, all subjects in language, as the price of entering into the symbolic order and acquiring identity, including sexual identity, are symbolically castrated; that is, they lack the phallus. The phallus must not be confused with the penis. Lacan states flatly that "the phallus is not . . . the penis or clitoris, that it symbolizes." "The phallus," Lacan further expounds, "is a signifier" (*Écrits* [Norton], 285). Thus the male child, like the female child, equally lacks the lost object, the unattainable phallic signifier. The difference between the male and female child is that the male child possesses vulnerable external sexual organs that symbolize the phallus. It should be remembered, however, that Lacan writes that the female's clitoris, too, is a symbol for the phallic signifier.

22. Mark Spilka ("Quentin Compson's Universal Grief") discusses the unmanning of Quentin Compson. Richard Feldstein ("Gerald Bland's Shadow") argues that Quentin exhibits homosexual tendencies.

23. For a full and clear discussion of castration anxiety, see Mitchell, *Psychoanalysis and Feminism*, 95–100.

24. While Bleikasten notes resemblances between Jason and Quentin in *The Ink of Melancholy* (108–11), in "Fathers in Faulkner" he maintains that, unlike Quentin, Jason is not threatened by feelings of impotence.

25. Freud, *SE* 11:207.

26. This quotation figures importantly in an essay by Polk. Whereas I contend that with this phrase Quentin blames his mother for the body he denies, Polk reads the line to mean that the mother does entomb her offspring: she is a "grotesque parody of the sexuality she abhors, fears, and represses in herself and in others . . . the country's resident genius of guilt and repression, the root of all problem" ("Dungeon," 66).

27. The equation of women with organic processes in Faulkner's fiction has been discussed by Karl E. Zink ("Faulkner's Garden") and David Williams (*Faulkner's Women*), both of whom appear to accept as a given that women are more closely tied to the flesh than are men. For example, Zink writes, "Man's ambiguous fear and hatred and love of woman must be explained in terms of his fear and hatred and love of the old Earth itself to which woman is related" (149).

28. Both Bleikasten (*Ink of Melancholy*, 79) and Irwin (*Doubling*, 43) recognize that Quentin's suicide simultaneously punishes and satisfies his incestuous desire for Caddy.

29. Boothby, *Death and Desire*, 39.

30. The use of mirror imagery is observed by Irwin and also by Lawrance Thompson ("Mirror Analogues"). Irwin, in particular, has analyzed this imagery perceptively (*Doubling*, 33–35). Irwin's study, however, is chiefly concerned with male pairings and repetitions forward in time.

31. Matthews, *Play,* 89–91; Dauner, "Quentin," 159–71.

32. Irwin, *Doubling,* 42.

33. In a discussion that focuses principally on the rhetorical strategies that enforce racial segregation, James A. Snead notes Quentin's desire for separateness from the female *(Figures of Division,* 31–32).

34. Eliade, *Patterns in Comparative Religion,* 188.

35. For probing discussions of the relationship between the appendix and the novel, see Polk (*Editorial Handbook*), Lester ("Market"), and Weinstein (*Faulkner's Subject,* 97–98).

36. In analyzing Faulknerian maternity, Weinstein convincingly demonstrates that Mrs. Compson is trapped between two defective male symbolic scripts: "a 'dry' virginal script that repudiates intercourse" and "a 'wet' adulterate script that concedes desire and equates the fertile womb with rot and drowning" ("Mother," 11–12). Building on Weinstein's sensitive reading, I attempt to reveal the psychic origins of these male scripts in phallic lack and desire of the m(other).

37. Cohen and Fowler, "Faulkner's Introduction," 277.

38. *FIU,* 77.

39. Ibid., 6.

2. THE DISPLACED MOTHER:
AS I LAY DYING

1. See: Rowan Oak Papers, box 3, folder 59.

2. Blotner, *Faulkner,* (1974) 634–35.

3. Irigaray, *Le Corps-à-corps,* 15–16.

4. Eagleton, *Literary Theory,* 165.

5. Homans, *Bearing the Word,* 7.

6. Cixous, "Castration," 52.

7. Gallop, *Daughter's Seduction,* 49.

8. Addie's role in *As I Lay Dying* has elicited various interpretations. André Bleikasten reads Addie as the embodiment of the maternal body, which is also the world body, "in which all boundaries between life and death are blurred" (*Ink of Melancholy,* 172). David Williams cites Erich Neumann's Jungian study *The Great Mother* and describes Addie as an incarnation of the mythic Great Goddess (*Faulkner's Women*). For T. H. Adamowski, Addie represents the phallic mother as described by Melanie Klein; that is, Addie does not resemble the early preoedipal mother, but rather "the later mother of oedipal fear and guilt," who appears to incorporate the father's penis ("Meet Mrs. Bundren," 226). In "Faulkner's *As I Lay Dying,*" Robert J. Kloss sees Addie as "a castrating

woman" (437) and the object of her sons' incestuous desire. According to Constance Pierce, Addie is seeking what Sartre calls "being-in-itself"; ironically, she finds it only in death ("Being, Knowing, and Saying"). In a study of revisionary repetition in the novel, Donald M. Kartiganer sees Addie's life as both repeating the past and revising it ("Faulkner's Art of Repetition"). According to Warwick Wadlington, Addie is pulled by two alternate strategies to deny death: a strategy "of contraction into a hidden sanctuary" and "a strategy of union with others" (*Reading Faulknerian Tragedy,* 114). In an insightful feminist reading, Deborah Clarke reads Addie as the repressed maternal referent (*Robbing the Mother*); similarly, Wesley and Barbara Morris see Addie as embodying "the voice of the authentic, of the body revealed in the gaps between the words, a voice previously silenced by Oedipus' monologues of monologues" (*Reading Faulkner,* 162).

9. Mellard, *Using Lacan,* 32.

10. Homans, *Bearing the Word,* 11.

11. In *Reading Faulkner,* the Morrises note Addie's sense of fulfillment in the birth of Cash and apply a Freudian interpretation: "Lurking in the background here is Freud, the child as completion of the woman, the child as phallus" (153). The Morrises seem to marry Freudian and Lacanian theory here. For Freud, the mother desires the child as a penis-substitute. The phallus, on the other hand, is a Lacanian concept. It refers not to the penis but to the paternal metaphor, which takes the place left by the absence of the mother. The phallus, also called the supreme signifier, stands for the separation of the mother and child as well as the father's presumed authority and completeness.

12. Bleikasten, *Ink of Melancholy,* 171.

13. Aeschylus, *The Eumenides,* 158.

14. Applying Lacanian theory to Addie's dissatisfaction with language, Karen Sass argues that Addie rejects the symbolic order and that this rejection "is the source of tragedy" in the novel ("At a Loss for Words," 20). I would counter this harsh reading, which seems to echo patriarchy's age-old rallying cry—Blame the mother. Addie does not, I think, so much reject the symbolic as she issues a healthy challenge to it; she gives a voice to the repressed other.

15. Lacan, *Feminine Sexuality,* 144. Jacqueline Rose cautions against interpreting Lacan's statement to mean that women are excluded from language. She writes: "Woman is excluded *by* the nature of words, meaning that the definition poses her as exclusion. Note that this is not the same thing as saying that woman is excluded *from* the nature of words, a misreading which leads to the recasting of the whole problem in terms of woman's place outside language, the idea that women might have of themselves an entirely different speech" (introduction, 49).

16. Lee, *Jacques Lacan,* 177.

17. Bleikasten notes that three of the four brothers successfully replace Addie with "animal totems or surrogate objects" (*Ink of Melancholy*, 182).

18. Eagleton, *Literary Theory*, 168.

19. Lacan writes that the *objet petit a* "takes the place of what the subject is—symbolically—deprived of" but "satisfies no need" ("Desire" 5:15). Catherine Clément offers this definition: "In the Lacanian lexicon the 'objet-petit-a' represents the little machine that unleashes desire" (*Lives and Legends*, 99). And Jonathan Scott Lee explains Lacan's word-choice for this formulation: "The *petit a*, the 'lower-case a,' stands for autre (other), as opposed to the *Autre* (Other)" (*Jacques Lacan*, 220). The Other is of course the place of speech, the domain of language.

20. Eliade, *Patterns in Comparative Religion*, 207.

21. Gallop, *Reading Lacan*, 59, 60.

22. Gallop, *Daughter's Seduction*, 149.

23. Laplanche, *Life and Death*, 125.

24. In this context, Jane Gallop's interpretation of infidelity seems particularly relevant to Addie's adultery. According to Gallop, "Any suspicion of the mother's infidelity betrays the Name-of-the-Father as the arbitrary imposition it is. The merest hint of the mother's infidelity threatens to expose what Lacan calls the symbolic (the register of the Name-of-the-Father), which is usually covered over, sutured, by the representations of what Lacan calls the imaginary, the imaginary of chivalry, the woman's presumed honour. Infidelity then is a feminist practice of undermining the Name-of-the-Father" (*Daughter's Seduction*, 48).

25. Bleikasten observes that Darl is bereft of solidity because of maternal rejection (*Ink of Melancholy*, 187–92). Other readings of Darl are noteworthy. According to Calvin Bedient, Darl and Cash represent two alternative responses to the human condition. Cash incarnates pride; that is, he struggles to define himself through his work; Darl embodies nakedness—the vacuum at the core of being ("Pride and Nakedness"). Carolyn Porter maintains that Darl Bundren embodies a widening chasm between seeing and being; Darl's dilemma "is precisely that he is nothing and he sees all" (*Seeing and Being*, xii). For Michel Gresset, Darl is the quintessential voyeur; he embodies "the symbolic function of the glance," and the object of his gaze is "the body of the mother" (*Fascination*, 225). Donald Kartiganer focuses on Darl as the "utterly ungrounded being"—and compares him to a modernist text. Like the modernist work, which subverts and challenges a past ground, raising the suspicion that we have dispelled it for good, so Darl has "no received structure *within* which or *against* which he can act" ("Faulkner's Art of Repetition," 43).

26. Bleikasten, *Ink of Melancholy*, 187.

27. Gallop, *Reading Lacan*, 60.

28. Chodorow, *Reproduction of Mothering*, 20, 199.

3. LAW AND DESIRE IN
LIGHT IN AUGUST

1. See Fadiman, *Faulkner's "Light in August,"* 31–32; and Ficken, "The Opening Scene," 175–84.

2. Wright, *Psychoanalytic Criticism*, 113.

3. For Carolyn Porter, Hightower plays a crucial role in *Light in August*. His detached, contemplative stance reflects the struggle of both the reader and the narrator to "appropriate the ceaseless flow of time into an ordered fiction within which man can find meaning" (*Seeing and Being*, 252).

4. Bleikasten, *Ink of Melancholy*, 251.

5. Irwin, *Doubling*, 66–67.

6. Jones, *Papers on Psycho Analysis*, 412.

7. Lacan, *Écrits* (Norton), 282.

8. Kristeva, *Revolution*, 47.

9. Bleikasten, *Ink of Melancholy*, 304.

10. Eagleton, *Literary Theory*, 165.

11. Joe's resistance to categorization has been interpreted in a number of interesting ways. In *Figures of Division,* James Snead argues compellingly that Joe refuses all of society's dividing figures; that is, the rhetorical strategies that enforce racial and gender divisions: Joe is "both masculine and feminine, both black and white, a 'tragic mulatto,' an American double-being, who breaks all the semiotic codes of society" (81). In a similar vein, André Bleikasten writes that Joe refuses to acquiesce to any "ready-made identity patterns" that Southern society would thrust upon him ("Closed Society," 83). Donald Kartiganer contends that Joe is searching for a myth or vision of reality that will allow him to "live out the entirety of his contradictory being" (*Fragile Thread*, 43). In a study that examines the perceptual habits of Faulkner's characters as well as narrators, Gail Mortimer convincingly demonstrates that Joe defends against an affinity for "all that is 'other' than the self . . . by repeatedly denying his ambivalence toward them by asserting his autonomy" (*Faulkner's Rhetoric of Loss*, 15). Eric Sundquist reads Joe as a figure of the monstrous double. As "a white nigger," he is both "inside and outside the community" (93); he contains "the community's own projected desires and fears as well as their reciprocal relation" (*Faulkner: The House Divided*, 94). In *Faulkner's "Negro,"* Thadious Davis finds Joe an unrealistic character, lacking in psychic depth, like a character in an early morality play. According to Davis, because in *Light in August* Faulkner is using race as a vehicle to probe questions of identity, he "specifically presents Negro as an abstraction" (176).

12. Mellard, *Using Lacan*, 28, 137.

13. Lee, *Jacques Lacan*, 47.

14. Lacan, *Écrits* (Norton), 4.

15. Neumann, *Origins,* 10.

16. Ibid., 105.

17. Bleikasten examines the dooming power of fathers in "Fathers in Faulkner" and in "*Light in August:* The Closed Society and its Subjects." For a discussion of the correspondences between the tragedy of Joe Christmas and the story of Sophocles' Oedipus, see Debra A. Moddelmog's "Faulkner's Theban Saga: *Light in August.*"

18. Everywhere in *Light in August* we see a blending of racial hatred and father-son rivalry. Perhaps the clearest example is Doc Hines, a white supremacist, who kills a father (Joe's father) and threatens his grandson. This merging of racism with father-son hostility is explained by Joel Kovel, who reads Southern white supremacy in terms of Freud's oedipal complex. According to Kovel, the Southern white male casts the Southern white woman as the forbidden mother and projects on the black man the dual role of son and rival father-figure: "the Southern white male simultaneously resolves both sides of the conflict by keeping the black male submissive, and by castrating him when submission fails. In both these situations—in the one symbolically, in the other directly—he is castrating the father, as he once wished to do, and also identifying with the father by castrating the son, as he once feared for himself" (*White Racism,* 71–72).

19. From behind a curtain, Joe witnesses (aurally, if not visually) the intercourse of parental substitutes: this episode constitutes yet another rendition in Faulkner's fiction of Freud's primal scene. In the primal scene, the father appears to be satisfying his desire for the mother and satisfying the mother's desire at the same time as, paradoxically, he appears to be punishing the mother, castrating her. The child takes from the scene (which may not be an actual event, but a fantasy or unconscious memory) this message: unless he (or she) obeys the father's injunction against incest, the child will be likewise castrated. See Freud's case history of the Wolf-Man (*SE* 17:7–122).

20. Bleikasten notes that Joe Christmas is haunted by Medusa figures throughout his life (*Ink of Melancholy,* 291).

21. Gallop, *Daughter's Seduction,* 147, 149.

22. In "Joe Christmas and 'Womanshenegro,'" I argue that Joe Christmas's racial ambiguity reflects gender indefiniteness; that is, the collapsing of the binary oppositions between male and female.

23. Neumann, *Origins,* 15.

24. Bleikasten interprets Joe's revulsed repudiation of menstruation in Freudian terms: "Menstrual bleeding, to him, can only be a reminder of woman's unhealable 'wound'; an anguishing confirmation of the deadly menace of female 'castration'" (*Ink of Melancholy,* 287).

25. Freud, *Civilization and Its Discontents,* 99.

26. Gallop, *Daughter's Seduction,* 27.

27. Neumann, *Origins*, 105.

28. Bahktin, *Rabelais and His World*, 341.

29. Citing Bahktin, Joseph R. Urgo notes Joe's "at homeness" with Bobbie. See "Menstrual Blood and 'Nigger' Blood: Joe Christmas and the Ideology of Sex and Race."

30. Lacan, *Écrits* (Norton), 282.

31. Gallop, *Daughter's Seduction*, 150.

32. Mitchell, introduction, 7.

33. Rose, introduction, 33.

34. In a sensitive reading of the novel, John Duvall cautions against calling Joe a murderer. He argues that if we call Joanna's death at Joe's hands murder, we participate in sexist and racist stereotyping that would classify Joe as a "nigger" rapist-murderer and would reduce Joanna to his passive object-victim (*Faulkner's Marginal Couple*, 19–36).

35. Freud does not read the Medusa as an image of the phallic mother, which is interesting, given that he discussses this figure elsewhere. Rather, in "Medusa's Head" he maintains that the Medusa represents "a terror of castration" because she is decapitated ("to decapitate = to castrate," Freud writes) and because "a multiplication of penis symbols [the snaky hair] signifies castration" (*SE* 18:273). It is possible that Freud is repressing the image of the phallic mother, which is so threatening to phallocentric culture. On the other hand, Freud's interpretation of the Medusa as an image of castration does not conflict with a reading of her as the phallic mother. The phallic mother is an image of a preconscious state before the rise of gender identity. She is imaged as possessing both male and female genitals to indicate a loss of gender meanings. This loss of gender difference is the symbolic equivalent in the unconscious of castration. In discussing the phallic mother, we must always remember that the phallic mother, like the phallic father, does not exist. Jane Gallop explains that "the Phallic Mother is undeniably a fraud, yet one to which we are infantilely susceptible" (*Daughter's Seduction*, 117) because "the need, the desire, the wish for the Phallus is great" (ibid., 130).

36. Arguing that Stevens's interpretation is incorrect, Polk maintains that Joe's running is "a desperate ultimate repudiation of the mother, one last attempt to get the punishment he deserves" ("Dungeon," 91).

37. Sundquist explains that Joe's death is a sacrifice because it depends on the "mechanism of reciprocal violence"; that is, a cycle of violence, which René Girard has shown to be the origin of ritual sacrifice. See Sundquist, *Faulkner: The House Divided*, 93–94.

38. Mellard, *Using Lacan*, 32.

39. In *The Ink of Melancholy*, Bleikasten writes that Percy Grimm, "the young frustrated warrior and would-be hero," is an ironic self-portrait of Faulkner's own youthful dreams of military glory (313). Bleikasten notes these correspon-

dences: like Faulkner, Grimm was "too young to have been in the European war" and was thought to be "just lazy and in a fair way to become perfectly worthless, when in reality [he] was suffering the terrible tragedy of having been born not alone too late but not late enough to have escaped first hand knowledge of the lost time when he should have been a man instead of a child" (450).

40. Lacan, *Le moi*. Séminaire 2, 233.

41. For an astute account of the dialogic structure of *Light in August*, see Martin Kreiswirth's "Plots and Counterplots: The Structure of *Light in August*."

42. For example, Malcolm Cowley writes that *Light in August* combines "two or more themes having little relation to each other" (Introduction to *Portable Faulkner*, 11); Irving Howe maintains that the novel "suffers from a certain structural incoherence" (*William Faulkner*, 209); and George Marion O'Donnell feels that the novel is a failure "because of the disproportionate emphasis upon Christmas" ("Faulkner's Mythology," 90).

43. The counterpoint of Lena Grove and Joe Christmas has been discussed by Michael Millgate (*Achievement*, 129–30) and Alfred Kazin ("Stillness," 247–52).

44. Ragland-Sullivan, *Jacques Lacan*, 134.

45. For a lucid analysis of Lena as the incarnation of the literal that threatens patriarchal power, see Deborah Clarke (*Robbing the Mother*, 92–108).

46. Possibly Joe Brown, alias Lucas Burch, doubles Joe Christmas because he, too, experiences ambivalent feelings toward the identificatory imago of the mirror stage that Lena seems to reflect. Faulkner signals this doubling by the use of the same name and by mirror imagery: a few hours before Christmas's fatal confrontation with Joanna Burden, he looks into the eyes of Joe Brown through the reflecting glass of a barbershop window (113). In "The Double in *Light in August:* Narcissus or Janus?," Joan Peternel notes the doubling of the two Joes.

47. LaLonde, "A Trap," 103.

48. Whereas most critics have not come to terms with Faulkner's introduction of a new narrator in the last chapter of *Light in August*, Christopher A. LaLonde offers an intriguing reading of Faulkner's last-minute narrative switch. He argues that Faulkner turns the narrative over to the voice of a traveling salesman "so that we might better see not Lena so much as the problem of figuring her" ("A Trap," 104). The problem that Faulkner had of figuring not only Lena but all female characters is a subject intelligently discussed in Philip M. Weinstein's *Faulkner's Subject: A Cosmos No One Owns*. Weinstein argues that Faulkner writes from the perspective of a white male and that his principal project is to "probe the deepest recesses of his men" (27). Consequently, Faulkner—and we his readers—can never know his female characters

as we know his male characters. While Weinstein draws on Lacan directly only in the third chapter of his book, his readings rely heavily on Lacan's notion of the subject.

49. Gallop, *Daughter's Seduction,* 22.

50. Eagleton, *Literary Theory,* 167.

51. Mellard, *Using Lacan,* 109.

52. Wright, *Psychoanalytic Criticism,* 108.

4. READING FOR THE REPRESSED:
ABSALOM, ABSALOM!

1. In an early essay, Floyd C. Watkins carefully examines the inconsistencies and contradictions among the three narrations and suggests that this disjointed narrative form may reflect "the impossibility of knowing history and the past fully and accurately, and perhaps even the method of development of myth" ("What Happens in *Absalom, Absalom!?*" 86). Another account of these contrary tendencies is offered by Gerald Langford in the introduction to his collation of the manuscript of *Absalom* with the Modern Library published text. Langford focuses on the issue of Mr. Compson's knowledge, or lack of it, of Charles Bon's identity as Thomas Sutpen's black son, and locates contradictory textual evidence. Examining Faulkner's revision of his manuscript, Langford finds in both the manuscript and published book a bewildering divergence of meanings—passages that plainly state Mr. Compson's ignorance of Bon's ancestry and others that signal Mr. Compson's awareness. Faced with such inconsistency, Langford concludes that Faulkner repeatedly altered the plan of his novel, writing at some times with the intention that Mr. Compson should know, and at other times with the intention that he should not: "It seems clear enough that Faulkner began with one intention, changed his mind, but then returned to his original intention. In revising the novel he changed his mind again but failed to alter several passages which indicate that the truth about Bon had been at least surmised all along" (*Faulkner's Revision of "Absalom, Absalom!"* 11). This explanation seems anything but "clear enough." Worse, it attributes to Faulkner indecisiveness and even negligence. Langford's conclusion proceeds from the faulty assumption that either Mr. Compson knows or does not know, and, if he seems both to know and not know, then the master must be nodding. Langford does not allow for the possibility that opposite tensions can coexist in the text; that Mr. Compson may be consciously unaware even as traces of disavowed meanings bubble to the surface; that undercurrents of meaning, Freudian slips, leak into the narrative, creating a subtext.

2. Lacan, *Écrits* (Norton), 297. Lacan echoes Freud. In his essay "Repression," written in 1915, Freud makes the point that "repression itself . . . produces

substitutive formations and symptoms, . . . indications of a return of the repressed" (*SE* 14:154).

3. My interpretation of *Absalom, Absalom!* builds on the work of others. It owes much to Donald M. Kartiganer's seminal chapter in *The Fragile Thread,* which first taught us that the needs and desires of the tellers shape their tale. I am also indebted to John T. Irwin, whose brilliant Freudian reading uncovered that *Absalom* maps repression; that Sutpen represents the ego struggling to repress the unconscious, incarnated in Charles Bon. Peter Brooks, in his penetrating Freudian analysis of the novel, anticipates my attempt to read for the repressed when he proposes that we should look for the truth of the novel, not in any fact or facts, but rather in "powerful formal patternings" (*Reading for the Plot,* 299). John T. Matthews also astutely addresses questions central to my attempt to trace hidden, unconscious meanings in *Absalom.* For Matthews, all of the narrations "oppose Sutpen's rigidly phallic and dynastic language with a playful language that disseminates meaning" (*Play,* 119). Philip Weinstein observes this slippage of meaning and reads it in a Marxist context. According to Weinstein, *Absalom, Absalom!,* unlike, for example, *Gone with the Wind,* dismantles the boundaries and social meanings that ideologies establish, revealing that individual identity is fluid (*Faulkner's Subject,* 92–98). Susan Donaldson, in an eloquent essay that focuses primarily on the women in the novel, also anticipates my approach. Donaldson advocates that we resist reading *Absalom* as a text about Sutpen and read for "the empty spaces, breaks, and margins" ("Subverting," 30).

4. According to Richard C. Moreland, the accounts of Miss Rosa and Mr. Compson fail to explain because they cling to the stance of a Southern modernist; that is, they view the Sutpen tragedy either with nostalgia for a past purity or with irony, and both aesthetic devices seek to distance and to protect, to reify distinctions of class, race, and gender. In later chapters of the novel, Moreland writes, Faulkner "looks again, more critically now, at both the nostalgia and the irony of modernism and Southern memory, looking especially for those other voices both have together excluded (though Faulkner is still not altogether ready to let those other voices speak)" (*Faulkner and Modernism,* 80). While I agree that Mr. Compson and Miss Rosa are consciously trying to cling to difference and distance, I contend that the interrelatedness they deny surfaces in the margins of their discourse.

5. Lee, *Jacques Lacan,* 110.

6. Freud, *SE* 19:239 and 235–36. Citing Freud's essay "Negation," François Pitavy discusses strategies of negation and denegation in the novel. See "Some Remarks on Negation and Denegation in William Faulkner's *Absalom, Absalom!*"

7. Leslie Heywood offers another reading of Judith. In an essay that draws on the work of feminist theorist Luce Irigaray, Heywood argues that Judith

refuses the role of reflecting mirror: she refuses to be the "other" that makes possible male identity ("Shattered Glass"). According to Deborah Clarke, Judith, despite "her lack of procreation," is aligned "with the maternal ability to erode clear distinctions and divisions" (*Robbing the Mother*, 146). Warwick Wadlington explains that, simply by virtue of being a daughter, Judith constitutes a threat to patriarchal power. She represents "a threshold, transitory phenomenon that constitutes a vulnerable point in the pure transmission of a patrilineal House over generations" (*Reading Faulknerian Tragedy*, 179).

8. Rosa Coldfield's role in the novel has generated wide-ranging debate. Judith Bryant Wittenberg contends that Rosa both uses and rebels against patriarchal language ("Gender," 100–105). Robert Con Davis maintains that Rosa's narrative unlocks the meaning of the novel: she articulates the thwarted desire of the human subject. Through her narrative, the novel investigates the repressed "'other' side, the feminine part, that forms the often inaccessible underside of authority" ("Symbolic Father" 39). For Minrose C. Gwin, Rosa is the uncanny hysteric; that is, in her text, there erupts "all that the symbolic order must repress in order to speak" (*The Feminine and Faulkner*, 71). According to Deborah Clarke, Rosa uses simultaneously two modes of discourse, the semiotic and the symbolic, both maternal and paternal language (*Robbing the Mother*).

9. Hades appears to be a mythic representation of what Lacan calls the Symbolic Father or phallic Other, and Sutpen is only one of many such Hades-figures in Faulkner's fiction. For an examination of Faulkner's use of the Demeter-Persephone myth, see my article, "The Ravished Daughter: Eleusinian Mysteries in *The Sound and the Fury*."

10. The cause of Sutpen's downfall has generated much critical commentary. In Lacanian terms, Sutpen is doomed to fail because the object of his desire, the phallus, a condition of complete invincibility, does not exist. In his Lacanian reading of *Absalom*, André Bleikasten eloquently explains that Sutpen "stands for . . . the quintessential *phallacy*: the omnipotence of infantile desire as projected onto the father" ("Fathers," 143). Using a Derridean approach, Matthews offers somewhat the same explanation when he attributes Sutpen's failure to his reliance on a phallic, paternal model of meaning (*Play*, 156–58). Carolyn Porter offers a revised formulation of this reading. Drawing on the theories of Marx and Georg Lukacs, Porter argues forcefully that Sutpen's downfall is the result of the contradiction within paternalism (*Seeing and Being*, 234–40). Another noteworthy interpretation is presented by Bernhard Radloff, who contends that Sutpen fails because he is attempting to transcend his own brutishness, his own animal nature ("An Ontological Approach"). In an early and important interpretation of the novel, James Guetti offers a related reading: Sutpen's design is doomed because his goal is unambiguous meaning (*Limits of Metaphor*).

11. Freud, *Beyond the Pleasure Principle,* 18.

12. As noted in my introduction, this hidden meaning may apply not only to Sutpen but also to Faulkner. Miss Rosa's name for Sutpen—"demon"—is a word Faulkner often used in reference to himself as artist. Repeatedly, Faulkner observed that the artist is "demon-driven" (*FIU,* 19). See also the interview with Jean Stein (*LIG,* 239). For interesting analyses of patterns of repetition in Faulkner's canon, see James B. Carothers's "The Road to *The Reivers*" and "The Myriad Heart: The Evolution of the Faulkner Hero." See also Donald Kartiganer's "Faulkner's Art of Repetition."

13. King, *Southern Renaissance,* 122.

14. Wright, *Psychoanalytic Criticism,* 108.

15. Reading Sutpen's hand-to-hand combat with his slave as analogous to the fight to the death for mastery (which, in *The Phenomenology of Spirit,* Hegel posits as constitutive of self-consciousness), Richard H. King identifies another kind of merging of slave and master: "[Sutpen] is master only under the condition of [the slaves'] recognition of his mastery. Insofar as the master needs the slaves, he is paradoxically their slave" (*Southern Renaissance,* 121).

16. According to Wesley and Barbara Alverson Morris, Quentin, no less than Rosa Coldfield or Mr. Compson, clings to repressive Southern mythmaking. The Morrises hold that it is Shreve, the outsider, who unmasks the repressed: "Shreve returns the Sutpen discourse to the unavoidable social issue of race; he supplies the dimension missing from all the other narratives with their Lost Cause apologetics in order to trace the fall of the Old South ideal to the unadorned fact of slavery" (*Reading Faulkner,* 217).

17. Irwin, *Doubling,* 119.

18. Jacqueline Rose writes that "Freud's most fundamental discovery" was "that the unconscious never ceases to challenge our apparent identity as subjects" (introduction, 30).

19. Langford, *Faulkner's Revision,* 268–69.

20. Mellard, *Using Lacan,* 27–28.

21. Lacan, *Écrits* (Norton), 2.

22. Mellard, *Using Lacan,* 12–13.

23. Quentin is also sullen and brooding as he listens to Miss Rosa's narration, where he repeatedly responds to Rosa with the phrase "No'me." Of course, Quentin's contraction stands for "No, ma'am"; however, "No'me" also could be read as a contraction for "not me,"; that is, an articulation of his desire to assert separate identity through negation.

24. For example, Ilse Dusoir Lind, "Design and Meaning," 283; Richard P. Adams, *Myth in Motion,* 194; and King, *Southern Renaissance,* 126. Duvall explores at length homoerotic desire in *Absalom.* See *Faulkner's Marginal Couple,* 110–16. See also Liles, "William Faulkner's *Absalom, Absalom!*"

25. In a letter to me (2 June 1994), James M. Mellard proposes that this

desire *is* homosexual, but "only because the mirror phase is also homosexual," in that in this early identificatory stage "there is no difference, gender or otherwise."

26. Duvall offers this explanation: "Quentin's orgasmic reaction to the completion of the narration of the story of Henry and Bon reminds us that good narration is like good sex and that it is metaphorically appropriate that formalists label the moment of greatest dramatic intensity of a plot its climax" (*Faulkner's Marginal Couple,* 115).

27. See, for example chapter 1 of Mark Bracher's *Lacan, Discourse, and Social Change.*

28. Lacan, *Écrits* (Norton), 319.

29. Ibid., 323.

30. Eric J. Sundquist, who reads *Absalom, Absalom!* in the context of other literary and extraliterary texts, observes that the novel moves toward a collapse of difference: "As in Poe's tales of incest and Melville's *Pierre,* the distinctions between narrators (or authors) and characters dissolve in a frenzy of nondifferentiation in which identity collapses along with almost every vestige of plot, chronology, and order" (*Faulkner: The House Divided,* 126).

31. Robert Con Davis ("Symbolic Father") and André Bleikasten ("Fathers in Faulkner") also read *Absalom, Absalom!* as the search for the paternal metaphor. For both critics, sons in the novel can never achieve paternal authority because Thomas Sutpen refuses to become the dead father; that is, he refuses to become a symbol. Bleikasten, for example cites Freud's myth of the primal horde and argues that, in death, the father comes to represent the Law "thus allowing the unrestricted violence of primitive paternal power to be replaced by the rules of patriarchal authority" (142).

32. Barthes, *Pleasure of the Text,* 10.

33. Lacan, *Écrits* (Norton), 199.

34. Brooks, *Reading for the Plot,* 306.

35. Two particularly eloquent and insightful readings of this climactic moment in the novel are worthy of note. For Kartiganer, this scene represents "the fusions of a supreme fiction now dissolved, as is necessary, back into the reality that fails to mean" (*Fragile Thread,* 105); for Stephen M. Ross, the long-deferred confrontation of Quentin and Henry "is a metaphor of speech itself, a virtual hieroglyph for all speech in its struggle with silence and death" (*Fiction's Inexhaustible Voice,* 233).

36. Freud, *Beyond the Pleasure Principle,* 47.

37. Ibid.

38. Anthony Wilden expresses this fundamental paradox of subjectivity this way: "the subject's profoundest desire to be 'One' again . . . is totally and absolutely irreducible. It is this desire for what is really annihilation (nondifference) that makes human beings human" (*Lacan,* 191). For a discussion of

the paradox of the death drive or death wish as a manifestation of the subject's desire for completion, see Kristeva, *Revolution*, 244; Laplanche, *Life and Death*, 103–24.

39. Guetti also holds that Jim Bond plays a pivotal role in the novel. According to Guetti, Jim Bond represents incomprehensibility. The novel is an attempt to render experience meaningful, but that goal is always beyond our reach. Like Jim Bond's howling, which ever eludes us, we can never "move beyond a language that is approximate" (*Limits of Metaphor*, 101). In an original reading that puts *Absalom* in the context of other literary texts, extraliterary texts, and history, Eric Sundquist offers another interpretation of Jim Bond's meaning. In *Faulkner: The House Divided*, Sundquist proposes that Jim Bond is the trace of Faulkner's own racism, his own dread of the other. With Jim Bond, Faulkner makes palpable the white Southerner's fear of miscegenation.

40. Langford, *Faulkner's Revision*, 40–41.

41. Kartiganer, for example, feels that Shreve's "comments on the mixed-blood Jim Bond . . . may be read as a reflection of Faulkner's own racism," but cautions against doing so, since the words are Shreve's and are a by-product of the "painful disintegration of the communion between Quentin and Shreve" (*Fragile Thread*, 104) that takes place at the novel's end. Arguing forcefully that *Absalom, Absalom!* undermines the reader's detached contemplative stance, Porter points to Shreve's closing remarks as a parody of the reader's attempt "to stand off and assemble a final interpretation, to detach himself from the talking, the telling" (*Seeing and Being*, 271).

42. Citing Sutpen's obscure and humble origins, James A. Snead writes that "Sutpen himself is the source of a certain censored blackness in the narrative" (*Figures of Division*, 113).

5. RENOUNCING THE PHALLUS IN
GO DOWN, MOSES

1. Lee, *Jacques Lacan*, 67.
2. Freud, *SE* 19:176.
3. Rose, introduction, 39.
4. Lacan, "Les formations de l'inconscient," 14.
5. Rose, introduction, 39.
6. Mitchell, introduction, 17.
7. Gallop, *Daughter's Seduction*, 22.
8. Rose, introduction, 48.
9. Ibid., 31.
10. See Chodorow, *Reproduction of Mothering*, 20, 199.
11. My essay, "The Nameless Women of *Go Down, Moses*," analyzes at length the subject of female and particularly maternal repression in *Go Down, Moses*. I

argue that a name signifies identity and that in a novel where two animals, Lion and Old Ben, are designated by names, women, with a very few exceptions, are denied names. Ike's wife and Roth's mistress are the two most notable examples; there are, however, others—in fact the great majority of female characters are unnamed—and this female namelessness is responsible for much of the genealogical complexity of the novel. The anonymity of these women signifies their exclusion: they are the absent center repressed to create a self. Denying the mother, the hunters then seek communion with a mother-surrogate, the wilderness.

12. Quite rightly, Weinstein notes that Miss Sophonsiba "has no narrative reality whatsoever as Ike's mother; this dimension of her being is simply omitted" (*Faulkner's Subject,* 25). However, Weinstein and I differ as to the cause of this omission. Whereas I contend that the exclusion of women in Faulkner's texts mirrors a cultural need to repress women as mothers, Weinstein holds that Faulkner bypasses the presentation of women as subjects because the novelist's focus is elsewhere—on the male subject. For example, Weinstein writes: "Seen for the most part from outside, deprived both vertically in time and horizontally in space of their own subjective history, Faulkner's women move through their world as 'wonderful' creatures, but considerably handicapped, from a narrative perspective, when compared with his men" (*Faulkner's Subject,* 28).

13. Relevant here is Annette Kolodny's study *The Lay of the Land.* Using a Freudian methodology, Kolodny analyzes the sexual meanings and gender implications of a female landscape. She theorizes that the hero, fleeing a society that has been imagined as feminine, then imposes on nature a child's fantasy of the mother. Thus the land becomes the all-gratifying mother over whom the child has power. Applying Kolodny's theory to *Go Down, Moses,* we recognize that this child's fantasy is the hunters' fantasy. In the wilderness, the hunters can act out their desires alternately to return to the mother and to disempower her. Read this way, "The Bear" conforms to a mythic paradigm identified by Nina Baym. In "Melodramas of Beset Manhood," Baym contends that underlying much of American literature is a myth that holds that men can achieve true self-realization only in the woods, far from civilization and women. In *Go Down, Moses,* the hunters seek to achieve a fully constituted self by seeking communion with the wilderness and then violating that oneness; that is, by representing the phallus, the locus of the constitution of the subject. Approaching the hunt motif by way of a theory of hunting formulated by José Ortega y Gassett, Eric Sundquist arrives at much the same conclusion as Baym and Kolodny. Sundquist writes: "The strategy of the hunt is to obliterate distinctions between hunter and beast, hold them posed in reflected postures as the ritual dance, the loving communion approaches its climax, and then to reassert those distinctions in an act of murderous volence. . . . The totem animal must

be killed in order for that intimacy to have existed at all and in order for his sacred status to be made manifest" (*Faulkner: The House Divided,* 145). Offering a somewhat similar interpretation of the goal of the hunt, John T. Matthews states: "The rite of the hunt passes the process of loss into one's loving control" (*Play,* 257). Other critics who have recognized that the hunters pursue a dream of freedom and complete self-identity in the wilderness include Patrick McGee, Karl Zender, and Stephen Barker.

14. Gallop, *Daughter's Seduction,* 96.

15. Matthews, *Play,* 254.

16. Lacan, "Le désir," 7:44.

17. Lacan, "Le désir," 4:31. Susan Donaldson also reads Ike's vision of the bear in the wilderness as the pivotal moment of his life. She interprets the bear's appearance as a mystical encounter with the sacred: "For one brief moment Ike has come face-to-face with something 'wholly other,' and in that moment he is at one with the wilderness" ("Possibilities of Vision," 39). This moment of Edenic unity "at radical odds with a world marked by history," a moment that leads to Ike's renunciation of history in favor of the timeless, is comparable, she claims, to the visions, the ecstasy, Faulkner experienced in the throes of artistic creation: "For [Faulkner] literature represented concerted attempts to capture and retain those fleeting instants of vision and wholeness" ("Possibilities of Vision," 40).

18. See, for example, Freud's "The Theme of Three Caskets," *SE* 12:289–301 and "The Interpretation of Dreams," *SE* 5:354.

19. Bowie, *Lacan,* 124.

20. Ike's dilemma corresponds to the quandary faced by the child passing through the oedipal phase. According to Freud, however the child chooses to satisfy his or her oedipal desire, the child's fate will be castration. For example, if the child chooses to take the father's place with the mother in the act of sexual intercourse, the child will suffer the father's punishment—castration. Alternatively, if the child chooses to take the mother's place and to be the father's love object, the child suffers castration as a precondition of assuming the mother's role, since the mother lacks a penis. See Freud's "Dissolution of the Oedipal Complex," *SE* 19:173–79.

21. Stephen Barker sensitively analyzes the doubling of Ike and Boon, arguing that the contrast between the two underscores Ike's alienation from the heroic. Barker draws from this pairing the same conclusion that I do, that neither Boon's action nor Ike's inaction achieves the desired relationship with the wilderness: "Boon cannot command and overpower it, while Ike cannot become one with it" ("From Old Gold," 11). For another view of Boon, see James B. Carothers, "The Road to *The Reivers,*" 118–24.

22. Given the similar contrast in Shakespeare's play between Laertes' heroic activity and Hamlet's inertia, the comparison of Boon and Ike to Shakespeare's

characters seems appropriate. This doubling of Laertes and Hamlet is analyzed at some length by Lacan. In "Desire and the Interpretation of Desire in *Hamlet*," Lacan argues that it is precisely because Laertes is Hamlet's counterpart, a mirror image and a rival, that Hamlet is at last free to act: "Here the man for whom every man or woman is merely a wavering, reeking ghost of a living being, finds a rival his own size. The presence of this customized double will permit him, at least for a moment, to hold up his end of the human wager: in that moment, he, too, will be a man" (34).

23. Wright, *Psychoanalytic Criticism*, 108.

24. For a full discussion of the primal scene, see Freud's case study of the "Wolf Man," *SE* 17:36–47, 77–80, 107–9. See also Brooks, "Fictions of the Wolf Man: Freud and Narrative Understanding" in *Reading for the Plot*. Noting that Freud admits that the primal scene may be a primal fantasy, Brooks points out that the "masterplot" on which "is conferred all the authority and force of prime mover" may well be a fiction (276).

25. In *Primal Scenes*, Ned Lukacher argues that the primal scene is "a constellation of forgotten intertextual events offered in lieu of a demonstrable, unquestionable origin" (24–25).

26. For discerning discussions of the *objet petit a*, see Lee, *Jacques Lacan*, 119–21, 143–46; and Clément, *Lives and Legends*, 97–101.

27. In a provocative discussion of *Go Down, Moses*, Michael Grimwood makes the case that the hunt is a "remote metaphor for the act of writing" and that the decline of the wilderness mirrors Faulkner's sense of his own declining ability to write. Within this paradigm, Grimwood locates Boon Hogganbeck's oddly hysterical beating of his disassembled gun, conjecturing that "Boon's scattered gun suggests the dismantling of Faulkner's creativity" (*Heart in Conflict*, 281).

28. Barker, "From Old Gold," 18.

29. Lacan, "Le désir," 4:30–33.

30. Gallop, *Daughter's Seduction*, 96.

31. Faulkner, "Appendix," *Portable Faulkner*, 710.

32. Lacan, *L'éthique*. Séminaire 7, 328–29.

33. Eliade, *Patterns in Comparative Religion*, 89. Matthews also invokes Eliade to explain Ike's mythic faith in the timeless world of the wilderness (*Play*, 245–46).

34. This scene is focal to Patrick McGee's illuminating essay on "The Bear," which has helped to shape my own reading of the novel. In "Gender and Generation in Faulkner's 'The Bear,'" McGee argues compellingly that "The Bear" represents Ike's search for a world outside of history and sexual difference, for "the subject's desire for immortality and deathless self-identity." According to McGee, only once in the novel—when he is confronted with the snake—does Ike seem to question this dream: "Isaac's parody of Sam's gesture,

substituting a 'snake' for a 'buck' or the symbol of the father of lies for the name of Isaac's real father, is as close as he ever comes to questioning the eternal presence and innocence of the wilderness" (54).

35. Freud, *Beyond the Pleasure Principle*, 47.

36. Lacan, *Écrits* (Norton), 105.

37. Critics who have addressed Ike's wife's brief appearance in the text include Matthews, McGee, and Barker. Matthews maintains that Ike's wife, who claps her hand over his mouth when he attempts to speak his repudiation, is trying to silence his voice of dissent (*Play*, 258–59). McGee, on the other hand, reads Ike's wife as victim: she represents the "feminine flesh" that Ike is sacrificing to "masculine spirit" ("Gender and Generation," 52). Barker seems to mediate between these two viewpoints. In his reading, Ike finds himself in an impossible position. Although his wife's desires are entirely justifiable, he cannot grant her request and still remain true to his dream of freedom ("From Old Gold," 20–21).

38. Mitchell, Introduction I, 7.

39. Lacan, *Écrits* (Norton), 289.

40. Ibid., 289.

41. Barker, "From Old Gold," 8.

42. Lacan, *Écrits* (Norton), 288.

43. Matthews also interprets the phrase "boundless conceiving" as a scarcely veiled reference to Old Carothers's incest with his black daughter. Without recourse to Lacanian terminology, Matthews draws a conclusion much the same as mine. He points out that by fathering his own grandchild, the old patriarch seeks to "reach toward immortality" (*Play*, 263).

44. Ike, then, is assuming the place of the father. It perhaps needs to be restated that, in Lacan's theory, the father is not a person or a presence; rather, the father is a function. Jacqueline Rose writes: "The father is a function and refers to a law, the place outside the imaginary dyad and against which it breaks" (introduction, 39).

45. Lacan, "Le désir," 10:25–26.

46. The identification of the female with castration is, of course, codified by Freud, who claims that when the male child first views the female genitals he is convinced that the female is castrated. See "The Dissolution of the Oedipal Complex," *SE* 19:174–78.

47. Lacan finds this identification of the phallus with nothingness in *Hamlet*. He observes that, when Hamlet says to Guildenstern, "The king is a thing— . . . Of nothing," we should replace the word *king* with the word *phallus* ("Le désir," 10, 27–29).

48. Mollie's name is spelled Mollie in "Go Down, Moses" and Molly in "The Fire and the Hearth." These variant spellings, I would argue, outwardly sign Mollie's remoteness from the symbolic order and her closer ties to the

tumultuous imaginary, an affinity that is also signaled by her illiteracy. She can not be bound by word-symbols; she overlaps them, resisting their attempt to create distinctions. She is both Molly and Mollie, both the one and the other. Matthews also notes these variant spellings and offers this explanation: "That Mollie's name is spelled differently than in 'The Fire an the Hearth' may also signal that the narrator is making visible the inaudible oddness with which her name is pronounced by one like Stevens who knows nothing of her legacy of loss" (*Play*, 273).

49. Lacan, "Le désir," 4:26.

50. Lacan, "Desire," 6:37.

51. Lacan, "Desire," 6:38.

52. Lee, *Jacques Lacan*, 118.

53. Here, as also in *The Sound and the Fury*, the allusion to Benjamin is incorrect. Joseph, not Benjamin, was sold by his brothers to Egypt. Benjamin is the youngest brother held for ransom during another episode of Joseph's Egyptian career. Like Mollie's/Molly's name, which is spelled two ways in the text, her inaccurate scriptural reference is in keeping with her role in the novel. Mollie/Molly represents the slippage, the indeterminacy of the imaginary, and thus she does not make nice distinctions between brothers; for her, Joseph and Benjamin merge.

54. In a typescript of this story, one name Faulkner used for Butch Beauchamp was Carothers Edmonds Beauchamp (Blotner, *Faulkner* (1974), 1055). This name, which Faulkner contemplated and discarded, underscores Roth Edmonds's role as surrogate-father.

55. In light of Mollie's identification with death, it is interesting to note that Mollie appears to be a portrait of Faulkner's mammy, Caroline Barr, who died in 1940 and to whom the novel is dedicated. For discussions of Mollie Beauchamp's resemblance to Caroline Barr, see Blotner, *Faulkner* [1974], 1034–37 and 1091; Minter, *Faulkner*, 183–84; and Wittenberg, *Transfiguration*, 193–94.

56. In a provocative essay, Zender argues that two characters in *Go Down, Moses* are Faulknerian self-projections: Roth and Lucas. In Roth, Faulkner represents the social and economic pressures put on him in the 1940s; in Lucas, Faulkner embodies his dream of freedom from constraints. See *The Crossing of the Ways*, 65–84.

57. The word *home* resonates importantly in Faulkner's life as well. On the day before his death, Faulkner, who had been drinking heavily, was half-carried, half-led out of his home to a car that would take him to Wright's sanitarium, where he would die. As he passed through the kitchen to the back door, Chrissie Price, the cook, asked him, "Mr. Bill, . . . do you want to go to the hospital?" To this, Faulkner replied, "I want to go home, Chrissie" (Blotner, *Faulkner* [1984], 712). Since Faulkner was at home, his family members dis-

missed his answer as the incoherent ravings of a man who had had too much to drink. But, given Faulkner's identification of home with a return to an original inchoate state, his reference to home here may articulate his desire for the death that was only hours away.

58. Between 25 May and 15 June 1960, Lacan delivered three seminars devoted to analyzing Sophocles' *Antigone*. This drama, Lacan claims, embodies "the tragic effect," or catharsis; that is, it encourages the audience to assume the full weight of their desire and to recognize the ineluctable otherness of human identity. See *L'éthique de la psychanalyse* (1959–60).

59. My linking of *Go Down, Moses* to *Absalom, Absalom!* gains credibility in light of textual evidence revealing that the 1936 novel was not far from Faulkner's mind when he wrote *Go Down, Moses*. In the typescript of the story "Go Down, Moses," the young black man executed for murder was first given the name Henry Coldfield Sutpen; this Henry Coldfield Sutpen was the grandson of Rosa Sutpen, one of Thomas Sutpen's slaves (Blotner, *Faulkner* [1974], 1055). Had Faulkner not changed this name, the story of Henry Coldfield Sutpen in "Go Down, Moses" would have been the final installment of the Sutpen tragedy. Sundquist discusses this convergence of *Absalom, Absalom!* and *Go Down, Moses* (Faulkner: *The House Divided*, 131–33).

60. Lacan, *Écrits* (Norton), 277.

EPILOGUE:
LACAN, FAULKNER, AND THE POWER OF THE WORD

1. Ferdinand de Saussure, *Course in General Lingistics*, 67.

2. Lacan, *Écrits* (Norton), 65.

3. Mellard, *Using Lacan*, 9–10.

4. Sarup, *Jacques Lacan*, 48.

5. Gallop, *Daughter's Seduction*, 12.

6. Lacan, *Écrits* (Seuil, 1966), 709.

7. Sarup, *Jacques Lacan*, 53.

8. In a stimulating essay, Richard Godden examines the dehumanizing effects of the word *nigger*. See "Call Me Nigger: Race and Speech in Faulkner's *Light in August*."

9. See Howe, *William Faulkner*, 203–4.

10. Gallop, *Daughter's Seduction*, 21.

11. Lacan, *Écrits* (Seuil, 1966), 709.

12. Lacan, *Écrits* (Norton), 234.

13. Mitchell, *Psychoanalysis and Feminism*, 397–98.

14. Lacan, *Écrits* (Norton), 65.

Works Cited

Adamowski, T. H. " 'Meet Mrs. Bundren': *As I Lay Dying*—Gentility, Tact, and Psychoanalysis." *University of Toronto Quarterly* 49 (spring 1980).

Adams, R. P. *Faulkner: Myth in Motion*. Princeton: Princeton Univ. Press, 1968.

Aeschylus. *The Eumenides*. Trans. by Richmond Lattimore. Chicago: Univ. of Chicago Press, 1953.

Bakhtin, Mikhail. *Rabelais and His World*. Boston: MIT Univ. Press, 1968.

Barker, Stephen. "From Old Gold to I.O.U.'s: Ike McCaslin's Debased Genealogical Coin." *Faulkner Journal* 3 (1987).

Barthes, Roland. *The Pleasure of the Text*. Trans. by Richard Miller. New York: Hill & Wang, 1975.

Baym, Nina. "Melodramas of Beset Manhood: How Theories of American Fiction Exclude Women Authors." *American Quarterly* 33 (1981).

Bedient, Calvin. "Pride and Nakedness: *As I Lay Dying*." *Modern Language Quarterly* 29 (1968). Reprinted in Brodhead, ed., *Faulkner: New Perspectives*.

Bezzerides, A. I. *William Faulkner: A Life on Paper*. Jackson: Univ. Press of Mississippi, 1980.

Bleikasten, André. "Fathers in Faulkner." In *The Fictional Father: Lacanian Readings of the Text*. Ed. by Robert Con Davis. Amherst: Univ. of Massachusetts Press, 1981.

———. *The Ink of Melancholy: Faulkner's Novels from "The Sound and the Fury" to "Light in August."* Bloomington: Indiana Univ. Press, 1990.

———. *"Light in August:* The Closed Society and Its Subjects." In Millgate, ed., *New Essays on "Light in August."*

Blotner, Joseph. *Faulkner: A Biography*. 2 vols. New York: Random House, 1974.

———. *Faulkner: A Biography*. 1 vol. New York: Random House, 1984.

Boothby, Richard. *Death and Desire: Psychoanalytic Theory in Lacan's Return to Freud*. New York: Routledge, 1991.

Bowie, Malcolm. *Lacan*. Cambridge: Harvard Univ. Press, 1991.

Bracher, Mark. *Lacan, Discourse, and Social Change*. Ithaca: Cornell Univ. Press, 1993.

Brodhead, Richard, ed. *Faulkner: New Perspectives*. Englewood Cliffs NJ: Prentice-Hall, 1983.

Brodsky, Louis Daniel, and Robert W. Hamblin, eds. *Faulkner: A Comprehensive Guide to the Brodsky Collection*. Jackson: Univ. Press of Mississippi, 1983.

Brooks, Peter. *Reading for the Plot*. New York: Knopf, 1984.

Works Cited

Broughton, Panthea Reid. "The Economy of Desire: Faulkner's Poetics, from Eroticism to Post-Impressionism." *Faulkner Journal* 4 (1988/89).

Capote, Truman. Personal interview. 11 April 1975.

Carothers, James B. "The Myriad Heart: The Evolution of the Faulkner Hero." In Fowler and Abadie, eds., *"A Cosmos of My Own."*

———. "The Road to *The Reivers.*" In Fowler and Abadie, eds., *"A Cosmos of My Own."*

Chodorow, Nancy. *The Reproduction of Mothering: Psychoanalysis and the Sociology of Gender.* Berkeley: Univ. of California Press, 1978.

Cixous, Hélène. "Castration or Decapitation?" *Signs* 7 (1981).

Clarke, Deborah. *Robbing the Mother: Women in Faulkner.* Jackson: Univ. Press of Mississippi, 1994.

Clément, Catherine. *The Lives and Legends of Jacques Lacan.* New York: Columbia Univ. Press, 1983.

Cohen, Philip, and Doreen Fowler, eds. "Faulkner's Introduction to *The Sound and the Fury.*" *American Literature* 62 (1990).

Cowan, Michael H., ed. *Twentieth Century Interpretations of "The Sound and the Fury."* Englewood Cliffs NJ: Prentice-Hall, 1968.

Cowley, Malcolm. *The Faulkner-Cowley File: Letters and Memories, 1944–1962.* New York: Viking, 1966.

———. Introduction to *The Portable Faulkner.* New York: Viking, 1946.

Dauner, Louise. "Quentin and the Walking Shadow." *Arizona Quarterly* 18 (1965). Reprinted in Cowan, ed., *Twentieth Century Interpretations of "The Sound and the Fury."*

Davis, Robert Con. "Critical Introduction: The Discourse of the Father." In *The Fictional Father: Lacanian Readings of the Text.* Ed. by Robert Con Davis. Amherst: Univ. of Massachusetts Press, 1982.

———. "The Symbolic Father in Yoknapatawpha County." *Journal of Narrative Technique* 10 (1980).

Davis, Thadious M. *Faulkner's "Negro": Art in Southern Context.* Baton Rouge: Louisiana State Univ. Press, 1983.

Diaz-Diocaretz, Myriam. "Faulkner's Hen-House: Woman as Bounded Text." In Fowler and Abadie, eds., *Faulkner and Women.*

Donaldson, Susan V. "Isaac McCaslin and the Possibilities of Vision." *Southern Review* 22 (1986).

———. "Subverting History: Women and Narrative in *Absalom, Absalom!*" *Southern Quarterly* 26 (summer 1988).

Dos Passos, John. "Faulkner." *National Review* 14 (15 Jan. 1963).

Duvall, John N. *Faulkner's Marginal Couple: Invisible, Outlaw, and Unspeakable Communities.* Austin: Univ. of Texas Press, 1990.

Eagleton, Terry. *Literary Theory: An Introduction.* Minneapolis: Univ. of Minnesota Press, 1983.

Works Cited

Eliade, Mircea. *Patterns in Comparative Religion*. Trans. by Rosemary Sheed. 1958. New York: New American Library, 1974.

Fadiman, Regina K. *Faulkner's "Light in August": A Description and Interpretation of the Revisions*. Charlottesville: Univ. Press of Virginia, 1975.

Faulkner, William. *Absalom, Absalom!* New York: Vintage International, 1990.

———. Appendix to *The Portable Faulkner*, "The Compsons, 1699–1945." Ed. by Malcolm Cowley. 1946. New York: Viking, 1967.

———. *As I Lay Dying. The Corrected Text*. 1930. New York: Vintage, 1987.

———. "As I Lay Dying." Faulkner Collection. Box 3, Folder 59, ts. Rowan Oak Papers. John Davis Williams Library, University of Mississippi.

———. *Faulkner in the University: Class Conferences at the University of Virginia, 1957–1958*. Ed. by Frederick L. Gwynn and Joseph L. Blotner. Charlottesville: Univ. of Virginia Press, 1959.

———. *Go Down, Moses*. New York: Vintage International, 1990.

———. "An Introduction to *The Sound and the Fury*." Box 2, Folder 39, ms. Rowan Oak Papers. Faulkner Collection. John Davis Williams Library, University of Mississippi.

———. *Light in August*. New York: Vintage International, 1990.

———. *Lion in the Garden: Interviews with William Faulkner*. Ed. by James B. Meriwether and Michael Millgate. Lincoln: Univ. of Nebraska Press, 1980.

———. *Mosquitoes*. (1927) New York: Boni & Liveright, 1951.

———. *Selected Letters of William Faulkner*, ed. by Joseph Blotner. New York: Random House, 1977.

———. *The Sound and the Fury. The Corrected Text*. New York: Vintage, 1987.

———. *Thinking of Home: William Faulkner's Letters to His Mother and Father, 1918–1925*. Ed. by James G. Watson. New York: Norton, 1992.

———. *The Wild Palms*. 1939; reprinted. New York: Vintage, 1966.

Feldstein, Richard. "Gerald Bland's Shadow." *Literature and Psychology* 31 (1981).

Felman, Shoshana. "To Open the Question." In *Literature and Psychoanalysis: The Question of Reading: Otherwise*. Ed. by Shoshana Felman. Baltimore: Johns Hopkins Univ. Press, 1980.

Ficken, Carl. "The Opening Scene of William Faulkner's *Light in August*." *Proof* 2 (1972).

Fowler, Doreen. *Faulkner's Changing Vision: From Outrage to Affirmation*. Ann Arbor: UMI Research Press, 1983.

———. "Joe Christmas and 'Womanshenegro.'" In Fowler and Abadie, eds. *Faulkner and Women*.

———. "The Nameless Women of *Go Down, Moses*." *Women's Studies* 18 (1993).

———. "The Ravished Daughter: Eleusinian Mysteries in *The Sound and the Fury*." In Fowler and Abadie, eds., *Faulkner and Religion*.

Fowler, Doreen, and Ann J. Abadie, eds. *"A Cosmos of My Own."* Jackson: Univ. Press of Mississippi, 1981.

Works Cited

———. *Faulkner and the Craft of Fiction*. Jackson: Univ. Press of Mississippi, 1989.

———. *Faulkner and Religion*. Jackson: Univ. Press of Mississippi, 1991.

———. *Faulkner and Women*. Jackson: Univ. Press of Mississippi, 1985.

———. *New Directions in Faulkner Studies*. Jackson: Univ. Press of Mississippi, 1984.

Freud, Sigmund. *Beyond the Pleasure Principle*. Trans. by James Strachey. New York: Norton, 1961.

———. *The Standard Edition of the Complete Psychological Works of Freud*. Ed. and trans. by James Strachey. 24 vols. London: Hogarth Press, 1961.

Friedman, Susan Stanford, ed. *Joyce: The Return of the Repressed*. Ithaca: Cornell Univ. Press, 1993.

Gallop, Jane. *The Daughter's Seduction: Feminism and Psychoanalysis*. Ithaca: Cornell Univ. Press, 1985.

———. *Reading Lacan*. Ithaca: Cornell Univ. Press, 1985.

Gilbert, Sandra M., and Susan Gubar. *No Man's Land: The Place of the Woman Writer in the Twentieth Century. Volume 1: The War of the Words*. New Haven: Yale Univ. Press, 1988.

Godden, Richard. "Call Me Nigger: Race and Speech in Faulkner's *Light in August*," *American Studies* 14, 2 (1980).

Gresset, Michel. *Fascination: Faulkner's Fiction, 1919–1936*. Durham: Duke Univ. Press, 1989.

———. "Faulkner's Self-Portraits." *Faulkner Journal* 2 (1986).

Grimwood, Michael. *Heart in Conflict: Faulkner's Struggles with Vocation*. Athens: Univ. of Georgia Press, 1987.

Guetti, James. *The Limits of Metaphor: A Study of Melville, Conrad, and Faulkner*. Ithaca: Cornell Univ. Press, 1967.

Gwin, Minrose C. *The Feminine and Faulkner. Reading (Beyond) Sexual Difference*. Knoxville: Univ. of Tennessee Press, 1990.

Hamblin, Robert W. "Saying No to Death": Toward William Faulkner's Theory of Fiction." In Fowler and Abadie, eds., *"A Cosmos of My Own,"* 1981.

Hegel, G. W. F. *The Phenomenology of Spirit*. Trans. and ed. by J. B. Baillie. London: Allen & Unwin, 1931.

Heywood, Leslie. "The Shattered Glass: The Blank Space of Being in *Absalom, Absalom!*" *Faulkner Journal* 3 (spring 1988).

Hoffman, Frederick, and Olga W. Vickery, eds. *William Faulkner: Three Decades of Criticism*. New York: Harcourt, Brace, 1963.

Homans, Margaret. *Bearing the Word: Language and Female Experience in Nineteeth-Century Women's Writing*. Chicago: Univ. of Chicago Press, 1986.

Honnighausen, Lothar, ed. *Faulkner's Discourse*. Tubingen: Max Niemeyer Verlag, 1989.

Howe, Irving. *William Faulkner: A Critical Study*. New York: Vintage, 1952.

Irigaray, Luce. *Le Corps-à-corps avec la mère*. Ottawa: Pleine Lune, 1981.

Works Cited

Irwin, John T. *Doubling and Incest/Repetition and Revenge*. Baltimore: Johns Hopkins Univ. Press, 1975.

Jones, Ernest. *Papers on Psycho Analysis*. Boston: Beacon, 1948.

Karl, Frederick R. *William Faulkner: American Writer*. New York: Weidenfeld & Nicolson, 1989.

Kartiganer, Donald M. "Faulkner's Art of Repetition." In Fowler and Abadie, eds., *Faulkner and the Craft of Fiction*.

————. *The Fragile Thread: The Meaning of Form in Faulkner's Novels*. Amherst: Univ. of Massachusetts Press, 1979.

Kazin, Alfred. "The Stillness in *Light in August*." In Hoffman and Vickery, eds., *William Faulkner: Three Decades of Criticism*.

King, Richard. *A Southern Renaissance: The Cultural Awakening of the American South 1930–1955*. London: Oxford Univ. Press, 1980.

Klein, Melanie. *Love, Guilt and Reparation and Other Works, 1921–1945*. London: Hogarth, 1975.

Kloss, Robert J. "Faulkner's *As I Lay Dying*." *American Imago* 38 (1981).

Kolodny, Annette. *The Lay of the Land: Metaphor as Experience and History in American Life and Letters*. Chapel Hill: Univ. of North Carolina Press, 1975.

Kovel, Joel. *White Racism: A Psychohistory*. New York: Vintage, 1971.

Kreiswirth, Martin. "Plots and Counterplots: The Structure of *Light in August*." In Millgate, ed., *New Essays on "Light in August."*

————. *William Faulkner: The Making of a Novelist*. Athens: Univ. of Georgia Press, 1983.

Kristeva, Julia. *Desire in Language: A Semiotic Approach to Literature and Art*. Ed. by Leon S. Roudiez. New York: Columbia Univ. Press, 1980.

————. *Revolution in Poetic Language*. Trans. by Margaret Waller. New York: Columbia Univ. Press, 1984.

Lacan, Jacques. "Desire and the Interpretation of Desire in *Hamlet*." Trans. by James Hulbert. *Yale French Studies* 55–56 (1977).

————. "Le désir et son interprétation." Séminaire 6, 1958–59. Sessions 1 & 2 in *Ornicar?* 24(1981); sessions 3 & 4 in *Ornicar?* 25 (1982); sessions 5, 6, 7 in *Ornicar?* 26/27 (1983). Text established by Jacques Alain Miller (seven sessions).

————. *Écrits*. Paris: Seuil, 1966.

————. *Écrits: A Selection*. Trans. by Alan Sheridan. 1966. New York: Norton, 1977.

————. *Encore*. Séminaire 20, 1972–73. Paris: Seuil, 1975.

————. *L'éthique de la psychanalyse*. Séminaire 7, 1959–60. Text established by Jacques-Alain Miller. Paris: Seuil, 1986.

————. *Feminine Sexuality: Jacques Lacan and the "École Freudienne."* Ed. by Juliet Mitchell. Trans. and ed. by Jacqueline Rose. New York: Norton, 1982.

————. "Les formations de l'inconscient" (1957–58), *Bulletins de Psychologie 2*.

————. *The Four Fundamental Concepts of Psycho-Analysis*. Ed. by Jacques-Alain Miller. Trans. by Alan Sheridan. New York: Norton, 1981.

Works Cited

———. *Le moi dans la théorie de Freud et dans la technique de la psychoanalyse.* Séminaire 2, 1954–55. Text established by Jacques-Alain Miller. Paris: Seuil, 1978.

———. *Les Psychoses.* Séminaire 3, 1955–56. Text established by Jacques-Alain Miller. Paris: Seuil, 1981.

———. *The Seminar of Jacques Lacan. Book 1: Freud's Papers on Technique, 1953–1954.* Ed. by Jacques-Alain Miller, trans. by John Forrester. New York: Norton, 1988.

LaLonde, Christopher A. "A Trap Most Magnificently Sprung: The Last Chapter of *Light in August.*" In Fowler and Abadie, eds., *Faulkner and the Craft of Fiction.*

Langford, Gerald. *Faulkner's Revision of "Absalom, Absalom!": A Collation of the Manuscript and the Published Book.* Austin: Univ. of Texas Press, 1971.

Laplanche, Jean. *Life and Death in Psychoanalysis.* Trans. by Jeffrey Mehlman. Baltimore: Johns Hopkins Univ. Press, 1976.

Lee, Jonathan Scott. *Jacques Lacan.* Amherst: Univ. of Massachusetts Press, 1990.

Lester, Cheryl. "To Market, to Market: *The Portable Faulkner.*" *Criticism* 29 (1987).

Liles, Don Merrick. "William Faulkner's *Absalom, Absalom!:* An Exegesis of the Homoerotic Configurations in the Novel." *Journal of Homosexuality* 8 (1983).

Lind, Ilse Dusoir. "The Design and Meaning of *Absalom, Absalom!*" In Hoffman and Vickery, eds., *William Faulkner: Three Decades of Criticism.*

Lukacher, Ned. *Primal Scenes.* Ithaca: Cornell Univ. Press, 1986.

MacCannell, Juliet Flower. *Figuring Lacan: Criticism and the Cultural Unconscious.* Lincoln: Univ. of Nebraska Press, 1986.

Martin, Jay. " 'The Whole Burden of Man's History of His Impossible Heart's Desire': The Early Life of William Faulkner." *American Literature* 53 (1982).

Matthews, John T. *The Play of Faulkner's Language.* Ithaca: Cornell Univ. Press, 1982.

McGee, Patrick. "Gender and Generation in Faulkner's 'The Bear.' " *Faulkner Journal* 1 (1985).

Mellard, James M. Letter to the author. 2 June 1994.

———. *Using Lacan, Reading Fiction.* Urbana: Univ. of Illinois Press, 1991.

Meriwether, James B., ed. "An Introduction for *The Sound and The Fury.*" *Southern Review* n.s. 8 (1972).

Millgate, Michael. *The Achievement of William Faulkner.* New York: Vintage, 1963.

———, ed. *New Essays on "Light in August."* New York: Cambridge Univ. Press, 1987.

Minter, David. *William Faulkner: His Life and Work.* Baltimore: Johns Hopkins Univ. Press, 1980.

Mitchell, Juliet. Introduction 1 to Jacques Lacan, *Feminine Sexuality.*

———. *Psychoanalysis and Feminism.* New York: Vintage, 1975.

Works Cited

Moddelmog, Debra A. "Faulkner's Theban Saga: *Light in August*." *Southern Literary Journal* 18 (1985).

Moi, Toril. *Sexual/Textual Politics: Feminist Literary Theory*. New Accents Series. Ed. by Terence Hawkes. London: Methuen, 1985.

Moreland, Richard C. *Faulkner and Modernism: Rereading and Rewriting*. Madison: Univ. of Wisconsin Press, 1990.

Morris, Wesley, with Barbara Alverson Morris. *Reading Faulkner*. Madison: Univ. of Wisconsin Press, 1989.

Mortimer, Gail L. *Faulkner's Rhetoric of Loss: A Study in Perception and Meaning*. Austin: Univ. of Texas Press, 1983.

Muhlenfeld, Elisabeth. " 'We have waited long enough': *Judith Sutpen and Charles Bon*." *Southern Review* 14 (1978).

Muller, John P., and William J. Richardson. *Lacan and Language: A Reader's Guide to "Écrits."* New York: International Universities, 1982.

Neumann, Erich. *The Origins and History of Consciousness*. 1949. Trans. by R. F. C. Hull. Bollingen Series 42. New York: Pantheon, 1954.

Nietzsche, Friedrich. *"The Birth of Tragedy" and "The Genealogy of Morals."* Trans. by Francis Goffing. New York: Doubleday, 1956.

O'Donnell, George Marion. "Faulkner's Mythology." In Hoffman and Vickery, eds., *William Faulkner: Three Decades of Criticism*.

Peternel, Joan. "The Double in *Light in August*: Narcissus or Janus?" *Notes on Mississippi Writers* 15 (1983).

Pettey, Homer B. "Reading and Raping in *Sanctuary*." *Faulkner Journal* 3 (1987).

Pierce, Constance. "Being, Knowing, and Saying in the 'Addie' Section of Faulkner's *As I Lay Dying*." *Twentieth Century Literature* 26.

Pitavy, François. "Some Remarks on Negation and Denegation in William Faulkner's *Absalom, Absalom!*" In Honnighausen, ed., *Faulkner's Discourse*.

Polk, Noel. " 'The Dungeon Was Mother Herself': William Faulkner: 1927–1931." In Fowler and Abadie, eds., *New Directions in Faulkner Studies*.

———. *An Editorial Handbook for William Faulkner's "The Sound and the Fury."* New York: Garland, 1985.

Porter, Carolyn. *Seeing and Being: The Plight of the Participant Observer in Emerson, James, Adams, and Faulkner*. Middleton CT: Wesleyan Univ. Press, 1981.

Radloff, Bernhard. "*Absalom, Absalom!:* An Ontological Approach to Sutpen's Design." *Mosaic: A Journal for the Comparative Study of Literature and Ideas* 19 (winter 1986).

Ragland-Sullivan, Ellie. *Jacques Lacan and the Philosophy of Psycho-analysis*. Urbana: Univ. of Illinois Press, 1986.

Rose, Jacqueline. Introduction 2 to Jacques Lacan, *Feminine Sexuality*.

Ross, Stephen M. *Fiction's Inexhaustible Voice: Speech and Writing in Faulkner*. Athens: Univ. of Georgia Press, 1989.

Works Cited

Safouan, M. *La sexualité féminine dans la doctrine freudienne, (le champ freudien)* Paris: Seuil, 1976.

Sarup, Madan. *Jacques Lacan.* Toronto: University of Toronto Press, 1992.

Sass, Karen R. "At a Loss for Words: Addie and Language in *As I Lay Dying.*" *Faulkner Journal* 6 (1991).

Saussure, Ferdinand de. *Course in General Linguistics.* Trans. by Wade Baskin. 1916; reprinted New York: McGraw-Hill, 1966.

Sensibar, Judith L. *The Origins of Faulkner's Art.* Austin: Univ. of Texas Press, 1984.

Snead, James A. *Figures of Division: William Faulkner's Major Novels.* New York: Methuen, 1986.

Snell, Susan. *Phil Stone of Oxford: A Vicarious Life.* Athens: Univ. of Georgia Press, 1991.

Spilka, Mark. "Quentin Compson's Universal Grief." *Contemporary Literature* 2 (1970).

Sundquist, Eric J. *Faulkner: The House Divided.* Baltimore: Johns Hopkins Univ. Press, 1983.

Thompson, Lawrance. "Mirror Analogues in *The Sound and the Fury.*" *English Institute Essays.* Ed. by Alan Downer. New York: Columbia Univ. Press, 1954. Reprinted in Hoffman and Vickery, eds., *William Faulkner: Three Decades of Criticism.*

Urgo, Joseph R. "Menstrual Blood and 'Nigger' Blood: Joe Christmas and the Ideology of Sex and Race." *Mississippi Quarterly* 41 (1988).

Wadlington, Warwick. *Reading Faulknerian Tragedy.* Ithaca: Cornell Univ. Press, 1987.

Watkins, Floyd C. "What Happens in *Absalom, Absalom!?*" *Modern Fiction Studies* 13 (1967).

Weinstein, Philip M. *Faulkner's Subject: A Cosmos No One Owns.* Cambridge: Cambridge Univ. Press, 1992.

———. " 'If I Could Say Mother': Construing the Unsayable about Faulknerian Maternity." In Honnighausen, ed., *Faulkner's Discourse.*

Wells, Dean Faulkner. "Dean Swift Faulkner: A Biographical Study." Oxford, Mississippi: University of Mississippi M.A. thesis, 1975.

———. Personal interview. 17 June 1990.

Wilde, Meta Doherty. "An Unpublished Chapter from *A Loving Gentleman.*" *Mississippi Quarterly* 30 (1977).

Wilden, Anthony. "Lacan and the Discourse of the Other." In *Speech and Language in Psychoanalysis* by Jacques Lacan. Trans. by Anthony Wilden. Baltimore: Johns Hopkins Univ. Press, 1981. Orig. pub. as *The Language of the Self: The Function of Language in Psychoanalysis,* 1968.

Williams, David. *Faulkner's Women: The Myth and the Muse.* Montreal: McGill-Queen's Univ. Press, 1977.

Works Cited

Williams, Joan. Personal interview. 5 August 1990.

Wittenberg, Judith Bryant. "Gender and Linguistic Strategies in *Absalom, Absalom!*" In Honnighausen, ed., *Faulkner's Discourse.*

———. *The Transfiguration of Biography.* Lincoln: Univ. of Nebraska Press, 1979.

———. "The Women of *Light in August.*" In Millgate, ed., *New Essays on "Light in August."*

Wright, Elizabeth. *Psychoanalytic Criticism: Theory in Practice.* New York: Methuen, 1984.

Wyatt, David M. *Prodigal Sons: A Study in Authorship and Authority.* Baltimore: Johns Hopkins Univ. Press, 1980.

Zender, Karl F. *The Crossing of the Ways: William Faulkner, the South, and the Modern World.* New Brunswick: Rutgers Univ. Press, 1989.

———. "Faulkner at Forty: The Artist at Home." *Southern Review* 17 (1981).

Zink, Karl E. "Faulkner's Garden: Woman and the Immemorial Earth." *Modern Fiction Studies* 2 (1956).

Index

Index

Index

211

Index

mirror-stage identification: in *Absalom, Absalom!*, 114–18; in *Light in August,* 71–72, 94

Mitchell, Juliet, 173n, 179n, 180n; definition of the phallus, 10; dilemma of subjectivity, 13, 36; on the female's oedipal passage, 151–52; as interpreter of Lacan, xv; on language, 172

Moddelmog, Debra A., 185n

Moi, Toril, 14, 15; on the imaginary, 7

Montrelay, Michelle, 80

Moreland, Richard C, 189n

Morris, Wesley, 182n, 191n

Mortimer, Gail L., 179n, 184n

Mosquitoes, ix, 17, 174n

mother: exclusion of, in *As I Lay Dying,* 48–49, 52–53, 54–56; —, in *Light in August,* 66, as identificatory imago, 7–8; identified with imaginary in *As I Lay Dying,* 51–53; identified with loss, in *The Sound and the Fury,* 33–34, 44–45; substitutions, 19; substitutions, in *As I Lay Dying,* 53–56

mother of the mirror phase relation, ambivalence toward, 16–23

mourning, 161–62, 164–66

Muhlenfeld, Elisabeth, 102

Neumann, Erich: congruence with Lacan, xii; and feminine repression, 49; and mythic representations of the unconscious, 75–76, 79, 81; origin of the ego, 3–4

objet petit a, 183n, 196n; in *As I Lay Dying,* xvii, 54–56; definition of, 12

O'Donnell, George Marion, 187n

Odyssey, The (Aeschylus), 48

oedipal complex: female's, 151–52; in *Go Down, Moses,* 140, 144; and race, 185n

oedipal conflict: in Faulkner's family, 24, 28; in *Go Down, Moses,* 128–30, 132–33; and narration, in *Absalom, Absalom!,* 111–12

oedipal moment, in *Light in August,* 92–94

oedipal passage: defined, 89; disruption of imaginary, 8–9; Lacan's reintrepretation, 8–10; in *Light in August,* 65–69, 71–74; reenacted, in *As I Lay Dying,* 57–58

Old Ben, as representation of symbolic Father, 128–29, 134–37, 140–43

Oresteia (Aeschylus), 48, 52

Orestes, 61

Other, the, xii; defined 9–12; desire of, in *Absalom, Absalom!,* 95–96, 105, 122–124; desire of, in *Go Down, Moses,* 138–45; and the other, 9. *See also* phallus

paternal signifier: ambivalence toward, 25; in "Delta Autumn," 157–59; intervention in mother-child dyad, 9; represented by Byron Bunch, 92–93; represented by Cash Bundren, 157–58; represented by Hightower's father, 66; represented by Old Ben, 138; as signifier of loss in *Go Down, Moses,* 131; as synonym for phallus, 10–11. *See also* father become Father; phallus

Perseus, as mythic representation of paternal metaphor, 86–88

Peternel, Joan, 187n

phallic lack, 23; projected onto women, 32–34; in *The Sound and the Fury,* 37–39

phallic mother. *See* preoedipal mother

phallic Other, 23; Sutpen as figure of, 106–8. *See also* Other, the

phallus: defined, 10–11; in "Delta Autumn," 157–58; distinguished from penis, 10, 152, 180n; distinguished from Real, 14; as forbidden signifier, 99–100; fraudulence of, xii, 197n; in *Go Down, Moses,* 130–32, 134–35; in *Light in August,* 67–69; 71–74; as lost object, 10–12; as marker of difference, in *Light in August,* 92

Pierce, Constance, 182n

Pitavy, François, 189n

Polk, Noel, 87, 180n, 181n, 186n

Porter, Carolyn, 183n, 184n, 190n, 193n

preoedipal mother, 7–9, 186n; in *Absalom, Absalom!,* 123–24; in *As I Lay Dying,* 50–56; in *Go Down, Moses,* 133–34; in *Light in August,* 60–70, 77–79, 92–94; in *The Sound and the Fury,* 35, 39–40, 46–47

preoedipal phase: defined, 6–10; in *Light in August,* 65–66

primal scene, 185n, 196n; in *Absalom, Absalom!,* 109–10; in *Go Down, Moses,* 139–43; in *Light in August,* 77–78

Psychoanalysis and Feminism (Mitchell), 173n

race: and the oedipal complex, 185n; as symbol in *Light in August,* 74, 83, 87–88

Index

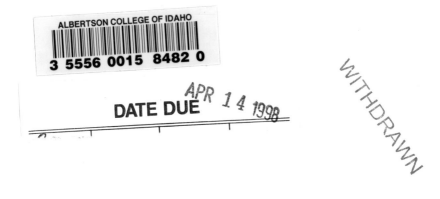